Nietzsche's
Moral Philosophy

Also by John Andrew Bernstein:

*Shaftesbury, Rousseau, and Kant: An Introduction to the Conflict
between Aesthetic and Moral Values in Modern Thought*

Nietzsche's Moral Philosophy

John Andrew Bernstein

Rutherford • Madison • Teaneck
Fairleigh Dickinson University Press
London and Toronto: Associated University Presses

Associated University Presses
440 Forsgate Drive
Cranbury, NJ 08512

Associated University Presses
25 Sicilian Avenue
London WC1A 2QH, England

Associated University Presses
2133 Royal Windsor Drive
Unit 1
Mississauga, Ontario
Canada L5J 1K5

The paper used in this publication meets the requirements
of the American National Standard for Permanence of Paper
for Printed Library Materials Z39.48-1984.

Library of Congress Cataloging-in-Publication Data

Bernstein, John Andrew, 1944–
  Nietzsche's moral philosophy.

  Bibliography: p.
  Includes index.
  1. Nietzsche, Friedrich Wilhelm, 1844-1900—Contributions
in ethics. 2. Ethics, Modern—19th century.
I. Title.
B3318.E9B47   1987   170'.92'4   85-46001
ISBN 0-8386-3283-1 (alk. paper)

Printed in the United States of America

Contents

Acknowledgments

The author is grateful to the following publishers for permission to quote extensively from copyrighted material:

Cambridge University Press: Nietzsche's *Daybreak: Thoughts on the Prejudices of Morality.* R. J. Hollingdale, translator, copyright © 1982.

Random House, Inc.: Nietzsche's *On the Genealogy of Morals*, Walter Kaufmann and R. J. Hollingdale, translators, copyright 1967 and Nietzsche's *The Will to Power*, copyright © 1967; Nietzsche's *Beyond Good and Evil*, Walter Kaufmann, translator, copyright © 1966, Nietzsche's *The Gay Science*, copyright © 1974, and Nietzsche's *Ecce Homo*, copyright © 1967.

Viking Penguin Inc.: *The Portable Nietzsche*, Walter Kaufmann, translator, copyright © 1954.

Abbreviations

A (The Antichrist)

BGE (Beyond Good and Evil: Prelude to a Philosophy of the Future)

D (Daybreak: Thoughts on the Prejudices of Morality)

EH (Ecce Homo)

G (On the Genealogy of Morals)

GS (The Gay Science)

KGA (Nietzsche Werke. Kritische Gesamtausgabe.)

M (Nietzsche Werke. Musarionausgabe.)

NCW (Nietzsche Contra Wagner)

T (Twilight of the Idols)

TSZ (Thus Spoke Zarathustra)

WP (The Will to Power)

A Note on Translations

The translation of *Daybreak* used here is by R. J. Hollingdale. Translations of *On the Genealogy of Morals* and *The Will to Power* are by Walter Kaufmann and R. J. Hollingdale. Translations from the other works are by Walter Kaufmann. Quotations giving a German edition as the source are translated by the present writer.

Introduction

The issues of morality are featured prominently in Nietzsche's works. Indeed, if one defines the sphere of moral philosophy to include both problems of conduct and the broader questions concerning the value of existence and the ends that make it worthwhile, issues which must obviously have a marked bearing on conduct, then his philosophical creativity was thoroughly dominated by "moral" issues. *Daybreak*, his first mature work, is subtitled *Thoughts on the Prejudices of Morality*. His most famous book, *Thus Spoke Zarathustra*, consists largely of a series of atheistic sermons. What has been called his most "systematic" book, the *Genealogy of Morals*, constitutes a massive attack on the Judaeo-Christian moral tradition, a campaign that reached even greater intensity in the *Antichrist*, while attempting to outline elements of a contrasting moral principle, that of "master" or aristocratic morality. *Beyond Good and Evil* foreshadows the same contrast and, as its very name implies, is dominated by moral and religious issues in its very effort to reach beyond them. So, to only a slightly lesser extent, are the other major books of Nietzsche's maturity, the *Gay Science* and *Twilight of the Idols*. All of these works were published in the 1880s.

The difficulties in expounding and criticizing this mass of material are enormous, but they do not lie primarily in its extensiveness. They rather lie in a combination of factors, some internal to the works themselves and another one external, dealing with the history of their influence in the twentieth century. Among the internal factors is the unsystematic and fragmentary character of Nietzsche's exposition. Even the *Genealogy* is anything but systematic as that word is normally understood. As is well known, Nietzsche's writings consist more of declarations than of arguments, and while he insisted upon the unity of his mature publications, there is a dearth of connective tissue even within individual works themselves, which usually consist of aphorisms ranging from single sentences to a few pages. This problem, however, is less serious than another one, the notorious contradictoriness of Nietzsche's writings, which is characteristic of his pronouncements on moral and nonmoral issues alike, and which does not permit any neat description in terms of different stages of his development. As a thinker and a writer, Nietzsche was extraordinarily volatile, and as emphatic as he was volatile. An example of these contradictions, of a nonmoral kind, but extremely important in terms of the philosophical attitudes that *appear* to be expressed, will be useful here. "They are no philosophical race, these Englishmen," Nietzsche wrote in the midst of an Anglophobic tirade in *Beyond Good and Evil*, "Bacon signifies an *attack* on the philosophical spirit; Hobbes, Hume, and Locke a debasement and lowering of the value of the concept of 'philosophy' for more than a century. It was *against* Hume that Kant arose, and rose...." (*BGE*, #252). Three years later, in the midst of a Teutophobic tirade in his autobiography, he declared, with reference to what can only be British empiricism: "Twice, when an honest, unequivocal, perfectly scientific way of thinking had just been attained with tremendous fortitude and self-overcoming, the Germans managed to find devious paths to the old 'ideal,' reconciliations of truth and 'ideal'—at bottom, formulas for a right to repudiate science, a right to *lie*. Leibniz and Kant—these two greatest brake shoes of intellectual integrity in Europe!" (*EH*, "Case of Wagner," 2).

The result of a body of writing that yields an infinite number of contradictions almost as neat as this one is that one can produce the most ringing declarations that seem to express the firmest and most settled convictions but which, in fact, do nothing of the kind. Not even Nietzsche's doctrine that everything profound loves a mask is really of any help here. While interpreters refer to this often enough, no one has really demonstrated with any clarity a way of distinguishing Nietzsche's mask from his face, or an esoteric from an exoteric teaching. In consequence, even writers who note Nietzsche's doctrine of masks pay no real attention to it in their interpretive practice.

This contradictoriness does not, of course, destroy the value of Nietzsche's writing. Some of his contradictions may have sprung from mere carelessness; others, from failings of a far more serious nature, including, as in the above examples on English and German philosophy, a need for feelings of contempt. But his works deal with many of the most complex and, at the same time, passion-stirring issues known to humanity. One could scarcely expect someone of his enormous sensitivity and passion not to register discordant responses to them in an extremely discordant age. And while the intensity of his internal conflict was unusual, perhaps unique, in the history of thought, the conflicts of the modern age as a whole are equally great, and find an extraordinarily instructive reflection in his writings. Unfortunately, the difficulties of summarizing his positions accurately are not made any easier by the advantages of doing so; and it has been hard for me to escape the feeling that no book on Nietzsche can be written that would entirely escape the charge of inaccuracy or sheer dishonesty in its treatment by unsympathetic readers unless it is so thorough as to be unreadable or so narrow as to be insignificant. Partly for this reason, I have largely refrained in this study from criticizing the selectivity of the quotations in specific works in the secondary literature, but it would be disingenuous not to say that it amazes me. I have sought in this study, at the risk and, I am afraid, at more than the risk, of pedantry, to provide enough of the range of Nietzsche's thought on each major issue treated here to present a fairly balanced picture in spite of the critical tone of this study. It is better for the reader to be confused than for him to have a clear and memorable impression of the half-false presented as the full truth.

The problem of inconsistency concerns every writer about Nietzsche, but it is all the more difficult when the issues are moral and the approach is critical. Inaccuracy is bad; injustice is worse. More important, while justice in the sense of well-founded criticism is good, forgiving may be better, and forgetting may be the best of all. One may question whether the concept of "beyond good and evil" can ever be much more than a pose when the issues involved are of immense existential import; but there is no denying that it is a very attractive, philosophical, large-minded, and, in its subtle way, an *edifying* pose. Perhaps for this reason many writers, even of comprehensive interpretations of Nietzsche, avoid concrete moral questions altogether. In other cases, they make only a passing reference to them, putting Nietzsche's views in the most favorable light, with or without the aid of a suitable group of quotations. The author of a book on Nietzsche's moral philosophy is placed in the uncomfortable position of choosing between the two attitudes of ostentatious self-righteousness suggested in the following delicious fragment of dialogue from *The Importance of Being Earnest*:

Cecily: When I see a spade I call it a spade.
Gwendolyn: I am glad to say that I have never seen a spade. It is obvious that our social spheres have been widely different.

The Nazi appropriation and misappropriation of Nietzsche, paradoxically, probably had a great deal to do with this entire, awkward situation. From the beginning, interpretations of the moral implications of Nietzsche's work varied, and the debate could be passionate enough, but it could also appear academic. The First World War made it seem less so, since echoes of Nietzsche could be and were found among the enthusiastic bellicose of both sides, while others were not wanting who insisted that the war had nothing to do with the real Nietzsche at all. In the Nazi era, the question of Nietzsche's moral philosophy ceased entirely to be merely academic. Some Nazis glorified him, or occasionally quoted him, and others, German and non-German alike, reaching for the intellectual background of Nazism both during and immediately after the Second World War, were led to believe that Nietzsche was a major part of that background. The result was the connection of

Nietzsche's name to the greatest catastrophe of modern history.

Meanwhile, however, Nietzsche had influenced, not merely a few members of the Nazi party and no doubt many more who accepted Hitler, and Mussolini too, for that matter, but practically everyone else of intellectual or artistic stature throughout Europe. This was only to be expected, given both the richness and contradictions of his ideas and the highly readable, at times magnificent, at times appallingly verbose, but never jargon-ridden style in which they were set forth. A substantial and very sophisticated fund of good-will for Nietzsche as well as ill will against him existed through the war and its immediate aftermath.

During that aftermath, some German writers wrote some sharply hostile or more temperate denunciations of Nietzsche as part of a process of national purification, and some of these works are not without continued value.[1] But it was easy to show that the Nazis, whose public use of Nietzsche was not all that extensive anyway, had used and abused him for their own purposes when they used him at all. They ignored material that sharply contested the value of their aims and beliefs, misquoted, and oversimplified. As a result of this, Nietzsche became the beneficiary of the sentiment he affected to despise more than all others, and which he was rarely able to transcend: righteous indignation. The way was cleared for the development of a vigorous, frequently excellent, international Nietzsche industry that, free from the domination of the war if not of its shadows, could expound upon the details of one of the most fascinating and elusive of thinkers. Some residual uneasiness, perhaps awakened by a polemic or by a particularly ghastly Nietzschean pronouncement, which might not be quoted but could not fail to be read, may have contributed to keeping most of this literature on the fringes of the moral issues of his work. But the abundant reasons to be grateful for the stimulation provided by Nietzsche, and the conviction, understandable in many ways, that he and his work were fundamentally decent, led many writers who treated his moral philosophy at all to oversimplify as grossly, and overlook as much, as the Nazis had done. The result is that, since the death camps, the author of many passages of a brutality unparalleled in the history of Western philosophy at its highest levels of sophistication has been attacked less frequently, and with far less venom by specialists, than Rousseau has been for two centuries, to say nothing of Marx. This is not to say, of course, that he has not been attacked at all.

In this general situation, Walter Kaufmann's *Nietzsche: Philosopher, Psychologist, Antichrist* occupies a special place and has played a special role. The work has had an unrivaled dominance in the English-speaking world (though one that may be challenged by Richard Schacht's recent, weightier, but perhaps no less misleading *Nietzsche*) and appears to have received much more respectful attention among continental Nietzsche scholars than any other work on Nietzsche ever written in English. In many ways it is a very

well-balanced book, for Kaufmann did not hide the importance of competition, struggle, and suffering in Nietzsche's thought. As a result, it has not been without appeal to some of Nietzsche's critics in their own attacks on the grosser oversimplifications of some Nietzschephiles. Originally published in 1950, its main aims were to exonerate Nietzsche from the charges of proto-Nazism on the one hand and excessive contradictoriness on the other. Both because of this first aim and Kaufmann's own passionate concern with moral issues, his work does not shove those issues to the side, but makes them central almost throughout. That fact, more than the magnitude of its influence, contributes to its being cited here more frequently than any other. But what contributes equally to this frequency is my conviction that Kaufmann overstated his case and oversimplified Nietzsche, whose basic moral attitudes were less coherent and frequently far less humane than one would gather from Kaufmann's distinguished book. In this conviction I am not alone. But the present book is a fuller study of Nietzsche's moral philosophy from a critical point of view than any other in English, and provides, I hope, a considerable supplement to works that have expressed a similar attitude on many individual points.[2]

The present study, however, was not solely nor even primarily written for the purpose of showing some of the limitations of Kaufmann's study and Nietzschean apologetics in general. It is intended to be a loosely connected sequel to an earlier book, *Shaftesbury, Rousseau, and Kant: An Introduction to the Conflict Between Aesthetic and Moral Values in Modern Culture*, in which I attempted to sketch an historical and theoretical background to some of the basic axiological disputes of modernity. As I suggested in that book, Nietzsche's thought expresses some of the most important features and serious consequences of the separation of the aesthetic from the moral. The consequences of this separation are particularly serious when morality has no regulative authority over the aesthetic, a situation that leaves the latter free, and leaves the individual whose inspiration is predominantly aesthetic similarly free, to be moral and immoral by turns. This is usually the situation in Nietzsche's thought, as I argue in this study. The present work does not presuppose any acquaintance with the earlier one, but it does develop many themes only suggested there.

The multiplicity of my purpose, especially when added to the inherent problems of writing about Nietzsche already mentioned, has made this study difficult to write and, more relevant to the reader, not, I fear, entirely easy to read. Exposition and criticism are always hard to combine, because a plan of organization that might most facilitate the one does not necessarily facilitate the other. When the writer under discussion is particularly contradictory, these problems are multiplied. There is also another consideration. As Ludwig Klages noted long ago, in spite of the surface wealth of subjects with which Nietzsche dealt, his works are actually focused very repetitively upon a comparatively small number of basic, multifaceted themes. Because these themes, however, are seen from so many angles and have such varied meanings and *levels* of meaning, anyone who would treat them with a richness that reflects some, at least, of Nietzsche's own must present similar ideas in different contexts. I think I have avoided much *exact* repetition, more successfully than Nietzsche himself, at any rate. But the reader is likely to have a sense of variations on a theme rather than the continuous unfolding of the new, and many of the arguments in this book are staggered across the whole of it.

This is said, not by way of excuse, but to explain why the organization of this study is not self-evident and requires some preliminary elucidation. The plan I have adopted is as follows. The short first chapter constitutes a kind of second introduction, in which aspects of Nietzsche's basic philosophic concept, the will to power, and those ambiguities which are particularly crucial to his moral philosophy, are presented. In each of the next two chapters, attention is focused upon one idea: Nietzsche's attempt to conceive an ideal that would combine power and goodness, and the moral purpose and implications of eternal recurrence, respectively. In both of these essays, the concentration is upon Nietzsche's view of the individual and his quest for affirmation and self-affirmation in substantial, though not complete, abstraction from society. It is this feature that makes them rather different from the remainder of the book that follows, in which social, political, and religious themes are more prominent, and that requires some explanation. By concentrating on the Nietzschean ideal of the individual, I hope to do justice to that important side of Nietzsche's thought which did not revolve entirely around the glorification of the few at the decided expense of the many, and which sought, in fact, not merely to *reconcile* goodness and power, but to *base* goodness upon a power rightly understood. I also seek to show, however, that, if this was truly Nietzsche's intention, he did not succeed in realizing it, and that there are reasons to believe that he was not permanently convinced of his success or even of the desirability of success.

Perhaps the most basic of the problems with which we shall deal in this study may be expressed in this way: the will to power is indisputably a will to power *over* something. The question is: over what, over whom, for what? In the *Genealogy*, Nietzsche propounded a very sketchy but justly celebrated theory of Judaeo-Christian morality and spirituality as internalized aggression, an aggression directed against the self and representing a will to power *over* the self. The polemical character of this construction is often obvious, but is nevertheless ambiguous when taken in the total context of Nietzsche's writing and even the *Genealogy* alone. Nietzsche can be viewed as both a rebel against and a continuator of the ascetic tradition. By the same token, he wrote much that praises will to power as primarily an ennobling discipline over the self, not merely a tyrannization of the self, and much that praises it as a domination over others as well. This domination, by turns, he viewed as primarily for the enhancement of the feeling of power of the great individual or primarily for broader, more "objective," but never very clear ends.

The chapters that follow the discussion of eternal recurrence explore these ambiguities by treating Nietzsche's social thought primarily as expounded in his last published works and notes. It is not my contention that he ever decisively abandoned the more humane ideas of the books of the early 1880s. But his social thought, which found fuller expression in his last writings than in earlier ones (themselves scarcely humane in a completely consistent way), was generally repressive, hierarchical, and frequently brutal in the extreme. The dialectic between various forms of internalized and of externalized will to power, however, runs throughout this study as it runs throughout Nietzsche's thought. For this reason, while I think the thesis that his philosophy became more brutal after *Zarathustra* might be defended, I do not wish to place any stress on this, but instead I attempt to do justice to the contrasts which can be found in his mature writings considered as a whole.

A few other comments by way of preliminary explanation and caution may be advisable here. One issue concerns the range of material on which this study is based. As already indicated, the emphasis will be upon the writings of Nietzsche's final decade of creative life. While there are discussions that directly or indirectly treat moral issues in his earliest works, those works are very different in most respects from his mature books. Consequently, I follow the practice of many other scholars in largely omitting them from consideration, though a few particularly apposite passages from them are cited here. A more complicated problem is raised by Nietzsche's notes. As every scholar of Nietzsche knows, Nietzsche's writings consist of books he himself published and a vast quantity of notes, the so-called *Nachlass*, or literary remains, which were gradually deciphered and published after his death. The advisability of using this latter body of material, and the question of whether much of it was intended to constitute the basis of a work he did not complete, or, instead, consists of expressly rejected material, are matters of much scholarly dispute. In keeping with the practice of most Nietzsche scholars, I use this *Nachlass* material. It is worth pointing out that one reason for not doing so is based on the view that it contains more morally reprehensible material than the published works, and that its use is misleading in a particularly serious way if, in fact, it contains rejected ideas. But, as Olivier Reboul has already observed, this view of the greater inhumanity of the *Nachlass* is simply erroneous.[3] There is very little, if anything, in the barbarism of some of the notes which exceeds, though it may embellish, the barbarism of parts of the published writings.

Another reason for not using the notes is rather weightier: that many of the arguments in them are simplistic or fail to prove their point and that

Nietzsche may have suspected this, and consequently did not incorporate them in his published works. The problem, however, is that Nietzsche's published works often do not even attempt to prove his most basic doctrines, such as eternal recurrence and the idea that will to power is the heart of reality, at all, but simply assume their truth, not always without vulgar abuse for the dishonesty or cowardice of those who think otherwise. For this reason, the notes are an indispensable source for anyone wishing to attempt to figure out why Nietzsche believed what he did.

I have quoted very frequently, like almost all writers on Nietzsche, and more extensively than most. But this seems to be particularly important in a highly critical book. Nor is the matter to be understood as giving Nietzsche enough rope to hang himself. Most of even the most outrageous quotations here, and certainly all of the very long ones, are invariably supremely *interesting*. Where Nietzsche was outrageous without being even moderately interesting, I have ignored the subject altogether. This is one reason that nothing is said here of Nietzsche's maunderings on women.

Finally, the criticism in this book is at times sharply expressed, and I have also, in one chapter, dealt with some issues of Nietzsche's personal psychology as revealed in his own published works. But, in spite of the moral subject of this work, criticisms of Nietzsche's ideas should not be taken as implying a total "verdict" upon the man's soul, but are intended to be *ad hoc* judgments of the particular passages under consideration. The psychological observations upon his personality, moreover, are in some ways as exonerating in their total import as they are reductive and disrespectful.

I issue this last caveat against misinterpreting or exaggerating the hostility expressed in this book for two reasons. First, because of the unique complexity and contradictory character of Nietzsche's writing on moral subjects, I am not sure even now, at the end of my labors, exactly what his real "intention" as a moralist was, supposing that, all appearances to the contrary, he had a unified intention. One of his very late notes declares that one helps morality by attacking it (*WP*, #329), and I cannot refute, nor do I wish to refute, anyone whose fondness for Nietzsche induces him to make the leap of faith that would pronounce that little jotting to be the key to the scriptures. But I cannot make it myself, and proceed on the assumption that the conflicting tendencies to which Nietzsche gave expression proceed from conflicts in himself.

Second, Nietzsche himself was sometimes extremely touchy and defensive, to the point of hideously bad manners, in response to possible criticism. "Verily, a strong wind is Zarathustra for all who are low; and this counsel he gives to all his enemies and all who spit and spew: 'beware of spitting *against* the wind!'" (*TSZ*, 2:6). This is far from being the worst specimen of its kind. And this defensiveness on Nietzsche's behalf animates some secondary material, especially Kaufmann's, though never so tastelessly expressed.

Yet Nietzsche himself, in the comparatively mild-mannered *Daybreak*, had intimated that he put contradictions in his work to encourage readers to think for themselves, and even to promote their pride at having found for themselves what they were intended to find (*D*, #449). When one places this expressly self-effacing, almost ostentatiously humble passage next to Zarathustra's animadversion upon spitting against the wind, one has some notion of how difficult it is to deal with Friedrich Nietzsche with a clear conscience. But one can do so only while insisting that it should be possible to criticize Nietzsche's philosophy and even his philosophic personality without attempting to consign him to hell, let alone to the everlasting contempt that would have bothered him much more.

In one sense, no doubt, this book may only increase the defensiveness of Nietzsche studies. But would it not be better to be less personally defensive toward Nietzsche and to make more *use* of him for the purposes of the advance of thought than the Nietzsche literature usually does? Anyone who compares the major explanations of Nietzsche with the major commentaries on Kant, in which it is taken for granted that Kant errs all the time, should be able to see that critique does more honor to a man, and makes him far more fruitful, than one-sided and selective defense. Many of the great modern works on epistemology and on morality have been written in the form of commentaries on Kant. Books on Nietzsche, by contrast, are often interpretations that are highly selective, yet in spite of that are only interpretations of Nietzsche rather than committed contributions to the subjects with which Nietzsche dealt. One of the oddest features of much writing on Nietzsche is that it "defends" him against "misunderstanding" without even subscribing to a judgment that Nietzsche, properly understood, was right. As a result of all this, studies on him are often neither sound as "history," since they simplify the ambiguities of Nietzsche, nor as philosophy, because they do not observe how arbitrary are Nietzsche's contentions, even at his best. The present study may help to clear the ground for a creative reconstruction of Nietzsche's philosophy or, alternatively, show that no moral philosophy that proceeds along the main lines laid down by Nietzsche can yield a worthwhile ethic. This is a matter, obviously, for the reader to decide for himself. For my own part, I shall attempt to show, especially in the last chapter of this book, that much that is most valuable in Nietzsche had already been expressed more adequately and nobly, if not always without ambiguities that are the mirror image of Nietzsche's own, in Christianity, especially in its Pauline formulations. If, in fact, I could accept the notion that there is a truly unified Nietzsche behind all the "masks," and that a very large part of his work does, in fact, constitute masks that are the direct opposite of his face, rather than expressions of a genuine and extraordinary variability of mood, I would unhesitatingly call him the subtlest Christian of modern times. Though I am not a Christian, that is intended as a most handsome compliment. But I am reasonably certain that it is not one Nietzsche deserved.

Nietzsche's
Moral Philosophy

1

The Will to Power

For Nietzsche, *"This world is the will to power—and nothing besides!"* (*WP*, #1067), and any account and criticism of his moral philosophy must be anchored in this basic conception. This is not true because Nietzsche achieved an ontological vision and then proceeded to deduce his concrete convictions on morality, society, and individual greatness from it. To say this would be both to overlook his existential passion and to forget the suspiciousness that his own philosophy inculcates. This suspiciousness recognizes that the will may be father to the thought, and that a conception of what reality is or may be can be inspired by the psychology of the philosopher and by the moral, social, or aesthetic convictions for which he seeks the highest or even just the most rhetorically effective justification. But without prejudging this possibility, we must begin with the abstract concept of the will to power, because all that Nietzsche wrote about moral subjects in the period of his intellectual maturity is related to it.

The will to power is a monism in that all is will to power; but it is also a pluralism in that the world is not unified by an overarching organization or divine organizer. Instead, it consists of a multitude of individual units of force that interact, overpowering one another and being overpowered in turn.[1] Nietzsche conceived these units of power as having a fixed quantum of force; but, while this may suggest a kind of atomism, he was not interested in the mathematical calculation of these forces and usually repudiated a dogmatic materialism (*BGE*, #12). "Will to power" was intended to suggest a spiritual "inside" to force, thus making possible a conception of reality in which desire and goal found a place.

The term "will to power," however, is misleading in that it implies that power is what the will wants but does not have. As we shall see a bit later in this chapter, there is an important aspect of Nietzsche's conception that corresponds to this, but for the present it should be emphasized that the will to power must *have* power in order to be at all. "A living thing seeks above all to *discharge* its strength" (*BGE*, #13). Specific goals and values are really only pretexts for this discharge, for a living thing, desiring to expend its force, requires a direction for this purpose. Nietzsche was attempting to grasp the purely positive essence of the units of reality, and this led him to define them in terms of the active power by virtue of which they existed and acted at all.

This purpose will become somewhat clearer if we note briefly his critique of Schopenhauer. As is well known, Nietzsche began his philosophic life very much under the influence of Schopenhauer and his pessimistic interpretation of the value of existence. According to that view, life was driven above all by *need*. This inherent neediness testified to life's valuelessness for Schopenhauer, since it reduced life to an endless and slavish quest to fill an unfillable void, a quest permitting only momentary satisfaction at best. "*Schopenhauer's* basic misunderstanding of the *will* (as if craving, instinct, drive were the *essence* of will) is typical:", Nietzsche charged, "lowering the value of the will to the point of making a real mistake" (*WP*, #84). "Schopenhauer spoke of 'will'; but nothing is more characteristic of his philosophy than the absence of all genuine willing" (*WP*, #95). The "absence of all genuine willing" means that Schopenhauer's will is nothing but a *re*action rather than an action, an effect of a need rather than an originating, commanding force. The concept of the will to power was itself in large part an effort on Nietzsche's part to construe existence in such a way that it would appear to have a positive value as active and creative, thus destroying the foundations of Schopenhauer's negative judgment.

The campaign against pessimism was continued along related lines in some of Nietzsche's criticisms of Darwin and modern biologists in general. Thus he attacked the tendency to place "'adaptation' in the foreground, that is to say an activity of the second rank ...; indeed, life itself has been defined as a more and more efficient inner adaptation to external conditions (Herbert Spencer). Thus the essence of life, its *will to power*, is ignored; one overlooks the essential priority of the spontaneous, aggressive, expansive, form-giving forces that give new interpretations and directions" (*G*, 2:12), adaptation only following this initial activity. The sense of offended pride, or more precisely, endangered *meaning*, as a result of the reign of the reactive in biological thought which is so clear in this passage, is also reflected in a note. "The influence of 'external circumstances' is overestimated by Darwin to a ridiculous extent: the essential thing in the life process is precisely the tremendous shaping, form-creating force working from within which *utilizes* and *exploits* 'external circumstances....'" (*WP*, #647). The effort to subordinate the reactive to the active and the needy to the forceful even induced Nietzsche to pronounce both nourishment and procreation to be "derivative" phenomena.

"Nourishment"—is only derivative; the original phenomenon is: to desire to incorporate everything.

"Procreation"—only derivative; originally: where one will was not enough to organize the entire appropriated material, there came into force an opposing will which took in hand the separation; a new center of organization, after a struggle with the original will. (*WP*, #657)

Nietzsche never published such a crass little exercise in biological myth-making as this, but it is important to emphasize that the will to power was not, for him, a purely anthropological or psychological term. He even considered it meaningful to declare that trees in their growth were reaching out for power (*WP*, #704). Nietzsche was far from thinking that he was reading an insatiability that presupposes a developed spirituality into the subhuman, and his notes abound in references particularly to protoplasm. This served his purpose because its activities seem, or seemed to him, to express a kind of open-ended activity which makes the basis for his claims about will to power more intelligible.

One cannot ascribe the most basic and primeval activities of protoplasm to a will to self-preservation, for it takes into itself absurdly more than would be required to preserve it; and, above all, it does not thereby "preserve itself," it falls apart—The drive that rules here has to explain precisely this absence of desire for self-preservation: "hunger" is an interpretation based on far more complicated organisms (—hunger is a specialized and later form of the drive, an expression of a division of labor in the service of a higher drive that rules over it). (*WP*, #651)

The idea of the last sentence, when interpreted in the light of others, appears to be that hunger, considered as a very specific need to replace expended material, develops as a subdivision of an originally more expansive and inclusive drive. For simple organisms there is only a general will to power, which finds expression in devouring whatever it can. In more developed organisms, hunger can exist in the usual sense because the process of expansion has been taken over by a more sophisticated process. This is obvious on the human level, where the goals of spirituality and aggression alike far outrun the demands of the belly. It is far less obvious in the case of much animal life, which frequently suggests a sphere of activity that, if not entirely limited to nourishment and reproduction, nevertheless displays no sign of an insatiable will. Nietzsche wished, understandably enough, to view life as a continuous dynamic process, not a static condition, and he was much concerned with the biological foundations of decadence. But the dynamic character of life does not presuppose the infinite ambition he apparently wanted to assign to everything.

The expansiveness of will to power, while it suggests the infinity of spirit, has an aggressive component, even an aggressive essence. This means that it is not a will to know or even a mere will to include, but what Nietzsche termed a "will to violate" (*WP*, #634). A clearer and less sensational formulation is given by the following: "The will to power can manifest itself only against resistances; therefore it seeks that which resists it—this is the primeval tendency of the protoplasm when it extends pseudopodia and feels about. Appropriation and assimilation are above all a desire to overwhelm, a forming, shaping and reshaping, until at length that which has been overwhelmed has entirely gone over into the power domain of the aggressor and has increased the same" (*WP*, #656). This aggressive character of a unit of will to power clarifies the assumption of the infinity of its aim. Were physiological need the decisive determinant of striving, it would seek only what satisfies the need. But since it desires the act of overwhelming as such, it seeks what resists it, anything that resists it that is not too strong. The purpose of this aggressive activity is what Nietzsche called *Machtgefühl*, the "feeling of power" that attends overcoming a resistance. This point is absolutely crucial to Nietzsche, and is made repeatedly in his mature work, published and unpublished. At times the emphasis falls upon the feeling of power that is simply the consequence of the expenditure of energy (e.g., *G*, 3:7), at other times upon the overcoming of resistance (e.g., *G*, 1:13); but at bottom Nietzsche thought these were the same. One can expend energy only *upon* something. If I mention this duality of emphasis, the reason is to avoid leading the reader to jump to the hasty equation of will to power with pure cruelty. Nietzsche usually stopped short of equating will to power with the desire to inflict pain as such. His emphasis, even when describing aggression, is on the feeling sought by the aggressor, not upon the feeling the aggressor feels as a result of the feeling he inflicts; and *Machtgefühl* can be enhanced without inflicting suffering. On the other hand, as we shall see shortly, pain and suffering were basic parts of his doctrine. The result is a tension that runs throughout his work between the obsession with cruelty and suffering and their sublimations, which he never satisfactorily resolved, and to which we shall have to return in several different contexts.

The desire for *Machtgefühl* should make it clear that while will to power presupposes power, it does not presuppose, but is instead a search for, an adequate *feeling* of power, which follows upon, rather than precedes, its activity. In this way, Nietzsche built a perpetual dynamism into his criteria of biological health without reducing that dynamism to a mere neediness. Will to power wants the feeling of power that comes only with the expenditure of power, but only because it has energy to expend. By means of this doctrine, superficially clear but at bottom profoundly ambiguous, Nietzsche could avoid a teleological, Aristotelian metaphysic predicated upon belief in a goal external to the organism that activates the will to power. Simultaneously, he could avoid the suggestion that the organism is entirely self-sufficient, like Aristotle's god, the prime mover. But the refusal to accept the adequacy of modern biology as an explanation of the phenomenon of life may be regarded as itself a vestige of Aristotelian teleological thinking, according to which all striving is a reaching beyond the purely "biological" to a perfection that is ultimately transcendent.

This entire construction doubtless seems arbitrary to the reader, either a lapse into a pre-Kantian dogmatic metaphysics or a pseudo-empiricism that leaps beyond the reality of change to a level of explanation the "facts" themselves do not sufficiently warrant. This is a subject to which it will be necessary to return in a later chapter. Suffice it to say here that Nietzsche believed that all knowledge was "interpretation,"[2] but that some interpretations were healthier, more dynamic and powerful, and hence more in love *with* power, than others, and therefore truer. Even if we believe in the arbitrariness of his interpretation, however, and the circularity implicit in its justification, it at least might seem to have the coherence that should always be possible when one can postulate whatever dogma one likes, such as the basic one that declares that all will desires objects that resist it. There is, nevertheless, an uneasy tension between the conception of will to power as pure discharge and will to power as a purposive drive toward *Machtgefühl*. The former can be viewed as an explosion, and regarded as a kind of original fact, presupposing an accumulation of force, but perhaps no more. But the drive for *Machtgefühl* cannot be conceived in that way. Its satisfactions have to be *learned*. Some of Nietzsche's notes imply this, though the consideration did not seem to trouble him or prompt a more comprehensive explanation of will to power. "'Useful' in the sense of Darwinist biology means: proved advantageous in the struggle with others. But it seems to me that the feeling of increase, the feeling of becoming stronger, is itself, quite apart from any usefulness in the struggle, the real *progress*: only from this feeling does there arise the will to struggle—" (*WP*, #649). This fragment, quoted in its entirety, is in part another reflection of Nietzsche's preference for the truly valuable as opposed to the superficially valuable, that which merely deals with utility and slavish needs. It is also an expression of his conviction that the basic fact of existence according to Darwin himself, the struggle for existence, presupposes a willingness *to* struggle. But the passage also claims that without what might be called a record of success, this struggle would not occur. How, then, did it begin in the first place? Can the initial will to power be conceived as a pure activity, or does it instead presuppose an element of reactivity? And does this not mean that the will to power does not *seek* what resists it until it first *encounters* what resists it?

Another note, a very late one, may help clarify the relevance of these questions.

Man does *not* seek pleasure and does not avoid displeasure: one will realize which famous prejudice I am contradicting. Pleasure and displeasure are mere consequences, mere epiphenomena—what man wants, what every smallest part of a living organism wants, is an increase of power. Pleasure or displeasure follow from the striving after that; *driven* [emphasis added] by that will it seeks resistance, it needs something that opposes it—Displeasure, as an obstacle to its will to power, is therefore a normal fact, the normal ingredient of every organic event; man does not avoid it, he is rather in continual *need* [emphasis added] of it; every victory, every feeling of pleasure, every event, presupposes a resistance overcome.

Let us take the simplest case, that of primitive nourishment: the protoplasm extends its pseudopodia in search of something that resists it—not from hunger but from will to power....

Displeasure thus does not merely not have to result in a diminution of our feeling of power, but in the average case it actually stimulates this feeling of power—the obstacle is the stimulus of this will to power. (*WP*, #702)

This note requires detailed comment.

(1) The famous prejudice Nietzsche was contradicting was, of course, the hedonistic assumptions of the English and French utilitarians. As Walter Kaufmann has shown with great clarity and force, Nietzsche was above all opposed to the sharp separation between pleasure and pain often made by this school.[3] His substitution of power for pleasure did not mean, as this quotation itself makes clear, that power was antithetical to or even different from pleasure, but that the intensest pleasures presuppose the overcoming of pain, not the mere avoidance of pain.[4]

(2) If every organism desires an increase of power, then comparison becomes crucial to the will to power. This is true in a double sense. First, there is a presupposition in favor of transitions from lesser to greater states of power and against the ideal of a fixed level of power, however exalted. As Nietzsche put it somewhat obscurely in a note from the same period: "If one level of power were maintained, pleasure would have only lowerings of this level by which to set its standards, only states of displeasure—not states of pleasure—" (*WP*, #695). Whatever he meant by this exactly, it is clear from many passages in his writing that life wants *more* life rather than a mere continuation of the same life, and that the setting of standards for the process of striving rather than of merely holding on to what one has was integral to will to power. Furthermore, the very aspiration for a fixed state of power, even one immeasurably transcending what one has, usually struck him as symptomatic of decadence. "The great confusion on the part of psychologists consisted in not distinguishing between these two kinds of pleasure— that of falling asleep and that of victory. The exhausted want rest, relaxation, peace, calm—the happiness of the nihilistic religions and philosophies; the rich and living want victory, opponents overcome, the overflow of the feeling of power across wider domains than hitherto" (*WP*, #703). On the basis

of this distinction, Nietzsche believed it legitimate to regard any aspiration for a fixed final state beyond the tensions of pleasure inextricably interwoven with pain as "weak," "sick," or "decadent," a sweeping condemnation that embraced Schopenhauer, Christianity, Buddhism, Platonism, and that verison of modern progressivism which sought to abolish all suffering.

Healthy life not merely presupposes the reality of different states that can be compared; it also presupposes the capacity to make comparisons and the crucial significance of doing so. "The will to grow is of the essence of pleasure: that power increases, that the difference enters consciousness" (*WP*, #695). Even if "consciousness' should not be understood strictly in a context discussing life as a whole rather than human life alone (and Nietzsche believed that even with regard to human life, the importance of consciousness was usually overdrawn), it seems impossible to escape the conclusion that the will to power predicates some sort of panpsychism. Nietzsche, like many more scientific thinkers, sought to abolish the idea of a radical distinction between the human and nonhuman. What should be stressed in the present context, however, is that if a difference enters consciousness, a mental act of comparison is presupposed. He referred in another note from the same period to "a feeling of more power (hence ... a feeling of difference, presupposing a comparison)...." (*WP*, #699). Immediately after quoting this passage, Martin Heidegger declared flatly: "Comparison is not presupposed. Rather, the disparity implied in being out beyond ourselves [in the act of willing] is first opened up and given form by joy."[5] This effort to understand Nietzsche's doctrine in a fashion different from the way Nietzsche understood it himself may have been inspired by an awareness of the havoc that the principle of comparison plays, as we shall see, in Nietzsche's moral and political philosophy (subjects Heidegger essentially ignored) and his axiology in general. Be this as it may, the emendation is anything but clear. Heidegger presumably meant that the joy which unfolds in the act of willing makes the individual aware of a new state, of his having transcended himself, and that only this joy introduces the suggestion of a comparison with the preceding state. But this line of interpretation and others related to it led Heidegger to imply that will to power itself simply unfolds from within, and to overlook the crucial role played by the incentive of the obstacle (and of pain) in the entire process.[6]

(3) Nietzsche also wrote in a part of note #702 not previously cited that nourishment was derivative, "an application of the original will to become *stronger*." Why does the protoplasm seek to be stronger? In other words, what process presents the terms of comparison to it? If this process is purely internal, then one naturally thinks of hunger and sexuality, to which, as we have seen, Nietzsche refused to reduce the will to power. Since hunger may be viewed as a pain that drives the organism to restore a lost state of satiety, it should be clear that it would not do as the explanation of a perpetual desire

for an increase of power. Sexuality would fare better, since the drive behind it corresponds to a "suffering from abundance," which Nietzsche regarded as healthy and strong in comparison with suffering from poverty, which suggests hunger. But, quite apart from Nietzsche's desire to avoid reducing will to power to sexuality as well as hunger, neither the one nor the other necessarily involves an obstacle as such, that is, an object which offers marked resistance.

The obstacle in this sense is crucial to will to power, but Nietzsche's presentation of it was confused. His declaration that the will to power *seeks* what resists it conforms to the idea that this will possesses power already and is essentially self-activated. But it is difficult to understand how one can seek an obstacle without having previously encountered one. At any rate, if it be possible, Nietzsche has not explained the ground of this possibility. Resistance must first, surely, be felt before this feeling (and the triumph that may follow) can be willed. The desire to become "stronger," therefore, cannot be explained with reference to a process occurring solely within the organism, but with reference to the clash of organisms occurring originally only on the basis of hunger, sexuality, or something else.

(4) The third paragraph of note #702 confirms that resistance must first be felt before it can be willed, although this paragraph, too, is confused. The feeling of power presupposes victory, and displeasure was normally associated by Nietzsche with a loss of the feeling of power. So, in the course of the paragraph, he amended "feeling of power" to the "will to power," which is stimulated by the obstacle. The will to power, then, is excited by a displeasure caused by encountering an obstacle. A feeling of power could, of course, well follow success in the encounter.

It should also be noted that while, in standard English usage, an *obstacle* is often merely something to go around or go over, and may play no significant role in stimulating desire for whatever it appears to block, Nietzschean obstacles are not of this character. They excite and incite the will to power. They must be conquered. This means that the obstacle seems to possess a strength that stimulates the desire to absorb it, in which case it is not an obstacle on the route to something else, but is itself the goal of will to power, or it presents a challenge to the will to power, an implicit or explicit threat to self-esteem or security that inspires the desire to prove oneself. Nietzsche never made this clear because it threatened the basis of his distinction between action and reaction. But he also did not make clear what makes an obstacle something *worth paying attention to*. Mere resistance would effect nothing, or otherwise all living beings would destroy themselves pounding against rocks.

Since on Nietzsche's showing the will to power is a dialectic between pleasure and pain, it obviously is important to determine as precisely as

possible how these feelings interact and which of the two may be said to predominate. Emphasis upon the obstacle is in danger of giving the decisive, motivating influence to pain. But not all of Nietzsche's remarks point in this direction, and sometimes they do so even less than he himself may have believed. Consider the following, in which Nietzsche disputed the common tendency to make "false opposites" out of pleasure and pain.

> There are ... cases in which a kind of pleasure is conditioned by a certain *rhythmic sequence* of little unpleasurable stimuli: in this way a very rapid increase of the feeling of power, the feeling of pleasure, is achieved. This is the case, e.g., in tickling, also the sexual tickling in the act of coitus; here we see displeasure at work as an ingredient of pleasure. It seems, a little hindrance that is overcome and immediately followed by another little hindrance that is again overcome—this game of resistance and victory arouses most strongly that general feeling of superabundant, excessive power that constitutes the essence of pleasure. (*WP*, #699)

One may wonder whether a rhythmic sequence of unpleasurable stimuli rhythmically overcome constitutes even an element of genuine *pain* or even *displeasure*, as those terms are usually understood. It is precisely the significance of gratifying rhythm, whether in sexuality or the arts, that it so continuously and reliably integrates the painful with the pleasurable and so clearly enhances the pleasurable by means of the painful, that the latter entirely loses the depressing and misery-producing character normally associated with the displeasurable.

A rhythmic sequence of little unpleasurable stimuli, constantly overcome, is not, however, the only way of subordinating the unpleasant to the pleasant. It could be said that, from the standpoint of a sufficiently gratifying success or victory *already attained*, any amount of pain or effort necessary to it, but now lying in the past, might be seen as "swallowed up in victory." In this case, definite knowledge successfully replaces rhythmically induced expectation. Even more important, any object or goal that is inherently attractive enough, that is, stimulates enough pleasure in the very contemplation of the prospect of reaching it, can have the same effect even before it is attained: that of making the pain and effort seem worthwhile.

These last considerations do not constitute any serious criticism of the doctrine of will to power, but at most a criticism of Nietzsche's misleading use of terms such as *pain, displeasure*, and, in other contexts, *cruelty*, which he was sometimes anxious to discern where others see little of the kind.[7] My main object is simply to show that one side of Nietzsche's doctrine points less to the importance of pain as such than to the centrality of the will to power's goal of subordinating pain to pleasure. By extension, this points to the primacy of the "affirmative" in general; and sometimes, in fact, Nietzsche could advocate this primacy normatively without any emphasis upon the negative or the obstacle, even with an explicit deprecation of it. The following aphorism is a beautiful example of this *via positiva*.

> *By doing we forego.*—At bottom I abhor all those moralities which say: "Do not do this! Overcome yourself!" But I am well disposed toward those moralities which goad me to do something and to do it again ... and to think of nothing except doing this *well*, as well as *I* alone can do it. When one lives like that, one thing after another that simply does not belong to such a life drops off. Without hatred or aversion one sees this take its leave today and that tomorrow, like yellow leaves that any slight stirring of the air takes off a tree. He may not even notice that it takes its leave; for his eye is riveted to his goal.... What we do should determine what we forego.... I do not wish to strive with open eyes for my own impoverishment; I do not like negative virtues—virtues whose very essence it is to negate and deny oneself something. (*GS*, #304)

Considered as a guide to morals, this paragraph begs many questions; and it asserts a criticism of ascetic traditions of dubious, or, at least, variable, relevance. But in the present context what is most important here is the claim made for the desirability of a positive goal and the deliberate avoidance of obsession with the negative. In fact, Nietzsche so denigrated the negative here, as he always did when traditional moralities were in question, that even the *obstacle*, so precious elsewhere, makes no appearance. Nietzsche appears to be pointing to a goal of desire that has no need of obstacles or of pain to heighten its attractions.

The paradox of Nietzsche's thought is, however, that while much of his criticism of ascetic traditions can be seen as a kind of extended and increasingly ill-tempered commentary on this comparatively early passage, his own doctrine of the will to power often placed such an emphasis upon pain and obstacles that the will to power could only seem, in its very essence, to be something *forced*. In addition to notes already cited pointing in this direction, the following solemn declaration from one of his last works should be emphasized: "The peoples who had some value, *attained* some value, never attained it under liberal institutions: it was great danger that made something of them that merits respect. Danger alone acquaints us with our own resources, our virtues, our armor and weapons, our *spirit*, and *forces* us to be strong. *First* principle: one must need to be strong—otherwise one will never become strong" (*T*, #38). The political implications of this are dismaying enough, but that is a subject for later chapters. What should be stressed here is that this "*first* principle" is completely incompatible with the entire spirit of "by doing we forego." The will to power to which it points seems entirely incapable of setting, let alone attaining, noble goals by itself. It needs the pressure of external forces impinging upon it. The desire for an original and originating will to power has yielded to a *derived* will to power under the conviction that a strength which is not forced will never fully develop itself. This distinction is similar to one that Nietzsche himself, as we shall see later, developed in relation to two kinds of moralities and social classes: the distinction between master and slave, to which the contrast between active and reactive forms corresponds on Nietzsche's analysis. In spite of his preference, not without ambiguity, for the masterful and active in that context, much that he wrote about the will to power in the abstract implies the reactive to a degree he never seems to have adequately appreciated, for the will to power often is quintessentially a *reaction to the obstacle*.

René Girard, in a brilliant and devastating essay on Nietzsche, declared that the final phase of the will to power is nothing less than the quest for the insuperable obstacle. The obsession with obstacles and the triumph over them invests them with a glamor that eventually leads to the search for the insuperable obstacle as the promise of a supreme power if only, *per impossibile*, it could be overcome.[8] Certainly Girard, in his short exposition, ignores some of the obstacles that Nietzsche's writings as a whole present for this thesis, but it is nevertheless a fair and illuminating summary of a facet of his thought that all too often rose to prominence. In support of Girard, one might note a line he did not discuss: "If the pleasure [i.e., feeling of power] is to be very great, the pains must be very protracted and the tension of the bow tremendous" (*WP*, #658). Where one side of Nietzsche's thought pointed to a pain so dependably overcome that it could only be called pain with some license,[9] and hence pointed to the complete dominance of pain by pleasure, the other side pointed to an interchangeability of pleasure and pain that threatened to make pain dominant by making it the indispensable inverted promise and premise of pleasure. This dominance was most conspicuous when any notion of a particular goal for which pain is endured is absent, and one is instead treated to a purely abstract praise of heroic endurance for no definite goal beyond the ability to endure itself.

2
Caesar and Christ

AFTER the introductory material just presented, the continuation of a critical study of Nietzsche's moral philosophy can only properly begin with the saintliest passage in the entire corpus of his writings:

> To be like a little inn which rejects no one who is in need but which is afterwards forgotten and ridiculed! To possess no advantage, neither better food nor purer air nor a more joyful spirit—but to give away, to give back, to communicate, to grow poorer! To be able to be humble, so as to be accessible to many and humiliating to none! To have much injustice done him, and to have crept through the worm-holes of errors of every kind, so as to be able to reach many hidden souls on their secret paths! For ever in a kind of love and for ever in a kind of selfishness and self-enjoyment! To be in possession of a dominion and at the same time concealed and renouncing! To lie continually in the sunshine and gentleness of grace, and yet to know that the paths that rise up to the sublime are close by!—That would be a life! That would be a reason for a long life! (D, #449)

How much, and how little, Nietzsche followed the letter and spirit of this beautiful passage from *Daybreak* in his later, better-known books will take the remainder of this study to show. Here only a few comments are in order. Whether one takes Nietzsche's imaginative sympathy to have been unusually broad or, instead, unusually narrow and deep, he was throughout his life an explorer of those modes of conflicting feeling his imagination could encompass which seemed to make life worth living. Although Schopenhauer had taught him to connect altruistic goodness with pessimism, and redemption with flight from life, he here saw goodness as a reason *for* life, for wanting to live. It is by no means a criticism of this quotation to say that its main point of departure is "self-centered" in this sense. This fact only becomes troubling in light of the awareness that Nietzsche so frequently let his imagination move in very different directions from the one followed here.

The questions "Why live?" and "Why be good?" are not perhaps entirely the same. The answers to them for any given individual may be the same or quite different, and it is perhaps dangerous for the naturally melancholy to demand of the pursuit of goodness that it constitute reason for long life. Goodness may come to suffer for it in their eyes.

Nietzsche includes egoism, power, and self-enjoyment in his ideal mixture and this, also, is unexceptionable at such a level of abstraction. But he does not tell us what the sources or character of these things are, and the presence of resignation, "renouncing," is particularly puzzling. Only a few years later, Nietzsche would counsel the complete rejection of any form of resignation (*TSZ*, 3:5, 3), and one must wonder whether resignation is present here as a part of the morally good, as a part of power, or as a subtle poetic touch needed to complete a portrait.

In an extraordinary passage from *Thus Spoke Zarathustra*, Nietzsche continued some of the lines of thought suggested in *Daybreak*, but with less sentimentality, less overt altruism, no resignation, and a greater concentration on the attribute of power. For all these reasons it is more characteristic of his mature thought than the material quoted above, and this chapter will be devoted to its direct and indirect elucidation and evaluation.

> His arm placed over his head: thus should the hero rest; thus should he overcome even his rest. But just for the hero the *beautiful* is the most difficult thing. No violent will can attain the beautiful by exertion....
> To stand with relaxed muscles and unharnessed will: that is most difficult for all of you who are sublime.
> When power becomes gracious and descends into the visible—such descent I call beauty.
> And there is nobody from whom I want beauty as much as from you who are powerful: let your kindness be your final self-conquest.
> Of all evil I deem you capable: therefore I want the good from you.
> Verily, I have often laughed at the weaklings who thought themselves good only because they had no claws. (*TSZ*, 2:13)

This speech, from "On those who are sublime," concerns the beautiful and the good, the latter signified by kindness and gentleness, as well as heroic force.[1] The central concept of value in Nietzsche, of course, was neither the good nor the beautiful, but power or strength (the two will be used interchangeably in this study). Yet that does not preclude the fruitfulness of approaching the ideal suggested here as a variety of what I have elsewhere termed "ethical-aestheticism," or a value system which attempts to unite morality with a principle of aesthetic attraction and fulfillment. Strength can have many meanings of both a moral and aesthetic nature, and the consideration that strength is not exclusively either moral or aesthetic only heightens the intriguing possibility that it might be a satisfactory synthetic term.

The idea that strength can have a moral reference surely does not need to be labored. The very etymology of *virtue*, "manliness," provides one obvious confirmation. Still more obvious is that any genuine moral code that makes serious demands requires some sort of strength or power to live up to it. The aesthetic character of strength is only slightly less obvious, if even that. Friedrich von Schiller, in a famous formulation, once defined beauty as "freedom in appearance." When we reflect that Nietzsche defined the will to power as, in part, a will to freedom (*G*, 2:17), we can propose emending Schiller in a Nietzschean spirit: beauty is power in appearance, power, in other words, made manifest.

The beauty that Zarathustra holds out as the goal of strength itself is moral in its graciousness and kindliness, but it is at the same time the supreme goal of individual passion, which finds fulfillment in it. Will to power at the level of the great man entails "self-overcoming," but this self-overcoming is not the annihilation of desire and will to power, but its supreme expression. Central to the wider issues underlying this great speech of Zarathustra, then, is a point on which Nietzsche and many of his interpreters have placed considerable emphasis: that passion should not be "extirpated," but should instead be "sublimated," or raised to a higher, more comprehensive goal.[2]

Strength requires passion. More precisely, power is the ability to bestow value and strive for the realization of value or *Machtgefühl*, and such ability is inseparable from passion in some sense of the term. Rather than spell out this sense, Nietzsche polemicized against any effort to extirpate the passions, an effort that for him constituted self-destruction.

> Formerly, in view of the element of stupidity in passion, war was declared on passion itself, its destruction was plotted.... The most famous formula for this is to be found in the New Testament, in the Sermon on the Mount.... There it is said, for example, with particular reference to sexuality: "If thy eye offend thee, pluck it out." ... *Destroying* the passions and cravings, merely as a preventive measure against their stupidity and the unpleasant consequences of this stupidity—today this strikes us as merely another acute form of stupidity....
>
> To be fair, it should be admitted, however, that on the ground out of which Christianity grew, the concept of the "*spiritualization* of passion" could never have been formed.... The church fights passion with excision in every sense: its practice, its "cure," is *castratism*. It never asks: "How can one spiritualize, beautify, deify a craving?" It has at all times laid the stress of discipline on extirpation (of sensuality, of pride, of the lust to rule, of avarice, of vengefulness). But an attack on the roots of passion means an attack on the roots of life: the practice of the church is *hostile to life*. (*T*, "Morality as Anti-Nature," 1)

It is far more difficult to find major moral and religious teachers who justify this sweeping diatribe by their sweeping hostility to the passions than it is to find those who do not. Nietzsche's tendency to see the intellectual history of mankind *sub specie Schopenhaueri* on this point as on some others produced grievous oversimplifications. There would be little point in listing all the modern secular thinkers who, though firmly committed to the control of passion, often wrote in praise of controlled passion, since the fire of Nietzsche's wrath was directed primarily against the Judaeo-Christian tradition on this issue. But it certainly is worth emphasizing that that tradition itself did not merit this polemic. The Puritans praised passion.[3] Aquinas wrote that there was nothing wrong with passion, only inordinate passion.[4] Since, in fact, the "soil out of which Christianity grew" was partially Platonic soil, it had inherited the Platonic concept of eros and made considerable use of it. This use is especially prominent in Augustine, one of Nietzsche's innumerable *bêtes noires*, whose entire thought centered upon the concept of the *ordo amoris*, the "order of love." Even that other plot of the soil out of which Christianity grew, Judaism, by no means bears witness to the truth of Nietzsche's contention. "Abraham made the evil inclination good," reads a passage in the Talmud. "David, unable to master the evil inclination, had to strike it dead."[5]

This brings us, finally, to the "most famous formula," "if thy eye offend thee, pluck it out." The text continues: "it is better for you to lose one part of your body than for the whole of it to be thrown into hell" (Matt. 5:29). A grim text, to be sure, but one that clearly has nothing to do with a mere "preventive measure" against the "stupidity" of the passions, but with the avoidance of concrete passions entailing "mortal" sin. One can suggest, in fact, that when preachers and moral philosophers have railed against "the passions," they had in mind not some amorphous, Protean drive like the will to power, the desire for happiness, or the Platonic eros, but a concrete passion that must be "extirpated," or from which the individual must be "freed" in its tyrannical particularity, in order to permit the "sublimation" of the broader drive for fulfillment of which it is an expression. Much "discipline," which Nietzsche could praise warmly, is often the elimination of particular desires, not war on desire as such.

In short, Nietzsche's campaign against the extirpation of the passions is both a platitude and a *petitio principi*. As the former, it amounts to the claim that it is better to employ the indeterminate raw energy of man's passions for the good, including, of course, one's own legitimate good properly understood, than to try to dispense, if possible, with such energy altogether, a proposition with which scarcely anyone would ever have disagreed. (Perhaps the secondary literature stresses a point such as this for this very reason. The stress on such a point serves to render Nietzsche's "immoralism" innocuous.) As a begging of the question, his campaign can only make us wonder what the criteria of successful and proper spiritualization in fact are.

But does not Zarathustra's exhortation provide such a criterion? The highest beauty and strength appear to be, unequivocally, kindness and gentleness. In fact, however, there is a very serious equivocation, and it concerns Zarathustra's laughter at those who are good only because they have no claws. The most important problem this raises, in the present context, is that goodness from strength and goodness from weakness are by no means always easy to distinguish from one another; and if we are to succeed in using Zarathustra's admonitions as any sort of concrete guide to self-perfection, this ambiguity is a serious matter.

Nietzsche's own assignment of epithets of strength and weakness to figures up and down the course of history, acts of evaluation that occur frequently enough, only serves to deepen rather than dispel perplexity. The most striking instance of all is the figure of Jesus. In a note Nietzsche referred briefly and cryptically to "the Roman Caesar with the soul of Christ" (WP, #983), and this celebrated formulation is perhaps the most vivid of Nietzsche's attempts to reduce the human ideal to a phrase. It has occasioned some controversy, though rather less than one might expect. The distinguished existential philosopher and Nietzsche scholar Karl Jaspers regarded this phrase as an attempt to imagine, "unconvincingly and unattainably—a synthesis of the ultimate antitheses...."[6] To this Walter Kaufmann replied that it was the "heart of Nietzsche's vision of the overman. Being capable of both sympathy and hardness, of loving and ruling, not using claws though having them...."[7] In a sense Kaufmann was perfectly right about the point he discerned in Nietzsche's apparent paradox, which repeats the idea of a gentleness with claws that we have already encountered, and erects it above both a gentleness without claws and the vicious use of claws.

But even if we gladly concede that the right kind of strength is decidedly better than the wrong kind of weakness, problems multiply as soon as we try to move beyond this empty truism. Behind Nietzsche's need to supplement the "soul of Christ" with the Roman Caesar was not an inordinate admiration for purely political power, at least in this particular context, but the conviction that Christ was *weak* in some basic psychological, even physiological sense. "Francis of Assisi, neurotic, epileptic, a visionary, like Jesus" (WP, #221) runs a representative verdict. In the *Antichrist*, one of Nietzsche's last books and certainly his most vehement one, this approach is followed at greater length. Assuming, as many more reverential scholars do today, that the Gospels attribute statements to Jesus that were in fact later interpolations reflecting struggles within the nascent Church (A, #31), Nietzsche did not hesitate to make Jesus into a veritable Ideal Type of weakness to whom not merely moralistic aggressiveness, but also anything else indicating strength, was totally foreign.

This way of dealing with Jesus enabled Nietzsche to accomplish two different purposes that were equally precious to him. On the one hand, by viewing Christ as weak, he could reject him as a guide, to say nothing of an object of faith. On the other hand, by viewing him as the very *perfection* of weakness, Nietzsche could use Jesus as a stick with which to beat Paul, the Church, and the whole theology of guilt and punishment which constituted, for him, the essence of Pauline Christianity. The respect that Nietzsche showed for the figure of Jesus amidst the violence of the *Antichrist* was consistent with the qualified respect he showed for other figures who exhibited, on his interpretation, a similar combination of weakness amounting to sickness and an absence of resentful hate against the strong, specifically, Epicurus and the Buddha.

Yet how well could one really serve both of these purposes at once? In order to complete the description of the weakness of Jesus, to deny him any ability to feel resentment in order to deny him any power to overcome it, Nietzsche had to predicate "an instinctive hatred of every reality" in Jesus, springing from a pathological excitability. This incapacity was mental, as well. Jesus was an *"idiot,"* a term that could possibly owe something to Dostoevski, but in the context is merely a reversal of Renan's claim that Jesus was a "genius" (*A*, #29). But if Jesus was an idiot and a weakling, he could not consistently be used as a means of denigrating even the rancorous vengefulness that Nietzsche ascribed to Paul, since on Nietzsche's account Paul was neither a weakling nor an idiot. This could only be done on the basis of a purely negative moralism of the kind that would hold that it is best not to feel resentment, even at the risk of turning oneself into an idiot. Such a negative moralism was the exact antithesis of Nietzsche's usual position, amounting to "castratism." If, by contrast, the freedom from resentment of Jesus and the Buddha deserves respect because it is connected to some positive power called love, or a rich as opposed to an empty internal freedom, then Jesus and the Buddha were not weak in a very important respect. To call them so because they did not think it worthwhile to conquer Gaul nor even think it worthwhile to prove that they might have done so in order to keep nineteenth-century philosophers from calling them weak, is to indulge in a highly unedifying sort of criticism.

To write about the weakness of Jesus in the first place was entirely arbitrary, and one might point out in passing that the combination of perfect strength with perfect gentleness was precisely what Christianity asked the faithful to believe Jesus possessed as the son of God. Thus Nietzsche used Jesus to criticize the Church and used an ideal aptly symbolized by Christian dogma to condescend to Jesus. But one need not press a debater's point of this sort. It suffices to observe that, if Nietzsche could criticize Jesus for weakness, he could just as easily criticize any imaginable embodiment of perfect goodness in the same unprovable, irrefutable way.

The point, be it emphasized strongly, is not what is or is not possible and even desirable to combine on some psychological or metaphysical level, but what is possible for a human being to allow to *appear*, both to others and to himself, in a fashion that admits of no doubt. When Zarathustra generously says in his exhortation, "of all evil I deem you capable," why does he say it? Of whom does he speak, and how does he know? Let it be rephrased then. "You who *are* capable of all evil, from you I want the good." Such people must know themselves and their capacity for all evil if this exhortation is to be of any use. They must, then, have committed all evil, and the "last and highest self-overcoming" that Zarathustra seeks must be nothing short of a conversion, a radical turning around. Those who have not committed all evil cannot even know that they are worthy, by reason of strength, to follow the good according to their lights. Those who have committed all evil have Nietzsche's permission to seek a "sublimation" of their will to power. What will be the principle of this sublimation? It can only be the ascetic principle that power is displayed in the difficult as such. The stronger the evil to be overcome, the more power is displayed in overcoming it. *Machtgefühl* can then be heightened if there is enough evil. If not, the desire for *Machtgefühl* is left unsatisfied.

This is not the grotesque caricature it may appear to be. It was Nietzsche himself, in *Zarathustra* itself, who identified the essence of the moral with the difficult as such. When, in the celebrated speech "On the Thousand and One Goals," Zarathustra discerns the variety of human ethical systems, he proclaims the will to power as the common root of this variety itself. "A tablet of the good hangs over every people. Behold, it is the tablet of their overcomings; behold, it is the voice of their will to power.

"Praiseworthy is whatever seems difficult to a people ... and whatever liberates even out of the deepest need, the rarest, the most difficult—that they call holy" (*TSZ*, 1:15). This contention that the praiseworthy is the difficult helps to justify the centrality of will to power in the entire process of valuing. There are two ways in which the validity of this contention can be provisionally defended. One is to concede that people scarcely bother exhorting one another to do what they would do without exhortation, or what they could do with ease. From this commonsensical standpoint one can even read Nietzsche's claim, elsewhere, that the Jews value love because they are the best haters in the world, without either stooping to be offended or accepting the statement as literally true (*D*, #377). What certainly is true is that people do not love all their neighbors as unthinkingly and effortlessly as they breathe.

Another approach would be simply to emphasize the way almost any historical system of values can be used, and continuously has been used, as a means of attaining personal distinction. Zarathustra pointed to this when, immediately after the last quotation, he continued: "Whatever makes them rule and triumph and shine, to the awe and envy of their neighbors, that is to them the high, the first, the measure, the meaning of all things." To believe in the validity of any particular system, however, is to believe that the validity of the personal distinction, or of the increase in the sense of power, is a consequence of obligation to the "law" of the system, and that one cannot found the fact of such obligation on the sense of power that can follow success in meeting its demands, still less upon the envy of one's neighbors. It might be asserted that, at his most sophisticated level of analysis, Nietzsche knew this, or something akin to it. The will to power is a doctrine that seeks to shed light on value systems as such without presupposing the ultimate validity of any of them. It suggests, therefore, that "obligation" presupposes a free act of evaluation which sets certain conditions for attaining the feeling of power.

But if the validity of power itself is determined by lawfulness, or, to use a less forbiddingly Kantian mode of expression, by an intuition of rightness, then power as such or even a specific form of the feeling of power cannot be the overriding aim, because the possibility remains that any given right action might in particular circumstances turn out to be strikingly easy or, at the least, totally unspectacular and capable of being confused with "weakness" without thereby losing its obligatory character. When Zarathustra demands kindness from the powerful as their "final self-conquest," he apparently places this noble exhortation within the sphere of thought that led him to define the good as the difficult. But suppose kindness should entail no self-conquest at all?

The question of this chapter is less the validity of the idea that will to power constitutes the essence of value systems in general than it is the possibility of analytically deriving a specifically Nietzschean ethic from the dualism strength/weakness, to which will to power points. When this possibility is examined afresh, however, the relevance of the objections just made to Nietzsche's procedure should become clear. For if the manifestation or, at the least, the self-consciousness, of power is the prime goal, or even an indispensable portion of the goal, then any possible confusion about the character of the psychological source of moral action, any doubt about whether it proceeds from strength or from weakness, would seem to threaten the very validity of the action concerned. Since, moreover, such doubt is often unavoidable, especially in the case of the "softer" virtues of kindness, the likelihood of founding an ethic that would resolutely require such virtues on Nietzschean premises appears bleak indeed. The individual is placed in the impossible position of having to live up to the demands of "strength" as defined by a particular moral code that includes kindness and gentleness, and having to be certain that he also lives up to the demands of strength in some broader sense. This would commit him to a veritable orgy of Puritanical introspection in order to be certain that his goodness was not the product of some secret weakness, or the vestigial remains of some pre-Nietzschean moral or religious doctrine that he never had the "courage" to renounce.

One way in which the particular character of the moral problem that will to power faces can be clarified is to compare it with a related difficulty in the philosophy of Kant, which Nietzsche could upon occasion praise specifically because of its alleged "cruelty," the severe asceticism that betokens both the presence of will to power and its spiritualization. The comparison I have in mind concerns the relation between consciousness of power as a goal of Nietzschean man and consciousness of morality, of acting for duty's sake alone, as a goal of Kantian man. The similarity between the two will do something to justify the connection Nietzsche drew between will to power and austere morality. The dissimilarity will help clarify the distinction between Nietzsche's analysis and a better, if not necessarily perfect, moral standpoint.

Much of Kantian morality centers around the conflict between rational obligation and personal inclination. The severity of Kant's ethics is due both to the desire to view ethics in such a way as to make this conflict intelligible and also, of course, to defend the authority of reason over purely personal caprice. The result of Kant's teaching was not to destroy the legitimacy of individual desire, but to subordinate it to a thorough principle of regulation that would separate legitimate from illegitimate ways of satisfying personal inclination. But it is also true that the highest moral and personal goal was, for Kant, acting for duty's sake alone rather than from personal inclination. This consideration placed considerable emphasis upon cases of conflict between duty and inclination because only in such cases of conflict would consciousness of duty as such be very clear. Where duty and inclination are one and the same, no specifically moral consciousness would be required. For the same reason, an action in which the individual chose duty *over* inclination would be more likely to indicate to both himself and others that he was moved by moral criteria than would an action that required no such choice. It is precisely this moral self-consciousness that gives rise to the Nietzschean suspicion that the root of the entire matter is a form of complex self-assertion and sublimated will to power, a suspicion only deepened by the consideration that the sole purely moral emotion Kant legitimized is *respect* (*Ehrfurcht*, i.e., honor-fear) for the law.

But consciousness of perfect dutifulness is not the aim of Kantian morality, not least because, for Kant himself, no one can ever possess such consciousness, since the determining ground of one's action always admits doubt even when the individual chooses duty over inclination. Kantian morality commands right action first and foremost, together with an effort at such moral self-consciousness as is conducive *to* right action. It does not command, and is indeed threatened by, a desire for a plentiude of moral *Machtgefühl*.[8] Partly as a consequence of this, partly out of hostility to any purely ascetic conception of personal fulfillment, the ultimate telos of Kantian man is not unitary, involving only consciousness of acting from duty alone, but dual, involving "worthiness" to be happy together with a happiness that derives from something other than awareness of having done one's duty. Nietzsche, by contrast, could synthesize the moral good with the aesthetic good in the concept of power only by making *Machtgefühl* into a truly indispensable ingredient of fulfillment, and this required what too often appears like the *subordination* of the morally good to the goal of the feeling of power.

Nietzsche never explicitly rejected the ideal outlined in Zarathustra's exhortation to the sublime, and he praised his *Zarathustra* in the most sweeping terms at the end of his creative life. But there is little that appears to continue the same line of thought, and much that implicitly rejects it. This can be gathered, even before we discuss his social thought in later chapters, from two very late notes.

> *Not* to make men "better," *not* to preach morality in any form, as if "morality in itself," or any ideal kind of man, were given; but to *create conditions* that *require stronger men* who for their part need, and consequently will *have*, a morality (more clearly: a physical-spiritual discipline) *that makes them strong!*
> Not to allow oneself to be misled by blue eyes or heaving bosoms: *greatness of soul has nothing romantic about it.* And unfortunately nothing at all amiable. (*WP*, #981)
> I should not like to undervalue the amiable virtues; but greatness of soul is not compatible with them. Even in the arts, the grand style excludes the pleasing. (*WP*, #1040)

The expression of regret in the first passage ("unfortunately") and the unwillingness to undervalue the "amiable virtues" in the second should certainly be noted. But these notes, by no means especially brutal for their period in Nietzsche's life, nevertheless bury Zarathustra's exhortation to the sublime and instead reinforce his notorious imperative, *become hard!* (*TSZ*, 3:12, 19). Caesar wins out against Christ, and the suggested synthesis, which predates these notes by several years, is almost forgotten.

There is, nevertheless, a line of thought in the period of *Zarathustra* and earlier upon which, perhaps more than on any other, the Kaufmann interpretation of Nietzsche's ethic rests, and which has not as yet been discussed. It is really a psychological argument, but with normative overtones, that true strength and true joy by nature exclude cruelty and even the desire to dominate. Faulty, or simply ambiguous and uncertain, as was Nietzsche's expression of this idea, too, it must be examined with the greatest care.

We may begin with a short aphorism from *Daybreak*: "*Feeling of Power*.—Be sure you mark the difference: he who wants to acquire the feeling of power resorts to any means and disdains nothing that will nourish it. He who has it, however, has become very fastidious and noble in his tastes;

he now finds few things to satisfy him" (*D*, #348). There is a hint here of the distinction between acting for power and from it, noted in the last chapter. But while Nietzsche seems to have believed in the dubious possibility that power is something one can simply have or not have, the aphorism also supports the reasonable view that power seeks more of itself, but at an increasingly high level of "taste." The meaning of "fastidious and noble," however, is not clear.

Another passage, from his notes, is of richer interest.

> I have found strength where one does not look for it: in simple, mild, and pleasant people, without the least desire to rule—and conversely, the desire to rule has often appeared to me as a sign of inward weakness: they fear their own slave soul and shroud it in a royal cloak; (in the end, they still become the slaves of their followers, their fame, etc.). The powerful natures *dominate*, it is a necessity, they need not lift one finger. Even if, during their life time, they bury themselves in a garden house.[9]

This ideal of effortless power, of domination *malgré lui*, certainly appealed to Nietzsche, and we shall encounter it again. But while this perception of a desire for power as a product of weakness is definitely edifying, the way in which powerful natures dominate, and the nature of that power which can be buried in a garden house, is left completely unclear. Do they, like Jesus, hate all sterner realities, and if not, how do we know? When other philosophers are edifying, they are pressed for details and demonstrations. Nietzsche's advantage as an "immoralist" was that he needed only to let fall a crumb of edification in order to be quoted with reverential relief.

A lengthier treatment of the relation between power and goodness appeared in the *Gay Science*.

> *On the doctrine of the feeling of power.*—Benefiting and hurting others are ways of exercising one's power upon others; that is all one desires in such cases. One hurts those whom one wants to feel [in] one's power, for pain is a much more efficient means to that end than pleasures; pain always raises the question about its origin while pleasure is inclined to stop with itself without looking back. We benefit and show benevolence to those who are already dependent on us in some way (which means that they are used to thinking of us as causes); we want to increase their power because in that way we increase ours, or we want to show them how advantageous it is to be in our power; that way they will become more satisfied with their condition and more hostile to and willing to fight against the enemies of *our* power....
> Certainly the state in which we hurt others is rarely as agreeable, in an unadulterated way, as that in which we benefit others; *it is a sign that we are still lacking power, or it shows a sense of frustration in the face of this*

poverty [emphasis added]; it is accompanied by new dangers and uncertainties for what power we do possess, and clouds our horizon with the prospect of revenge, scorn, punishment, and failure. It is only for the most irritable and covetous devotees of the feeling of power that it is perhaps more pleasurable to imprint the seal of power on a recalcitrant brow—those for whom the sight of those who are already subjected (the objects of benevolence) is a burden and boredom. What is decisive is how one is accustomed to *spice* one's life: it is a matter of taste whether one prefers the slow or the sudden, the assured or the dangerous and audacious increase of power; one seeks this or that spice depending on one's temperament. (*GS*, #13)

In a footnote to the words in the second paragraph that I have italicized, Kaufmann wrote: "Hurting others is a sign that one lacks power!" Surely in the light of the passage as a whole this apologetic enthusiasm is misplaced. To be sure, that Nietzsche was writing here in a spirit of psychological exploration rather than ethical prescription is not an objection to the aphorism or to Kaufmann's interpretation. Furthermore, the opinion that what we desire when we help others is the feeling of power, while problematic enough, could be taken as evidence that goodness and a kind of self-fulfillment can go hand in hand, very much in the fashion of eighteenth-century sentimentalism. But there are, nevertheless, grave problems with any clearly moralistic interpretation of this passage and its implications.

In the first place, that hurting others may be "accompanied by ... failure" is nothing but an argument from weakness, and to such an extent that one might think that whoever does not hurt others can never give an adequate display of strength.

Second, if "hurting others is a sign that one lacks power," then so, by the psychological presuppositions of the aphorism, is positive goodness toward others a sign that one lacks power. Either course appears as a need for self-confirmation which is equally suspicious. Nietzsche did not consider the alternative possibility in this simplistic exercise in reductionism that one "power" an individual might possess is the ability to judge whether his aid is desirable or not entirely in relation to the welfare of the other and not in relation to his own need for *Machtgefühl*. If the "sublimation" of the will to power is ever to proceed very far in a moral direction, it should be capable of this much. In *Zarathustra*, Nietzsche at least succeeded in briefly deflecting the emphasis away from the helper to the helped sufficiently to declare that pity humiliates (*TSZ*, 2:3). This is itself rather one-sided, but it is an improvement over the aphorism in the *Gay Science*. Still later, in *Beyond Good and Evil*, he did not consider this humiliation, and went back to the evaluation of moral action purely and simply in relation to the psychic state of the strong man (*BGE*, #293). Since, moreover, Nietzsche had earlier said in the same chapter of the same book that the noble man acts "not, or almost not, from pity, but prompted by an urge begotten by an excess of power" (*BGE*, #260), the entire emphasis remained misplaced, and Nietzsche would seem to endorse exactly what Zarathustra had proscribed.[10]

The aphorism "On the doctrine of the feeling of power" is not, then, very cogent in depicting, let alone advocating, a humane conception of strength. But in *Zarathustra*, Nietzsche had written: "Verily, I may have done this and that for sufferers; but always I seemed to have done better when I learned to feel better joys. As long as there have been men, man has felt too little joy: that alone, my brothers, is our original sin. And learning better to feel joy, we learn best not to hurt others or to plan hurts for them" (*TSZ*, 2: 3). Here, surely, is a passage that admits, even requires, an edifying interpretation. The desire to hurt others may require strength to be acted upon, but its innermost spring, Nietzsche appears to say, is a frustration for which the cruel person is in need of compensation. As such, it is weak. The "fastidious and noble taste" possessed by those who *have* power is given something of a moral content, even if it is limited and negative, and Nietzsche hence arrived at what has become, because of the central position of this doctrine in the psychological theories of Alfred Adler, a widely accepted observation that a mean and nasty aggressiveness is a sign of "insecurity."

But this achievement remains, from a moral point of view, grossly inadequate, because in the works of Nietzsche as in the life of mankind, overt cruelty is far less important than the cruelty that is rationalized in the name of some creative purpose. The individual who delights in inflicting brutal torture is less common, or, at any rate, less dangerous on a large scale than the individual who will trample upon large numbers of the human race, not for the self-magnification that comes directly from inflicting pain as such, but for the indirect self-magnification that comes from the subordination of others to an end he wishes to promote. Nowhere in Nietzsche's later works is such ruthlessness clearly condemned, and it is applauded directly or indirectly many times. Even Zarathustra himself, by explicitly recommending love of the "farthest" rather than love of the neighbor (*TSZ*, 1:16), undermines the humanity of much of his teaching. And when later he says: "Do love your neighbor as yourself, but first be such as *love themselves*—loving with a great love, loving with a great contempt" (*TSZ*, 3:5), he only worsens the situation and doubles the confusion. Both true self-love and self-contempt come together as a kind of creative spur to the creation of a higher man in a nobler future. But in this ambivalent mixture of love and contempt, what neighbor can escape the fear that he will be victimized by a love-contempt that is, from the victim's perspective, indistinguishable from pure contempt, even if the sacrificer himself has a more complex view of the matter? His fears would be reasonable, and it is not twentieth-century totalitarianism which alone informs us of this. "The magnitude of an 'advance' can even be measured by the mass of things that had to be sacrificed to it; mankind in the mass sacrificed to the prosperity of a single *stronger* species of man—that *would* be an advance" (*G*, 2:12).

There is another, more complicated problem. Zarathustra demands that we learn to feel more joy. Unfortunately, given the importance of pain and the conquest of pain in the theory of will to power, it is neither too obvious nor too pedantic to note that the joy that is to get us beyond cruelty cannot be a joy *in* cruelty. Triumph over pain presupposes pain, and this fact creates the greatest problems for the coherence of Nietzsche's total position, as will be seen shortly. These problems are not necessarily made less serious by assuming, as befits the focus of this chapter, that the cruelty of will to power is internalized rather than directed outward in its quest for victories. Internalized cruelty can be, as Nietzsche himself was exceedingly well aware, destabilizing in the extreme. In order to do justice to one of Nietzsche's more promising trains of thought, therefore, it is advisable to treat some of the evidence that suggests that he endorsed precisely the imposition of a measure of stability on the self and the creation of an enduring joy and self-satisfaction which, because no longer buffeted by the violent and exhausting oscillation between pain and triumph over pain, might issue in a reliable graciousness. The material relevant to this question, especially when the indirectly relevant is included, is enormous and, as always, ambiguous. An adequate survey would swell the length and tortuousness of this chapter to unpardonable dimensions. But the most important points can be summarized.

One of the most successful ways of demonstrating that the philosophy of the will to power was not conceived simply as a paean to barbarism is to show that Nietzsche's "taste" in both men and art frequently ran to the severely restrained and the majestically calm, as we should expect from the exhortation of Zarathustra to the sublime. It is worthy not merely of note but also of emphasis that the sometimes noisy and frequently melodramatic author of the *Antichrist* should have praised Goethe for the strength exhibited in his Olympian affirmations, to give only one example.

Yet at bottom judgments of this sort can be made to look as arbitrary, on Nietzsche's premises, as his judgment on the weakness of Jesus. Nor does this arbitrariness depend on whether the judgments are favorable or unfavorable. An example or two will suffice to show this. Nietzsche's doctrine that the capacity to suffer boldly and courageously, and overcome suffering, is one of the clearest indications of an individual's "rank"[11] is, at first sight, helpful in the evaluation of the personalities of artists and thinkers. But if we use this criterion to explicate some of Nietzsche's own evaluations, their rationality is made no less obscure. When he denigrated no less a sufferer and affirmer than Beethoven in comparison with Goethe by writing of them, respectively, "the man in need of comfort next to the man who *is* comforted" (*GS*, #103), one can ask whether Beethoven needed more comfort because he suffered more deeply and whether Goethe was comforted because he turned away whenever he could from whatever he could not bear. Evidence is not lacking for the latter belief. As Nietzsche was well aware, Goethe *could* not write a genuine tragedy, no mean failing in Nietzsche's eyes.[12] When, similarly, he praised Emerson above Carlyle because the former "nourished himself only on ambrosia, leaving behind what is indigestible in things" (*T*, "Skirmishes," 13), we are left wondering why an insight used to praise Emerson could not as easily be turned against him, as it surely would have been had Nietzsche not found Emerson attractive,[13] and found him useful to vent his own spleen against the splenetic, suffering, but upon occasion noble Carlyle.[14] Certainly Nietzsche was aware that the very same characteristics in a work of art or system of thought, whether calm or turbulent, could answer the needs of both the "strong" and the "weak" among their creators and spectators alike. The calm could be the need of those whose weakness needs comfort, or the need of the strong who love to *impose* order (and then become weak?) Or the turbulent could be the refuge of the undisciplined, undisciplinable weak, or else the favorite object of the strong who have faith in their "restorative" powers, and shrink from nothing (*GS*, #370).[15] From such inscrutable and relative standards as Nietzsche employed, Zarathustra's "All-too-small, the greatest!" (*TSZ*, 3:13) follows as a matter of course. "All have sinned, and fallen short of the glory of God."

If one says that Nietzsche wanted the absolute maximum of suffering, internal contradiction (which made for richness in his eyes), honesty in relation to life, and then the triumphant resolution of all the tensions thus produced, one could say of any given example in life or art that the triumph was only possible, especially when it is expressible with the greatest appearance of *ease*, because the obstacles overcome were not sufficiently great. But suppose that, notwithstanding the fierce judgmentalism of so much of his writing, Nietzsche was really after something different: that what is important is that the individual attain his own inward reconciliation, that he surmount such obstacles as he is burdened with, and that only in this way can he attain a poise that will enable him to be good. This is suggested in a remarkable aphorism from the *Gay Science*.

> *One thing is needful.*—To "give style" to one's character—a great and rare art! It is practiced by those who survey all the strengths and weaknesses of their nature and then fit them into an artistic plan until every one of them appears as art and reason and even weaknesses delight the eye. Here a large mass of second nature has been added; there a piece of original nature has been removed—both times through long practice and daily work at it....
>
> It will be the strong and domineering natures that enjoy their finest gaiety in ... constraint and perfection under a law of their own; the pas-

sion of their tremendous will relents in the face of all stylized nature, of all conquered and serving nature. Even when they have to build palaces and design gardens they demur at giving nature freedom.

Conversely, it is the weak characters without power over themselves that *hate* the constraint of style. They feel that if this bitter and evil constraint were imposed upon them they would be demeaned; they become slaves as soon as they serve; they hate to serve. Such spirits—and they may be of the first rank—are always out to shape and interpret their environment as *free* nature: wild, arbitrary, fantastic, disorderly, and surprising. And they are well advised because it is only in this way that they can give pleasure to themselves. For one thing is needful: that a human being should *attain* satisfaction with himself, whether it be by means of this or that poetry and art; only then is a human being at all tolerable to behold. Whoever is dissatisfied with himself is continually ready for revenge, and we others will be his victims, if only by having to endure his ugly sight. For the sight of what is ugly makes one bad and gloomy. (*GS*, #290)

The psychological interpretation of strength and weakness here is less cogent, and far less interesting from the standpoint of moral psychology than the way in which Nietzsche transcends, as he so often did not, the temptation to treat the antithesis strong/weak as a synonym for good/bad. Instead, he pointed to the internal resolution of the individual's conflicts, substituting a goal of self-contentment, which might serve an absolute moral purpose, the transcendence of revenge and of the victimization of anyone, for the hopeless relativities of strength/weakness. Does the dialectic of this chapter, then, have a suitably happy ending? Unfortunately, it does not.

The problem with regarding this fine piece of writing as truly definitive of Nietzsche's position is twofold. If, on the one hand, the artistic self-formation and stabilization of the character is defended because of its *moral fruits*, then will to power, to say nothing of personal autonomy, is not the supreme principle, but is instead subordinated to a regulative moral ideal that requires harmony between people and, by extension, harmony within individuals as a means to that end. This is clearly an illegitimate reading of Nietzsche as a whole. If, on the other hand, what is praised is the power required to give "style to one's character," from which beneficial moral consequences might flow as a side-effect that here unquestionably pleased Nietzsche, then we are faced with the problem of determining how and why any particular "style" and self-limitation is really the product of strength or weakness, a problem suggested by the aphorism itself. We must also wonder whether the mood of stable self-contentment is, in Nietzsche's eyes, always as appealing, or as noble, as more dialectical, tension-filled joys, those springing from power as an open-ended lust for victories. Zarathustra castigated "the most despicable man …, he that is no longer able to despise himself" (*TSZ*, Prologue, 5). Nietzsche also praised those whose faith in themselves was entirely unshakable. The result was that he could be interpreted with equal legitimacy as pointing toward noble discontent or noble complacency.[16]

Plato had, in the *Philebus*, long ago stigmatized what he termed the "impure pleasures," those involving a mixture of pleasure and pain, and above all those involving a dependence of the former on the overcoming of the latter, as inherently immoderate. And certainly they suggest a constant process of transition to which no end can be readily assigned, while the very act of continuous comparison made by the mind and feelings between pleasure and pain serves to stimulate desire to dreams of an ever greater intensification. When pleasure and pain are synthesized in a will to power that wants victory and the feeling of power, this open-endedness becomes obvious. The early Nietzsche had explicitly warned against stretching oneself to a dangerous degree (*D*, #559). The later Nietzsche, by contrast, largely justifies the view of Werner Dannhauser that "the transvaluation of all values [Nietzsche's polemical term for his philosophical project] seems to be above all intended to abolish moderation."[17]

"*Measure* is alien to us," he wrote in *Beyond Good and Evil*, just after writing of the splendid nobility of classical calm: "let us own it; our thrill is the thrill of the infinite, the unmeasured. Like a rider on a steed that flies forward, we drop the reins before the infinite, we modern men, like semi-barbarians—and reach *our* bliss only where we are most—*in danger*" (*BGE*, #224). That Nietzsche was writing about himself here, and not excoriating *other* moderns, is clear.[18] The bold self-exposure to danger, which in his own case meant dangerous ideas, was for him strength. The problem is that any truly bold self-exposure must, if truly radical, endanger that poise apparently recommended by the aphorism "One thing is needful" (from a work that also says "*live dangerously!*") (*GS*, #283). The triumphant *resolution* of conflict, inner or outer, might testify to power for the moment, but it seems to promise death for the next moment. The acceptance of measure on moral grounds would then appear to be an illicit importation of a moral principle into a will to power by nature adverse to it.

> What is good? Everything that heightens the feeling of power in man, the will to power, power itself.
> What is bad? Everything that is born of weakness.
> What is happiness? The feeling that power is *growing*, that resistance is overcome.
> Not contentedness but more power; not peace but war; not virtue but fitness. (*A*, #2)

One could still say that power is of many kinds, and is not necessarily over other people. Yet Nietzsche's difficulty in conceiving, or at least describing, a will to power at once stably triumphant over its own sufferings and sublimated above any need to inflict harm on others is brought out with excruciating vividness in the following very late note.

> The value of a man (apart from his morality or immorality, naturally; for with these concepts the value of a man is not even touched) does not reside in his utility; for it would continue to exist even if there were no one to whom he could be of any use. And why could not precisely that man who produced the most disastrous effects be the pinnacle of the whole species of man: so high, so superior that everything would perish from envy of him? (*WP*, #877)

There are more ghastly quotations to be found in Nietzsche, but perhaps none more subtle or more instructive in its ghastliness than this one. It illuminates both the artificiality of this entire chapter's focus upon Nietzsche's idea of individual power in abstraction from his social thought and, at the same time, the necessity of making the fruitless attempt to maintain such a focus. For there is a kind of "innocence" here. If the greatness to which Nietzsche points in this passage does not require someone to whom to be of use, it also, presumably, does not require someone to dominate. But Nietzsche could not make intelligible what this supreme being is going to do with his time, and in what his power really consists. Instead, following a well-known precept of Lessing that, since beauty cannot be described in words, it is best to describe its *effect*, he proceeded to give the measure of the power of this self-enclosed, presumably by-no-means-malicious being, by describing his effects, his baneful effects, on the envious. This, then, is a proper "sublimation" of the will to power. The sublimated one is too powerful, too fulfilled, to deign either to dominate or to love. But he creates ruin in his path anyway. Someone has to suffer somehow. Only then can it remain clear that the most sublimated consummation of will to power is still will to power, and not the consummation of love.

But, on the other hand, Nietzsche also wrote: "*Type*: True graciousness, nobility, greatness of soul proceed from abundance; do not give in order to receive—do not try to exalt themselves by being gracious;—prodigality as the type of true graciousness, abundance of personality as its presupposition" (*WP*, #935). This note, quoted in its entirety, is from the same late period as the one quoted above. It expresses a leading conviction of Zarathustra, one which holds, in essence, that only those who have can give away. But where is the lust for victories?

Yet one could argue that these two quotations, though not compatible in their moral tenor, nevertheless proceed from the same style of thought: one which attempted to define individual greatness without regarding the way in which the individual relates to the other as being really crucial, but of secondary significance. When strength and greatness are conceived this way, they permit the thinker, the *spectator*, to relish their perfection by heaping up a congeries of attributes that enhance the total effect. But as long as the effect in question is not regulated by some principles that relate individual greatness to a mode of being with the other, the moral character of this greatness will fluctuate hopelessly from the strength that issues in graciousness to the strength that issues in the other's death, a death not necessarily from envy. What is termed "morality" need not by any means be regarded as the sole constituent of the "good life." But only the "pure in heart" can smuggle it in through the back door. Nietzsche was not, and did not want to be, pure in heart. Are not the pure in heart those who desire such strength as they need for what they want and for what they ought to do, being content to leave the rest alone? And if one should maintain, determined to rescue and moralize Nietzsche's method at all costs, that those who are beyond the need for *Machtgefühl* are precisely the strongest of men, then one must add that these are also those who do not care if they appear weak unless there is some compelling reason for them to appear otherwise. Such a view, so far from rescuing Nietzsche's method, destroys it root and branch. The ideal of Caesar and Christ becomes not so much unthinkable as not worthy of being thought. More precisely, the ideal, if worthy, describes a being worthy of worship, not one which one can very clearly aim to embody in oneself or create in a future humanity. To load predicates of perfection on an object of worship may be legitimate, provided they are not logically incompatible. But the perfect does not have to strive to become perfect. Imperfect beings, by contrast, must strive; and they can only do so with the aid of principles that sometimes force a choice between being good and appearing strong, or between being strong in a purely moral sense and being strong in an extra-moral sense. For this reason, an imperative that is to be morally meaningful cannot have the hopeless ambiguity that the synthesis of "Caesar and Christ" must possess for anyone who strives to embody it and seeks to choose his course of action accordingly.

The ultimate ground of this ambiguity in Nietzsche already appeared clearly disclosed, if tentatively and politely expressed, at the beginning of the 1880s; and this chapter, which began with the discussion of a saintly aphorism from *Daybreak* can conclude with the discussion of another from the same work. In an aphorism entitled *"The realm of beauty is bigger,"* Nietzsche asked:

Is it then forbidden to *enjoy* the *evil* man as a wild landscape possessing its own bold lineaments and effects of light, if the same man appears to our eyes as a sketch and caricature and, as a blot in nature, causes us pain, when he poses as good and law-abiding?—Yes, it is forbidden: hitherto

we have been permitted to seek beauty only in the *morally good*—a fact
which sufficiently accounts for our having found so little of it and having
had to seek about for imaginary beauties without backbone!—As surely
as the wicked enjoy a hundred kinds of happiness of which the virtuous
have no inkling, so too they possess a hundred kinds of beauty: and many
of them have not yet been discovered. (*D*, #468)

Here Nietzsche referred unmistakably to the tradition I have termed ethical-
aestheticism, a tradition that, albeit in varying ways, identified the highest
beauty and happiness with the moral life. His criticism was that the expo-
nents of this tradition had implicitly begun with a selective criterion for
beauty and happiness that ensured their compatibility with moral requirements at the very start. While no attempt need be made here to assess the
truth of this contention fully, there is much to be said on its behalf.[19] Equally significantly, Nietzsche accepted one of the cardinal assumptions of the
main destroyer of this tradition, Immanuel Kant. For in defending the necessity of deriving the moral law from a pure practical reason that abstracts
from all empirical conditions, Kant insisted that the criteria of happiness are
discovered empirically and, most important, vary according to the constitu-
tions of different individuals. Consequently, no universally binding law
could be based upon the nature and implications of "happiness." Nietzsche's claim, already cited, that whether one's happiness includes or excludes
the exercise of aggressive domination is entirely a matter of how one wishes
"to spice one's life," is in a sense in complete conformity with this Kantian
doctrine. But, of course, Kant's critique of the ethical-aesthetic tradition had
been accompanied by making explicit what ethical-aestheticisms had left implicit: the primacy of the moral. In other words, where ethical-aestheticisms
had asserted that all "true" happiness required conformity with humane
morality, Kant's separation of the moral law from individual happiness
involved recognizing the multiple sources of happiness for different individuals; but in isolating the demands of morality from the question of happiness, Kant wished to place those demands in a position where they could
regulate all action undertaken to achieve happiness, however defined, permitting what was compatible with morality and prohibiting what was not.
Nietzsche, however, did not follow this procedure or an alternative one that
would accomplish the same result. On the contrary, as we have seen, his
efforts to redefine the quest for happiness as the desire for *Machtgefühl*, and
to redefine beauty as "power," did not permit him more than fleeting efforts
to achieve a consistent moralization of the concept of power, because there is
no power that is infallibly humane, just as there is no beauty that is infallibly
humane, unless morally relevant predicates are introduced into the concept
of power or of beauty from the start. Thus it was only a step, if not necessarily a step Nietzsche took without hesitation, from the polite language of

Daybreak to the final verdict Nietzsche pronounced on Plato, the philosophic father of all ethical-aesthetic syntheses, at the close of his career:
"Plato is boring" (*T*, "What I owe to the Ancients," 2).

3
Affirmation, Self-Confirmation, and Selection: Thoughts on the Concept of "Eternal Recurrence"

THE famous Nietzschean doctrine of the eternal recurrence of the same is a philosopher's doctrine expressing a contemplative ecstasy and supposedly resting on objective demonstration. But it is also meant to be personal, both for Nietzsche himself and for all those who accept it, related to concrete experience and capable of being relished accordingly. As the supreme expression of strength, eternal recurrence recapitulates and intensifies rather than dissolves the moral and psychological tensions we have already found in that concept. Yet the true greatness and depth, not of the doctrine itself, which is dubious in the extreme and has been criticized even by some who find little else in Nietzsche to criticize,[1] but of the intention behind it, can scarcely be grasped in purely moralistic terms. Eternal recurrence attempts to unite time and eternity, striving and being, action and contemplation in a way that is truly impossible. But Nietzsche's uniqueness and profundity as a spiritual personality are perhaps best revealed in his desire to attain these reconciliations.

Eternal recurrence has at times been interpreted in exceedingly rarefied, not to say far-fetched, terms. Here I assume, along with the majority of scholars, that Nietzsche meant by it exactly what he said: that all things that happen now have happened before and will happen again an infinite number of times in the future (*TSZ*, 3:2, 2). Nietzsche never published any attempt to prove this teaching, and it is probably misleading to regard it as having been forced upon him by sheer scientific honesty. He may, in fact, have been highly dissatisfied with the proof his notes contain.[2] But he did at least seriously flirt with a scientific proof based upon what he took to be essential verities of modern cosmology, finite matter and infinite time. When these were taken together, he believed they necessitated the perpetual reappearance of any given concatenation of forces (*WP*, #1066). The only alternative possibility, a state of permanent equilibrium, was excluded, Nietzsche believed, by the consideration that if such a state were possible, it would already have been reached. Since it has not been reached, it must be impossible, an argument that seems to presuppose an extremely simplistic metaphysic of time. While the logical underpinning of eternal recurrence has long been found inadequate[3] and has seldom found supporters, the very character of the proof employed for it indicates the advisability of a straightforward and literal interpretation of what the doctrine claims. The existential purposes on which Nietzsche most insisted in connection with recurrence indicate a similar advisability.

These purposes, their interrelation with one another, and the complex questions they raise about the affirmation of life that the affirmation of recurrence was intended to express are all far more intriguing than the proof. First and foremost, as many scholars have noted, Nietzsche intended that eternal recurrence should act as a kind of imperative, one which would induce the individual to choose a life and a mode of action he would *want* to recur. This imperative character is clear from the memorable first introduction of the idea in Nietzsche's published work.

> *The greatest weight.*—What, if some day or night a demon were to steal after you into your loneliness and say to you: "This life as you now live it and have lived it, you will have to live once more and innumerable times more; and there will be nothing new in it, but every pain and every joy and every thought and sigh and everything unutterably small or great in your life will have to return to you, all in the same succession and sequence—even this spider and this moonlight between the trees, and even this moment and I myself. The eternal hourglass of existence is turned upside down again and again, and you with it, speck of dust!"
>
> Would you not throw yourself down and gnash your teeth and curse the demon who spoke thus? Or have you once experienced a tremendous moment when you would have answered him: "You are a god and never have I heard anything more divine." If this thought gained possession of you, it would change you as you are or perhaps crush you. The question in each and every thing, "Do you desire this once more and innumerable times more?" would lie upon your actions as the greatest weight. Or how well disposed would you have to become to yourself and to life to *crave nothing more fervently* than this ultimate eternal confirmation and seal? (*GS*, #341)

Recurrence owed part of its appeal to Nietzsche from its being, not merely an imperative, but also an immanent one, coming from and referring solely to this life rather than to a beyond, and yet exacting precisely that infinite affirmation which Christianity had reserved for God and the heavenly life alone.

The status of eternal recurrence as an imperative, however, renders any dissatisfaction Nietzsche may have felt with his scientific proof readily understandable. Even if his demonstration were valid, it would prove too much. The necessary return of all things because of objective truths about time, force, and matter would mean that anything that *could* happen would happen an infinite number of times and nothing else would happen at all. In this scheme of things, the individual creative will does not create and, almost more important, it does not exclude. What the individual does not want will return as inevitably as what he does want if both are possible in the nature of things, and neither will occur at all if it is not so possible. The objective guarantee of recurrence is at variance with the reality of choice that guarantee is supposed to encourage.[4]

Let us suppose, however, that Nietzsche has demonstrated what he sought to prove: that what one chooses will recur and what one is capable of avoiding in one's life will be eternally excluded from reality. This only opens the prospect of subtle but no less serious problems for the existential significance of the doctrine. The depth of the eternal return is its attempt to fuse an imperative inspiring a life of open process with a timeless perspective of affirmation in which one steps outside process in order to bless it, savor it, and welcome the prospect of its perpetual return. But can one really fuse the moment of choice, burdened by "the greatest weight," with a blessing that can only be *retrospective* if it is to have any concrete meaning? Eternal recurrence as an "existential imperative" addresses an individual in the full insecurity of becoming. If the imperative is to exert any influence, he must be engaged in choosing his future. This means that he should be exerting himself to realize a specific content and specific values that he can affirm, and he must be continually anxious that circumstances beyond his control will threaten them. How does he bestow infinite affirmation on this very insecurity itself and on the very possibility of failure that it denotes?

The concept of play, of which Nietzsche was fond, might seem to offer an answer to this question. For play is in its essence often an affirmation of risk itself, and the enjoyment of the challenge and the activity involved is often as important as the outcome. But while this helps make Nietzschean affirmation intelligible, that affirmation remains inevitably problematic. What is at stake, after all, is not a more or less tolerable existence, that of the good loser, but total affirmation. One can affirm in the abstract the general conditions of life and logic alike which decree that there must be losers for there to be winners, or that the possibility of failure must be real for the prospect of success to be meaningful; but one cannot affirm one's own particular existence with the same concrete sense of joyous triumph regardless of whether one wins or loses, succeeds or fails. To do so would be to remove oneself from access to the very personal *Machtgefühl* that Nietzsche extolled and approach instead the nonattachment that is the gateway to the nihilism (often known as wisdom) he fought. Nietzsche strongly emphasized courage, chance, and risk as positive values to the healthy man; and this was not entirely unreasonable. But the abstract affirmation of risk is not the same thing as the concrete affirmation of something that has already been experienced; and it is precisely Nietzsche's most ecstatic, amorous evocation of eternal recurrence that is most expressly tied, not to the future, but to the past.

> Have you ever said Yes to a single joy? O my friends, then you said Yes too to *all* woe. All things are entangled, ensnared, enamored; if ever you wanted one thing twice, if ever you said, "You please me, happiness! Abide, moment!" then you wanted *all* back. All anew, all eternally, all entangled, ensnared, enamored—oh, then you *loved* the world. Eternal ones, love it eternally and evermore; and to woe too, you say: go, but return! *For all joy wants—eternity.* (*TSZ*, 4:19, 10)

In contrast with this gracious affirmation of the already attained, which eternal recurrence permits and encourages, the same doctrine considered as an imperative directing the future must have a different emotional quality. Obviously, I am not speaking here of any logical contradiction. To love something in the past in such a way as to enable one to want its eternal return, and to accept the eternal return of even the most painful for its sake, can be an inducement to live the future in a way that will invite the same affirmation. But the psychological gap remains wide. For retrospective affirmation, eternal recurrence is wish-fulfillment; considered in respect to the future, it is promise marching hand in hand with *threat*. And in concrete existence, either retrospection or an anxious orientation toward the future can devour the other. The burden of the future may seem so great that the bliss of relishing the past, and affirming all for its sake, may seem something for which one cannot spare the time. Or one can use the past as a means to cease willing the future by dubbing it worth returning and constituting, by itself, a fulfillment of one's existence. The former alternative is no doubt healthier, but it is the latter in which recurrence comes into its own as what Nietzsche wished it to be, the "highest formula of affirmation that is at all conceivable" (*EH*, *TSZ*, 1).

Eternal recurrence is thus poised uneasily between compulsive vitality and decadence. The one points to more life, the other may emanate from death. At issue here is not Nietzsche's personal psychology but the question of whether the affirmation of eternal recurrence really provides what Nietzsche intended it to provide, an objective touchstone of personal strength that cannot be misused by the unconsciously morbid for morbid ends. In order to clarify this possible misuse of recurrence from a specifically Nietzschean perspective, it will help to note Nietzsche's philosophy of death briefly. He believed in the desirability of "free death," one which would convert the "stupid physiological fact into a moral necessity. So to live that one can also

will at the right time to die!" (*WP*, #916, cf. *TSZ*, 1:21, "On Free Death").
But Nietzsche could never give any concreteness to this demand.[5] From the
stand-point of his own philosophy at its most humane, he was probably
much wiser when, in the *Gay Science*, he wrote: "It makes me happy that
men do not want at all to think the thought of death! I should like very much
to do something that would make the thought of life even a hundred times
more appealing to them" (*GS*, #278). Even the loss of creative energy does
not preclude a genuinely enriching spectatorial old age, as Zarathustra
himself seemed to recognize (*TSZ*, 1:21). Nietzsche's dilemma was that the
very idea of a meaningful movement from birth to a death that was not
to be regarded as entrance into eternal life presupposes the possibility of
experiencing "enough" of life. But the requirement of "health" and eternal
recurrence was that one should regard life as something of which one could
not possibly have enough. This contrast permits a restatement of the alternatives. A healthy, hopeful individual will charge into the future in search
of the maximum experience of power, undeterred by anything in his past,
positive or negative. A declining will, by contrast, will search through his
past for something upon which he can bestow an ultimate affirmation. But
this very retrospective graciousness may be prompted by fatigue, and the
affirmation itself may serve only to give a good Nietzschean conscience to
suicide at the "right time." The healthy will has no sense of consummation
at all. The declining will has a sense of consummation that might be a complete delusion. Neither can make something meaningful of life as a whole, as
a spiritual movement from life to the acceptance of death. Yet Nietzsche
himself seems to have recognized the reality and the importance of just such
a progress in meaning. A beautiful aphorism from *Beyond Good and Evil*
(a book that makes no mention of recurrence) reads in its entirety: "One
should part from life as Odysseus parted from Nausicaa—blessing it rather
than in love with it" (*BGE*, #96). This is completely at variance with the
mood of Zarathustra's famous "Was *that* life? ... Well then! Once more!"
(*TSZ*, 4:19). To view life as a movement toward a state from which one
blesses life while no longer in love with it can only mean searching for the
transcendence of that relentless dynamism which was usually the essence of
will to power and the essence, as well, of eternal recurrence when viewed as
an imperative directed toward the future.

There is another, if closely related, issue. To attempt to consider life as a
meaningful affirmative movement through life toward death may require a
fundamental distinction between two different kinds of joy that Nietzsche
never made: between those which are primarily superficial in nature and
those which are spiritual and cumulatively progressive, and which may, for
that very reason, lend themselves less to the desire for repetition than to the
desire for consummation and completion. One can imagine affirming an
eternal recurrence of a magnificent feast, provided hunger also eternally re-

curs, because the pleasures of dining, for most of us, do not involve stages in
a gustatory education that recurrence would threaten to turn into an exercise
in Sisyphusan futility. Because superficial joys are not primarily cumulative
in nature, they do not contribute to a larger synthetic happiness from whose
perspective joys that were once intense now strike one as a bore. The most
deeply meaningful joys, by contrast, may be those which lead to a sense of
having lived a life one can bless without any desire to live it again. Or, such
joys may appear to be capable of an infinite enrichment, like those of knowledge, art, and love; but this very infinitude must make the prospect of start-
ing over again profoundly unattractive. For this reason, to find eternal recurrence unappealing need not be the result of weakness or a hatred of life,
but may instead spring from a love of life that is rooted in the linear character of spiritual progression. Such a love, whether of goodness or knowledge,
wants more goodness and more knowledge, not the eternal return of one's
original sin or pristine ignorance. From this point of view, it scarcely matters
whether one accepts death as the gateway to a greater life or instead makes
the acceptance of death into the final, consummating phase of the wisdom of
life and the acceptance of life, parting from life with a blessing rather than in
love with it. Either way, recurrence may seem equally meaningless. Given
the spirituality of Nietzsche's own conception of joy, one might be able to
conclude that his attempt to reconcile that conception with the circularity
suitable to raw and unsublimated vitality rather than the linearity suitable to
spirit was an attempt to reconcile the irreconcilable and doomed to failure.

Nietzschean affirmation has a dual focus. It refers to the self on the one
hand, the strong will that manifests itself in the strength of its affirmation,
and, on the other, to life, the earth, and the concrete blessings they contain
for the self. One difficulty of that affirmation is that a gap and even a conflict
threaten to appear between these two poles; and this is the most serious
consequence of the self-deception which that affirmation invites. To put the
point more circumspectly, it provides the most serious ambiguity between
self-deceptive and authentic affirmation. Clarification of this ambiguity and
its basis should clarify as well the gravity of the possible self-deception
entailed in the concept of the eternal return.

Nietzsche recognized that a concrete individual does not will power as
such, but a particular goal or a particular form of power. But as the philosopher of the will to power, he believed, as we have seen in an earlier
chapter, that particular goals are willed for the sake of power as such.
Human life then presents the following broad possibilities:

Man can be an instinctive animal, attaining goals not consciously chosen,
in sheer stupidity.

Or he can attain them intelligently, but only with the aid of an objective
axiology that denies the absolute freedom of the value-creating self. This
alternative, the post-animal, pre-Nietzschean stage of humanity, is repre-

sented by false philosophy and all religion.

Finally, in true or Nietzschean philosophy, man recognizes his absolute freedom and recognizes, simultaneously, that concrete goals exist for the sake of power and the *feeling* or self-manifestation of power. This means that he affirms his abstract ability to affirm more than he affirms the concrete goals of freedom.

The affirmation of affirmation has a distinct advantage over concrete affirmations as a principle of life. The individual is removed from dependence on continual success. Moreover, it both permits diversity of goal according to the diversity of individuals and, equally important, it permits diversity for the same individual who, in essence, affirms not a particular condition, but his capacity to make the most of *any* condition. The strong man is he who is less dependent upon favorable circumstances to make something worthwhile out of life. Unfortunately, this very advantage, in which the abstractness of the principle of will to power is ultimately shown to be partially valid as a reflection of the freedom of the human condition, becomes a threat to coherence. To the degree that the individual focuses his affirmation, not upon a particular object or condition, but upon his capacity to make the most of any condition, to that degree he is paradoxically dependent upon nonsuccess. Affirmation of affirmation becomes affirmation in *spite* of, an affirmation of what one is profoundly tempted to negate. Only with the aid of such self-mortifying, ascetic affirmation can the individual feel his own strength and independence at their maximum intensity. "Unsterblich ist der Augenblick, wo ich die Wiederkunft zeugte. Um dieses Augenblickes willen *ertrage* ich die Wiederkunft," runs a complete note. "Immortal is the moment when I begot recurrence. For the sake of this moment, I can *bear* recurrence" (*M*, 14:132). Only because of the moment when Nietzsche could triumph over his own immense sufferings with their ultimate affirmation was his life sweet enough to enable him to bear its return. But one must wonder whether this triumph is real, constituting a genuine joy, or is merely what Ludwig Klages called a "negation of negation."[6]

One should not base too much upon an isolated note, however characteristic it appears to this author to be. One might also argue that, while Klages's contention that eternal recurrence was a kind of desperate counterweight to a suicidal inclination has considerable plausibility,[7] such a biographical fact has little relevance to the philosophical critique of Nietzsche's doctrine. This is perhaps true. But two things should be said. First, Nietzsche is often presented as a kind of *hero* of affirmation, as if there could be no question of the sincerity and authenticity of his "everlasting yeas," if a Carlylean phrase might be permitted in this context. One need not begrudge Nietzsche any distinction to which he was entitled or begrudge his admirers any valuable edification they can derive in order to question this authenticity. The reason for raising this question is simply that Nietzsche as a philosopher took it upon himself to provide valid criteria by which to distinguish the true from the false, the self-deceptive from the honest. I would argue only that there are good reasons for doubting this in the case of the idea of eternal recurrence, as with many other Nietzschean propositions.

Second, the works Nietzsche himself published afford reason to question the character of his affirmation and reinforce this skepticism. Precisely when affirmation of eternal recurrence and the related doctrine of *amor fati* (love of fate) are elevated to the rank of touchstones, they most invite use as a means whereby the individual can prove himself to himself. "My formula of greatness in a human being is *amor fati*: that one wants nothing different, not forward, not backward, not in all eternity. Not merely bear what is necessary, still less conceal it—all idealism is mendaciousness in the face of what is necessary—but *love* it" (*EH*: "Why I am so clever,"10). Is it graciousness and a genuine joy or desperate self-assertion that predominates here? The use of *amor fati* to prove strength can easily become abuse as the individual endeavors to convince himself of the reality of his strength by a deceptive affirmation of his life. The deception is *invited* by the very weight of information the affirmation is supposed to reveal about the self. All affirmation becomes difficult to distinguish from a pose of health when it is a matter only of sweeping words that cost nothing and hence prove nothing. What makes this whole line of inquiry reasonable and fair, and not simply an exercise in unsympathetic cruelty, is that Nietzsche himself remarked in the *Genealogy of Morals*, that celebrated treatise on resentment and its self-deceptions, that an individual is not healthy just because he feels healthy (*G*, 3:16), a remark applicable *a fortiori* to those who only *say* they are healthy. Elsewhere in the same work he insisted that all men of resentment are in the habit of attempting "to persuade themselves, *deceive* themselves, that they are happy" (*G*, 1:10). Nietzsche did not invite any consideration of whether these remarks might be applicable to himself, but the possibility cannot be ruled out arbitrarily. Worth noting in this connection is the extraordinary defensiveness with which he insisted that his endless negations were merely the corollary of his affirmations rather than the reverse, that he was the very opposite of a negating spirit, a point he thought it necessary to make three times in various ways (*EH*: *TSZ*, 6; *EH*: "Why I am a Destiny," 1; *T*; "What the Germans Lack," 6). But repetition is particularly unconvincing in an issue of this kind. The fact remains that almost every affirmation in Nietzsche concerns either himself, the universe as a whole, an as yet unrealized ideal, or some other individual or group the affirmation of whom is immediately and directly employed to degrade someone else. The negation of negation may seem better than pure negation; but when one realizes that for Nietzsche negation of negation merely facilitates negation and gives it an air of righteous indignation, it is difficult to be certain even of that.

The difficulty is only increased when we reflect that Nietzsche intended the idea of recurrence to be, not merely a powerful inducement to people to make the most of their lives, but also a selective force that would destroy those who could not bear the prospect of the eternal return of their misery (*WP*, #462, 1053, 1056, 1058). One should not overemphasize this selective intention, which was mentioned briefly, vaguely, and only in notes. Perhaps Nietzsche rejected the idea altogether. This sinister aspect of recurrence was probably not a very serious contribution to "breeding" a stronger humanity. Still less does it demonstrate any depth of personal malice on Nietzsche's part. But it does testify to the necessity of taking his quest for self-affirmation and self-justification seriously when considering the reasons for his attachment to recurrence. For if he imagined, however fitfully, that the thought of the eternal return of one's misery would destroy anyone, surely it is not unwarranted to surmise that at times the doctrine must have inspired nothing short of terror in Nietzsche himself. And if this was so, then at least part of the attraction of affirming recurrence must have consisted in the opportunity such affirmation afforded to affirm himself in spite of and also, paradoxically, *because* of that terror. So regarded, eternal recurrence threatens to become, not the highest principle of affirmation ever conceived, but the most guilt-ridden inspiration ever received, born of a need to escape an appalling threat of failure. One need not accept such an interpretation as decisive (I certainly do not myself) in order to appreciate with its aid how ambiguous Nietzsche was, or, to put it less personally, how ambiguous Nietzscheanism is.

If one cannot exclude the possibility that "guilt" in a psychological rather than a theological-moral sense operates in eternal recurrence,[8] one must immediately add that the doctrine was intended explicitly to counter theological-moral notions of guilt. Nietzsche associated it, perhaps because of the principles of determinism employed in its proof, with the *innocence* of necessity. Recurrence was coupled in his mind at times with a kind of tolerance toward the "mistakes" (*Irrthümer*) of others as opposed to the intolerance visited upon "evil deeds" (*M*, 11:187–88). Zarathustra, in one of his most justly celebrated speeches, "On Redemption," had defined the essence of the will's misery as the inability to "will backwards." "This, indeed this alone, is what *revenge* is: the will's ill will against time and its 'it was.'" Carried to its highest pitch, this ill will turns against life as a whole.

> For "punishment" is what revenge calls itself; with a hypocritical lie it creates a good conscience for itself.
> Because there is suffering in those who will, inasmuch as they cannot will backwards, willing itself and all life were supposed to be—a punishment. And now cloud upon cloud rolled over the spirit, until eventually madness preached, "Everything passes away; therefore everything de-

serves to pass away. And this too is justice, this law of time that it must devour its children."

"Things are ordered morally according to justice and punishment....

"Can there be redemption if there is eternal justice? Alas, the stone *It was* cannot be moved: all punishments must be eternal too." Thus preached madness....

I led you away from these fables when I taught you, "The will is a creator." All "it was" is a fragment, a riddle, a dreadful accident—until the creative will says, "But thus I willed it." (*TSZ*, 2:20)

One need not deny the magnificence of either the insight or the intention revealed here. But the will cannot will backward any more genuinely with the aid of recurrence than without it. The past cannot be willed but only accepted, detested, or forgotten, and there is perhaps little to be gained by dignifying one's helplessness by an illusion of power indistinguishable from mere submission.[9] It might be replied that Nietzsche understood the commonsense point that the past as such is out of our power, and that his entire aim was simply to lend a redemptive depth to the notion that one should so live the present as to want the return of the entire past for its sake. That can only mean, however, that one uses recurrence and the idea of the highest principle of affirmation to bestow an idolatrous infatuation upon personal experience that can be trivial in the extreme from any objective standpoint, an infatuation that scarcely makes any sense even from a subjective standpoint. Eternal recurrence as pure affirmation implies that nothing except what was in the past and is in the present will do, that nothing greater can be conceived. As a result, one "wills" every past calamity that has ever been inflicted upon humanity for the sake of the eternal return of this or that moment of joy it might have been quite possible to live affirmatively and unresentfully without because without those calamities one's world would be different and one's joy different. But one cannot even have any assurance that the joy in question, though different, would have been any less. Even Dr. Pangloss might have balked.

4

The Master and the Slave

THE core of the *Genealogy of Morals* is contained within a famous distinction, that between master and slave moralities, and an equally famous theory, that the "bad conscience," or moral guilt-feeling, originates from an internalization of the will to power. I shall present both very briefly and uncritically before proceeding to amplification and critical comment.

Master-morality belongs to a dominant, warlike horde or race. It represents, first and foremost, their self-affirmation and joy in life. The "good" is whatever they believe belongs to them and to their conquering instincts. Because the essence of master-morality is constituted by affirmation, its negatives, such as "bad," "unhappy," and "base," are only derivative, and are ways of designating the opposite of its affirmations (G, 1:10).

In slave-morality, by contrast, the negative is of fundamental importance. The overpowered slave who revolts ideologically against his condition does so by inventing a series of distinctions by which to condemn his master as "evil" and to affirm himself, not directly and spontaneously, but indirectly and "reactively," as the one who does *not* do the evil the conquerors perpetrate. (Since, in fact, he cannot do this evil, the pejorative connotations of this way of defining the essence of slave-morality are a continuation of Zarathustra's contempt for those who are good only because they have no claws.) The morality of the slave is in its essence resentment and hate, and develops religions, Judaism and Christianity, and philosophical tenets, such as free will, in order to enjoy a revenge in thought that is denied in reality (G, 1).

Much later Nietzsche gave his "hypothesis" concerning the origin of the "bad conscience," the self-torment undertaken with the aid of moral ideas. The background for this was the sudden change effected by the forcible incorporation of previously free beings into a tightly organized society.

I regard the bad conscience as the serious illness that man was bound to contract under the stress of the most fundamental change he ever experienced—that change which occurred when he found himself finally enclosed within the walls of society and of peace. The situation that faced sea animals when they were compelled to become land animals or perish was the same as that which faced these semi-animals, well adapted to the wilderness, to war, to prowling, to adventure: suddenly all their instincts were disvalued and "suspended." From now on they had to walk on their feet and "bear themselves" whereas hitherto they had been borne by the water: a dreadful heaviness lay upon them. They felt unable to cope with the simplest undertakings; in this new world they no longer possessed their former guides, their regulating, unconscious and infallible drives: they were reduced to thinking, inferring, reckoning, co-ordinating cause and effect, these unfortunate creatures; they were reduced to their "consciousness," their weakest and most fallible organ! I believe there has never been such a feeling of misery on earth ...—and at the same time the old instincts had not suddenly ceased to make their usual demands! Only it was hardly or rarely possible to humor them: as a rule they had to seek new and, as it were, subterranean gratifications.

All instincts that do not discharge themselves outward *turn inward*—this is what I call the *internalization* of man: thus it was that man first developed what was later called his "soul." ...

The man who, from lack of external enemies and resistances and forcibly confined to the oppressive narrowness and punctiliousness of custom, impatiently lacerated ... and maltreated himself; this animal that rubbed itself raw against the bars of its cage as one tried to "tame" it ... this fool, this yearning and desperate prisoner became the inventor of the "bad conscience." (*G*, 2:16)

It is very natural to take this hypothesis on the bad conscience as a further development of the concept of slave-morality. External inhibition plays a key role in both. More important and profound is another consideration. Nietzsche presented slave-morality as undergoing a development. Both in the *Genealogy* and more clearly in the *Antichrist*, he distinguished between the comparative health of Old Testament Judaism and the advanced Jewish "decadence" of Christianity, which grew out of Judaism only after mounting political misfortune. Now the theory of internalized will to power seems to explain precisely this, since it admits of degrees. The genuine profundity of Nietzsche's hypothesis, an aspect of which, incidentally, had been intimated in an obscure work of Kant's,[1] is that it presents a way of viewing an entire continuum running from comparatively low levels of social restraint all the way up to such strangling inhibition that the caged beast must attack himself because no other outlet for his energy is available. When such a stage is reached, then indeed "negativity" may take over, any form of spontaneous joy becomes worse than suspect, and asceticism reaches heights little if at all short of madness.

It is natural in thinking about slave-morality and internalized will to power to link resentment, the bad conscience, and moral law together. But Nietzsche's exposition both confirms and denies the validity of this. At one point he wrote: "one can see who has the invention of the 'bad conscience' on his conscience—the man of *ressentiment!*" (*G*, 2:11). Some pages later he wrote that "among the presuppositions of this hypothesis concerning the origin of the bad conscience is ... that the change referred to was not a gradual one and did not represent an organic adaptation to new conditions but a break, a leap, a compulsion, an ineluctable disaster which precluded all struggle and even all *ressentiment*" (*G*, 2:17). The former quotation seems to link the bad conscience to the Judaeo-Christian religions, the latter to a wider, perhaps much earlier development, with the original internalization out of which (again one must say perhaps, since Nietzsche left the issue so unclear,) resentment evolved. If this is so, however, we are left wondering exactly what the bad conscience is that is not capable of resentment, and how it differs from the bad conscience that is.

Equally mysterious is the relation among the bad conscience, resentment, and law. Nietzsche bestowed warm praise on law for bringing order and control into the chaos of resentment and the reactive feelings in general. The frustration of that chaos was regulated and at least partially overcome by taking revenge out of private hands, by focusing those feelings against the public enemies, and by codifying what is permitted and what is not (*G*, 2:11). There is a curious and no doubt unintended Lockean overtone in this, since the disadvantages of the purely private settlement of grievances and the spirit of vengeance were crucial to Locke's theory of the justification of government, but Nietzsche's points are none the worse for that. What is surprising, however, is that Nietzsche should present slavish resentment, law, and the bad conscience as unconnected with one another and, still more mysterious, that he should regard the first as quintessentially Jewish, and not mention the Jews at all in the later discussions. At issue here is not the question of Nietzsche's ambivalent attitude toward the Jews, which will be discussed in a later chapter, but the historical unclarity of the entire complex of theories. The Jews, the people of resentment, were also the people of law; but when law and its effectiveness against resentment are discussed, they make no appearance. Furthermore, they make no appearance when the bad conscience is discussed. Instead of presenting the Christian bad conscience as a deepening and darkening of the Jewish bad conscience, which might have some plausibility if only because ascetic practices have been rather more characteristic of Christianity than Judaism, Nietzsche presented the origin of the bad conscience in such general terms that one is left wondering why it did not flourish in all sorts of places where it evidently did not exist in an articulated form at all. One also must wonder how the bad conscience can exist without law, or how resentment can exist with law if law is such an effective means of channeling resentment.

Considered as criticism, these points are comparatively minor, and simply point to the lacunae in Nietzsche's argument. From both the conceptual and the historical point of view, there are problems both more serious and more interesting.

The bad conscience culminates in an orgy of self-torment.

> In this psychical cruelty [of religious guilt] there resides a madness of the will which is absolutely unexampled: the *will* of man to find himself guilty and reprehensible to a degree that can never be atoned for; his *will* to think himself punished without any possibility of the punishment becoming equal to the guilt; his *will* to infect and poison the fundamental ground of things with the problem of punishment and guilt so as to cut off once and for all his own exit from this labyrinth of "fixed ideas"; his *will* to erect an ideal—that of the "holy God"—and in the face of it to feel the palpable certainty of his own absolute unworthiness. Oh this insane, pathetic beast—man! What ideas he has, what unnaturalness, what paroxysms of nonsense, what *bestiality of thought* erupts as soon as he is prevented just a little from being a *beast in deed!* (G, 2:22)

There is enough self-flagellating hysteria in religion to justify something of Nietzsche's own hysteria, but there are nevertheless serious oversimplifications here. The great masters of the religious bad conscience have frequently turned out to be those who testify to it most eloquently because they sought to break out of it, as I shall note in more detail in the final chapter of this study. Here it suffices to observe that the doctrines about man's nothingness, helplessness, worthlessness, and infinite indebtedness were central to early Protestantism, for example, as was the wallowing in verbiage to relieve the feelings, which Nietzsche both contemned and exhibited. But what was also central to Luther and his followers, in whose light, one can argue, Nietzsche saw Christianity as a whole, was that the bad conscience was only truly posited as a preliminary to the liberation of grace. Indeed, it was the first stage *of* such grace. Who, then, *had* a bad conscience in the sense of this quotation, that is, was devoutly convinced, not that he deserved to be damned when his own unaided "merit" was weighed (many certainly believed as much), but that he *would* be damned? Nietzsche mentioned no one. And while he knew that violent religious feelings could constitute a relief from pain, the product of the priest who first makes sicker in order to administer his little balm of comfort, he evidently wished to obscure the significance of the Christian dialectic in order to render plausible the view that the bad conscience is nothing but the offspring of the individual's natural *cruelty* internalized. Only in this way could he make the self-laceration of the individual appear to be an end in itself, and the realm of the "negative" an end in itself.

That there have been men who have been beasts may be conceded; and it may also be true that certain kinds of cages induce them to flail at themselves. But how plausible is this theory as a sweeping explanation of the phenomenon of moral guilt-feeling? Guilt is normally understood as the consequence of a misrelation between the individual and an other. To the believer, this other is God; to the sociologist, society; to the psychologist, frequently, one's parents. Different though these may be, they possess much in common, as theologians, sociologists, and psychologists often recognize. Each theory presupposes an initial positive relation, in which the individual recognizes the other as an object of love or at least support. Guilt is then the feeling of having violated this positive relation, and entails the internalization, not necessarily of will to power in an abstract sense, but of the negative judgment of an other, who is at least partially loved. Nietzsche's own claim that punishment frequently produces no guilt-feeling (*G*, 2:14), which has considerable plausibility, but which he left curiously unexplained, might possibly be explained in this light. A punished individual may simply be able to view his punisher, even "society," as an enemy. Precisely because the positive bond has been thoroughly destroyed, he can retreat into the sullen hostility Nietzsche described as the effect of punishment, without ever developing a bad conscience at all. The theory of the caged beast then turns out, on Nietzsche's own showing, not to produce guilt when men-beasts are actually caged, when we should expect them to become heroes of asceticism in their cells. More important, the theory of internalized will to power simply assumes what must be proved and yet is so inherently implausible, that guilt-ridden man can be understood as not having any positive connection to something other than himself at all.

Nietzsche's argument entails, on the religious level, which it primarily treats, that the positive view of the holy God is merely the product of the will to self-torment, an invention of the self to heighten anguish. Religious guilt does, of course, involve a comparison between what God is and expects, and the unworthiness of the self. But it is at this point that the historical looseness of Nietzsche's construction becomes a source of serious perplexity. According to the *Antichrist* (#25), where the metamorphosis of Israelite faith is most explicitly treated, the original Jewish God was the expression of the warlike faith and good conscience of the people. When the national hopes remained unfulfilled, He became something else, a "god only under certain conditions," a "god who *demands*—in place of a god who helps ... who is at bottom the word for every happy inspiration of courage and self-confidence." At this point, morality ceases to be "the expression of the conditions for the life and growth of a people," but becomes "abstract," the "'evil eye' for all things."

There are a host of ambiguities here. The last stage of this development clearly is reminiscent of the bad conscience and resentment of the *Genealogy*. But at what point is this transformation accomplished, and how could it develop out of so healthy a condition as that enjoyed by the early Israelites? One could maintain that neither the beginning nor the end of this religious "history" was what Nietzsche claimed it was. It is gratuitous to assume that the God of the Jews was ever conceived as one who made no "demands." The Jewish religion may have been formed at its earliest stages as part of a struggle against empires,[2] a struggle that from the start involved some internalization of will to power, a term used "for the sake of argument" here.

By the same token, the evil eye for all things is not descriptive of either Judaism or Christianity, but a pathological extreme which individuals under the influence of those faiths have perhaps exhibited often enough, but which cannot be identified with the essence of either faith for the simple reason that even the severest moralists of both have so often warned against it. Calvin himself could be cited in this regard.[3] At least as plausible as Nietzsche's construction in the *Genealogy* and the *Antichrist*, and one that presupposes no religious commitment, is that the internalization accomplished by both Judaism and Christianity involved the same *ordering* of the "reactive pathos" by means of religious law as Nietzsche praised with regard to law in general, and that this entire process was not pure negativity, but presupposed the background of the affirmation of God and His world, which Nietzsche praised in the earliest Jewish faith. The early Christians, who were so busy pointing out the woes of earthly existence to complacent pagans, were simultaneously engaged in defending the beauties of God's creation to the Gnostics, who maintained that the world was created by an evil deity, the God of the Jews.

What, then, does the whole construction, this "ideal type" of slave-morality, really add up to (since there can be little question of either refuting or affirming a doctrine so historically and even psychologically nebulous)? Nietzsche had noted a power of the negative spirit to spread like cancer; he noted it in Schopenhauer, in himself, in various and assorted flagellants of one description or another, also in anarchists and anti-Semites! (*G*, 2:11). At the same time, committed to the monocausal theory of the will to power, he brilliantly connected this triumph of negativity to a frustration of energy and positive self-expression. But the price exacted by this theory, a price Nietzsche obviously thought well worth paying and, indeed, perhaps a positive advantage in itself rather than a price at all, was to tar all generous humanitarianism, all neighborly love and recognition of the dignity of the other found in the Judaeo-Christian traditions, with the brush of his own hatred by deriving them all from hatred itself. The ascetic extreme was used to define the essence, the heart and soul of the entire Judaeo-Christian tradition, with a not very touching exception made for Christ, the "idiot." The result may be a catastrophic misunderstanding of the nature and function of morality, even in its most "slavish" form. One can say at the least that in identifying the origins of morality with the hypertrophied bad conscience,

Nietzsche left the "genealogy" of the nonascetic aspects of the Judaeo-Christian moral traditions, the simple precepts of humane love of the neighbor, unexplained by his theory and certainly irreducible *to* that theory.

If Nietzsche's slave-morality is an ideal type consisting of an abstract depiction of a disease, his master-morality is an ideal type of health, although the question of the degree to which this health is unequivocally affirmed and the corresponding disease unequivocally condemned must not be prejudged by such a description. Still less can one rule out the possibility that no genuinely clear answer to this question can be obtained that does justice to all the evidence.

Nietzsche emphasized both the cruelty and the "innocence" of master races. Their cruelty he understood in the usual sense of a tendency to inflict the grossest harm on others. Their "innocence," however, must be put in quotation marks, because he did not tend to use the word *innocence* as the opposite of cruelty or as an incapacity for it, but as the absence of a bad conscience about it. For this reason one must be wary of interpreting one stated aim of his thought, the furtherance of a new innocence, as being necessarily humane in intention. Such a reading depends for its cogency upon regarding guilt-feeling as the sole cause of evil, which can scarcely be justified, even if on Nietzsche's own showing, as we saw in the second chapter, it may be one cause of evil.

If there is, nonetheless, a kind of moral claim made for the master that might be respected from the perspective of slave-morality itself, it is his lack of hate. On this point, as on so many others, the image of the triumphant master is used to denigrate the viciousness of the impotent. Nietzsche uses the image this way in a remarkable passage rich in insight and sentimentality.

> When the noble mode of valuation blunders and sins against reality, it does so in respect to the sphere with which it is *not* sufficiently familiar, against a real knowledge of which it has indeed inflexibly guarded itself: in some circumstances it misunderstands the sphere it despises, that of the common man, of the lower orders; on the other hand, one should remember that, even supposing that the affect of contempt, of looking down from a superior height *falsifies* the image of that which it despises, it will at any rate still be a much less serious falsification than that perpetrated on its opponent—*in effigie* of course—by the submerged hatred, the vengefulness of the impotent. There is indeed too much carelessness, too much taking lightly, too much looking away and impatience involved in contempt, even too much joyfulness, for it to be able to transform its object into a real caricature and monster.
>
> One should not overlook the almost benevolent nuances that the Greek nobility, for example, bestows on all the words it employs to distinguish the lower orders from itself; how they are continuously mingled and sweetened with a kind of pity, consideration, and forbearance. (*G*, 2:10)

There is, surely, a real truth here. The resentful, to the degree that they are such, cannot look down upon their oppressors. Resentment means, in Nietzsche's analysis, in part the internalization of the image of the masters' power and its terror. This internalization makes them into monsters, while the very contempt of the fortunate may, as long as their position is secure, prevent any such attitude toward their victims. But since, as Nietzsche has just demonstrated, what makes masters what they are is a refusal to regard the lowly as human beings like themselves, the kindly epithets in which they can indulge need not be greeted with great enthusiasm. As Nietzsche himself observed unequivocally, if in a different work and a different context, hatred *honors* more than contempt (*GS*, #379).

In spite of this consideration, the issue of the innocence of the master in comparison with the hate of the slave suggests at least the possibility that Nietzsche's critique of Christianity, both in the *Genealogy* and elsewhere, was essentially an attempt to purify morality rather than simply eliminate slave-morality and reenthrone master-morality. Whether this is true or not is the essential subject of the remainder of this book. At present I shall simply focus on those aspects of the critique of Christianity and the "moral view of the world" which appear to be in the interest of a more humane (as opposed to a more dominating) moral ideal.

We may start with what appears to be an unambiguous and straightforward example. Near the end of the first essay of the *Genealogy*, so placed in order to bring the polemics of the whole essay to their climax, Nietzsche discussed the Christian conception of Heaven. "These weak people," the Christians, "some day or other *they* too intend to be the strong...." They will be "indemnified." Dante, he noted, "with a terror-inspiring ingenuity," had "placed above the gateway of his hell the inscription 'I too was created by eternal love'—at any rate, there would be more justification for placing above the gateway to the Christian Paradise and its 'eternal bliss' the inscription 'I too was created by eternal *hate*'...." The positive goal of Christian bliss was invented as the supreme expression of Christian vengeance. The proof of this contention is given by citing the doctrine that the happiness of the saved will be magnified by their ability to see the punishments of the damned. Nietzsche referred to Aquinas, "meek as a lamb," to this effect. He then added a much longer, more detailed, and more blood-thirsty passage from Tertullian's *De Spectaculis*, observing first that Tertullian was "adjuring his Christians to avoid the cruel pleasure of the public games—but why? 'For the faith offers us much more ... *something much stronger*; thanks to the Redemption, quite other joys are at our command...'" (*G*, 1:15). Among these are the blood of Christ and the martyrs, and, above all, the supreme delights of contemplating the shrieking misery of the damned.

The passage cited by Nietzsche is, quite frankly, disgusting. But what was his real purpose in quoting it? Walter Kaufmann, in a long note to this section of the *Genealogy*, assumed that Nietzsche, like Gibbon before him (who had cited it with more merciful brevity in the *Decline and Fall*), was "outraged" by it. But one may wonder whether the whole section, especially when taken in the context of related material elsewhere in Nietzsche's work, really expresses outrage or something more complex. One can make the case for "outrage" plausible by viewing the treatment of Tertullian as a continuation of the comparison between the personal hatred and vindictiveness characteristic of those whose power has been forcibly internalized and the less personal, less hate-ridden aggressiveness of the masters.

But it is worthy of remark that in a note of late 1884, before his distinction between the master and slave was fully developed, but when his (qualified) opposition to revenge was already clear, Nietzsche specifically praised the Christian Church for spiritualizing cruelty (*Grausamkeit*) with its doctrine of hell, the auto-da-fé, and so on, great advances, he maintained, over the "splendid but half-idiotic massacres in the Roman arenas" (*KGA*, 7:3, p. 170). This attitude is quite as reasonable as any outrage over Tertullian, especially if we reflect that Roman gladiatorial spectacles, which sometimes amounted to nothing short of mass murder, were themselves hardly examples of "healthy" or "natural" aggression.

A passage written after the *Genealogy*, moreover, also sheds a very revealing light on the issue at hand. In *Twilight of the Idols*, Nietzsche, in a rare expression of praise for his own time, commended what he took to be a characteristically modern "spiritualization of *hostility*." "It consists in a profound appreciation of the value of having enemies ..." unlike previous ages, especially under the Church. "[W]e immoralists and Antichristians find our advantage in this, that the church exists." In politics, also, practically "every party understands how it is in the interest of its own self-preservation that the opposition should not lose all strength.... A new creation in particular— the new *Reich*, for example—needs enemies more than friends: in opposition alone does it *feel* itself necessary, in opposition alone does it *become* necessary." The same is true, Nietzsche continued, with regard to the "'internal enemy,'" for "the price of fruitfulness is to be rich in internal opposition.... Nothing has become more alien to us than that desideratum of former times, 'peace of soul,' the *Christian* desideratum..." (*T*, "Morality as Anti-Nature," 3). Enemies keep one alive; they also help define one's *identity*. According to one of Nietzsche's very last notes, Christianity was necessary, for the greatest "no" to life provokes the greatest "yes" (*KGA*, 3:3, p. 455). What Nietzsche had just finished denouncing in the *Antichrist* as "the one eternal blemish of mankind" is eternally needed, even if at times one has to fight it as if one wanted to destroy it, the better to know who one is. Christianity must last, or at least recur eternally, and be combated eternally, for the greater *Machtgefühl* of Nietzscheans, who need it as the blessed need the damned.

One could still maintain, however, that the Christian doctrine has an element of personal vindictiveness that is absent from Nietzsche's combative pathos. The latter could then be regarded as a *further* spiritualization of the *Grausamkeit* that Christianity had spiritualized incompletely. Even this, however, turns out to be dubious, especially if we leave aside Tertullian himself, whose imaginative enthusiasm on the issue was hardly typical. Thus Augustine, who certainly was most emphatic about the eternity of the punishment awaiting the damned, made the particular point about the knowledge the saved have of this punishment in an offhand and convincingly impersonal manner. After insisting at greater length that the saved have knowledge of their own past life and its wretchedness, he continued: "But their intellectual knowledge, which shall be great, shall keep them acquainted not only with their own past woes, but with the eternal sufferings of the lost. For if they were not to know that they had been miserable, how could they, as the Psalmist says, for ever sing the mercies of God?"[4] This passage from the *City of God* was undoubtedly the principal source of Thomas Aquinas's affirmation of this knowledge. The essence of the doctrine, however unpleasant, is not vindictiveness as such but the eminently Nietzschean principle of comparison. Thus Aquinas wrote elsewhere in the *Summa Theologica*, with no reference either to damnation or salvation: "Sad things, called to mind, cause pleasure, not in so far as they are sad and contrary to pleasant things; but in so far as man is delivered from them."[5] Meek as a lamb.

Behind this entire line of thought may well have stood some of the more ferocious elements of Jewish Apocalyptic. But an equally plausible source is a very celebrated passage from Lucretius's *De Rerum Natura*, well known to the Latin fathers:

> How sweet it is, when whirlwinds roil great ocean,
> To watch, from land, the danger of another,
> Not that to see some other person suffer
> Brings great enjoyment, but the sweetness lies
> In watching evils you yourself are free from.
> How sweet, again, to see the clash of battle
> Across the plains, yourself immune to danger.
> But nothing is more sweet than full possession
> Of those calm heights, well built, well fortified
> By wise men's teaching, to look down from here
> At others wandering below, men lost,
> Confused, in hectic search for the right road,
> The strife of wits, the wars for precedence,
> The everlasting struggle, night and day,
> To win towards heights of wealth and power. O wretched,
> O wretched minds of men. O hearts of darkness.[6]

Christianity had thus inherited from pagan as well as Jewish sources the perception that we think, and still more, *appreciate*, with the aid of contrasts, and it is certainly arbitrary to emphasize vindictive resentment as the really determining ingredient involved. The possibility cannot be ruled out, in fact, that Nietzsche was less concerned to express indignation at Christianity's expense than to indicate the pervasive importance of struggling contrasts, or the will to power, even in Christianity's own conception of joy. Seen in that light, his point against Tertullian is merely a kind of *tu quoque*. The real ambiguity arises, however, when we realize that the sublimation of cruelty could be both an exaggeration and an attenuation of cruelty in Nietzsche's eyes, a process that pointed away from coarse violence yet one that also meant a more intense, personal hate. That Nietzsche disapproved of this hate is certain, one of the few points in his moral philosophy that admits no argument. But insofar as the will to power is itself deepened and made more consciously egotistical in Nietzsche's philosophy, the problem of the moral effects of "sublimation" is not really solved by such a consideration, for ruthlessness does not require hate. One thing certainly should be clear; it is scarcely possible to take even a small detail from Nietzsche and examine it with some care without encountering one ambiguity after another.

This has been, perhaps, an unduly elaborate treatment of a small portion of Nietzsche's discussion of "slave-morality" and a minuscule doctrine of Christianity. Yet a number of things have, I hope, been demonstrated by it: first, and most obviously, the typical unfairness of Nietzsche's polemical procedure, which oversimplifies whatever it touches, especially by asserting a more radical cleavage between the Judaeo-Christian and the pagan than is in all respects warranted. Second, however, is that his own attitudes show themselves to be far more complicated, if not in this instance more utterly contradictory, when all relevant material is adduced, than might at first appear. Third, and most interesting of all, is the reason for this complexity. Nietzschean sublimation and spiritualization seem to point to a superior moral stance in the recognition of the *need* for enemies, and the "consideration" that can go with this recognition. But it simultaneously points to the need for *enemies*, and hence at the least to a *possible* deepening of hostility and contempt. A far more intrinsically important topic can serve as another example of the same points.

Were Christian hate and vindictiveness, on Nietzsche's account, merely expressed in imaginary triumphs over their enemies, they could be laughed to scorn. But Nietzsche viewed Christianity as actively dangerous in weakening the strong, although it is notorious that he could never explain satisfactorily how the strong ever became Christian in the first place.[7] This weakening was accomplished with the aid of doctrines that divided the individual against himself. The most important of these were belief in free will and in the necessity of remorse, which free will seemed to justify. At the same time, however, free will also expressed vengeance by justifying moral disapprobation. Thus Nietzsche's criticism of it was intended to have the force of a double censure, against both the motives behind and the effects of the doctrine of freedom of the will.

The *Genealogy* attacked this doctrine, with special emphasis upon the motive of vengeance, not long before the treatment of Tertullian already discussed.

> To demand of strength that it should *not* express itself as strength, that it should *not* be a desire to overcome, a desire to throw down, a desire to become master, a thirst for enemies and resistances and triumphs, is just as absurd as to demand of weakness that it should express itself as strength. A quantum of force is equivalent to a quantum of drive, will, effect— more, it is nothing other than precisely this very driving, willing, effect- ing, and only owing to the seduction of language (and of the fundamental errors of reason that are petrified in it) which conceives and misconceives all effects as conditioned by something that causes effects, by a "subject," can it appear otherwise. For just as the popular mind separates the light- ning from its flash and takes the latter for an *action*, for the operation of a subject called lightning, so popular morality also separates strength from expressions of strength, as if there were a neutral substratum behind the strong man, which was *free* to express strength or not to do so.... [N]o wonder if the submerged, darkly glowering emotions of vengefulness and hatred exploit this belief for their own ends and in fact maintain no belief more ardently than the belief that *the strong man is free* to be weak and the bird of prey to be a lamb—for thus they gain the right to make the bird of prey *accountable* for being a bird of prey. (*G*, 1:13)

This is a brilliant piece of writing, but, as with so much of Nietzsche's bril- liant writing, it establishes nothing, and much of it is, in fact, altogether beside the point. Moral freedom of the kind attacked here does not require any such entity as a "neutral substratum," but merely an absence of strict determination of the will by forces beyond the subject's control. Nietzsche himself, much later in the same work, declared that "man is more sick, un- certain, changeable, indeterminate than any other animal" (*G*, 3:13). And in *Beyond Good and Evil* he had referred to man as "the *as yet undetermined animal*..." (*BGE*, #62). It is possible that he meant by "indeterminate" something other than free to choose. (One cannot be certain, since he did not say what he did mean.) But any form of indeterminacy, that is, anything that led to conflict of "instincts" and to the need for deliberation, would suffice to explain how the belief in freedom could arise without having to resort to the seduction of language, much less to Wagnerian melodrama con- cerning "glowering emotions of vengefulness and hatred." And needless to say, regardless of the manner in which man can be said to be free or not free, determined or undertermined, the nature of lightning and the behavior of eagles offer no instruction on the issue. That a quantum of strength must express itself may be true, but the whole question is: how?

In his next work, *Twilight of the Idols*, Nietzsche repeated his attack on free will, insisting again on the claim of the *Genealogy* that the desire to judge, punish, and impute guilt was the determining fact in the genesis of the doctrine. He added to what we have seen a new emphasis on the priestly drive for power as responsible for the doctrine; a new insistence that his own aim was "to take the concept of guilt and the concept of punishment out of the world again"; and an emphasis upon the erroneous belief that all action originates in consciousness as the crucial presupposition of defenders of freedom (*T*, "The Four Great Errors," 7).

That a large number of philosophers and theologians have defended free will in order partly to defend responsibility, and responsibility partly in order to defend judgment, positive or negative, cannot be denied. Even Epicurus, no lover of priests and normally treated very gently by Nietzsche as an antithesis, if hardly the *best* antithesis, to slave-morality, exhibited this.[8] But that a doctrine can be used for a certain purpose tells us a good deal less about the complex origin of a complex doctrine than Nietzsche's typically reductionist polemic would have us believe. One way of demonstrating this is to adduce strong arguments against free will precisely because the concept *undermines* rather than strengthens the case for condemnation. Such arguments were advanced by David Hume in a passage which, to my knowledge, has received remarkably little attention, and whose presuppositions afford a striking contrast to Nietzsche's own.

> Actions are by their very nature temporary and perishing; and where they proceed not from some cause in the characters and disposition of the person, who perform'd them, they infix not themselves upon him, and can neither redound to his honour, if good, nor infamy, if evil. The action itself may be blameable; it may be contrary to all the rules of morality and religion: But the person is not responsible for it; and as it proceeded from nothing in him, that is durable or constant, and leaves nothing of that nature behind, 'tis impossible he can, upon its account, become the object of punishment or vengeance. According to the hypothesis of liberty, therefore, a man is as pure and untainted, after having committed the most horrid crimes, as at the moment of his birth.... 'Tis only upon the principles of necessity, that a person acquires any merit or demerit from his actions, however the common opinion may incline to the contrary.[9]

Nietzsche had assumed that guilt can only follow from conscious intention, which has certainly played a major role in legal conceptions of responsibility. But it is by no means clear that one cannot judge and condemn what does not originate in consciousness. Furthermore, the more embedded an action is in a man's "instinct," the more a condemnation of the action appears as a total condemnation of the very being of the actor. Hume made this point. Side-stepping the entire question of conscious intention, he simply wanted to demonstrate that all action proceeds from what a man *is*, from a totality of character which, regardless of whether that character be "caused" by conscious intention or unconscious instincts mirrored in consciousness, renders each action the genuine expression of its performer. Brought up a Calvinist, though hardly remaining one, Hume was in a position to see that predestination and judgment could easily go hand in hand.

The reason the contrast between Hume and Nietzsche is so instructive is that Hume, in his very *moralistic* hostility to the notion of freedom, points to the connection between freedom and something other than guilt: the belief in the openness of the human personality, which can mitigate, not reinforce, vindictiveness. In saying that, on the hypothesis of freedom, a man is as untainted after crimes as a newborn child, he criticized what many believers in freedom have expressly believed, if they have put it in a somewhat less radical way: that no man simply *is* his own past, be it good or bad, since the capacity for a change in the fundamental direction of moral character is coextensive with life. And it is this insistence on the capacity to change, on free will as an encouragement to inner effort, that has probably had as much to do with the popularity of the doctrine with moralists as the desire to impute guilt in any vindictive spirit. However much the doctrine of free will encourages punishment and blame for individual transgressions, there is no denying that it also renders final and total judgment on people impossible. One of the things that the doctrine of freedom resists, for example, is just that sort of final judgment explicit in any permanent division of men into two classes, "the strong" and "the weak," a division usually central to Nietzsche's own philosophy.

Because, according to Nietzsche, free will exists to justify the imputation of guilt, Nietzsche's attack on guilt-feeling and its debilitating effects is a continuation of the campaign against free will, but with a new emphasis.

Against remorse and the purely psychological treatment of it.—To be unable to have done with an experience is already a sign of decadence. This reopening of old wounds, this wallowing in self-contempt and contrition, is one more illness, out of which no "salvation of the soul" can arise but only a new form of soul sickness—....

The entire practice of psychological healing must be put back on to a *physiological* basis: the "bite" of conscience as such is a hindrance to recovery—one must try to counterbalance it all by new activities, in order to escape from the sickness of self-torture as quickly as possible. (*WP*, #233)

Nietzsche's indictment of remorse hinges upon an understanding of the "bite of conscience" as a truly enfeebling, not to say envenomed, bite. As such, it may not be entirely irrelevant to the history of religious practice. But by defining guilt-feeling as *essentially* obsessive ("wallowing" is the key word of the indictment), as a morbid incapacity to move beyond one's past to a new life, Nietzsche was able to score a very easy triumph. Surely no serious philosopher or theologian has ever approved, let alone counseled, such obsessiveness. The question remains open, moreover, even without casting doubt on the possible merits of "physiological" therapy, whether a man can become morally good without a capacity for self-criticism, which inevitably entails some feeling of contrition, however brief, and however much that feeling is viewed as a mere phase in self-transcendence and self-reform. Because Nietzsche did not even consider the possibility of such a nonmorbid guilt-feeling, he could slide into a denunciation of guilt sweeping enough to preclude any degree of regret at all. "I do not like this kind of cowardice toward one's own deeds; one should not leave oneself in the lurch at the onset of unanticipated shame and embarrassment. An extreme pride, rather, is in order. After all, what is the good of it! No deed can be undone by being regretted ..." (*WP*, #235). That a deed cannot be undone by being regretted may be true, but is of questionable relevance. The problem involved concerns less the past than the *future*. All attempts at reaching a morally new future would seem to be impossible in the face of this recommended intransigence about the past. The culmination of this line of thought was reached when Nietzsche denounced the folly of any exhortation to change oneself. "The single human being is a piece of *fatum* from the front and from the rear, one law more, one necessity more for all that is yet to come and to be. To say to him, 'Change yourself!' is to demand that everything be changed, even retroactively" (*T*, "Morality as Anti-Nature," #6).

Moral judgment is a terrible weapon, at least when wielded against moral individuals. It is possible to read much of Nietzsche, including much of what has been quoted above, as a kind of extreme tenderheartedness in the face of human shame from which it would be difficult to withhold all sympathy (even if one must wonder why the suffering of guilt should be the only form of suffering for which Nietzsche had no praise when it is obvious that it can be as fruitful as any other form of suffering). *Zarathustra* had frequently demonstrated this concern. "'Enemy' you shall say, but not 'villain'; 'sick' you shall say, but not 'scoundrel'; 'fool' you shall say, but not 'sinner'" (*TSZ*, 1:6). One may ask, even without any especially fervent zeal for the theological terminology of guilt, whether words matter so much, or, if they do, whether Nietzsche's alternatives are any better than the ones he opposed. To say "enemy" may betoken a kind of respect in comparison to moral condemnation, but it also means that one is fully content simply to suppress or eliminate the enemy rather than transform him into a friend. "Sick" can be as galling to pride as "scoundrel," perhaps more so. Had

Nietzsche written "weakling" the point would be only slightly more obvious. Nor do most care to be called "fool," even if Nietzsche could sometimes ironically apply related terms to himself.

This concern for the shamed is demonstrated again by Zarathustra when he declared: "if you have an enemy, do not requite him evil with good, for that would put him to shame. Rather prove that he did you some good.

"And rather be angry than put to shame. And if you are cursed, I do not like it that you want to bless. Rather join a little in the cursing" (*TSZ*, 1:19). That this was intended to raise moral sensitivity, not to lower it, is clear. Presumably it is an allusion to the Christian doctrine that, by returning good for evil, one may awaken repentance in the evildoer.[10] But surely nothing is more galling to an enemy than proof that his malice resulted in benefit. Nietzsche, therefore, probably meant that one should prove this benefit only to *oneself*, which may or may not be possible or in accord with the most elementary honesty.

The possibility of intense moral shame indicates the parallel possibility of intense moral pride, as Nietzsche knew full well, but it did not meet with a parallel condemnation from him. "'Freedom of the will'—that is the expression for the complex state of delight of the person exercising volition, who commands and at the same time identifies himself with the executor of the order—who, as such, enjoys also the triumph over obstacles, but thinks within himself that it was really his will itself that overcame them" (*BGE*, #19). This sympathy with the triumphant will was repeated still more openly and enthusiastically in the *Genealogy*, where Nietzsche considered the ultimate *telos* of the moralization of man in a positive light, the "*sovereign individual*,"

> the man who has his own independent, protracted will and the *right to make promises*—and in him a proud consciousness, quivering in every muscle, of *what* has at length been achieved and become flesh in him, a consciousness of his own power and freedom, a sensation of mankind come to completion. This emancipated individual, with the actual *right* to make promises, this master of a *free* will ...—how should he not be aware of his superiority over all those who lack the right to make promises and stand as their own guarantors, of how much trust, how much fear, how much reverence he arouses—he "*deserves*" all three—... The "free" man ... also possesses his *measure of value*: looking out upon others from himself, he honors or he despises; and just as he is bound to honor his peers, the strong and reliable (those with the *right* to make promises) ... whose trust is a mark of *distinction* ... he is bound to reserve a kick for the feeble windbags who promise without the right to do so, and a rod for the liar who breaks his word even at the moment he utters it. The proud awareness of the extraordinary privilege of *responsibility*, the consciousness of this rare freedom, this power over oneself and over fate, has in his

case penetrated to the profoundest depths and become instinct, the dominating instinct. What will he call this dominating instinct, supposing he feels the need to give it a name? The answer is beyond doubt: this sovereign man calls it his *conscience*. (G, 2:2)

The freedom praised in both these quotations is not, perhaps, inconsistent with the freedom Nietzsche denied, but something very different, a power of self-control that presupposes a strength one simply has or develops, which must be possessed *in embryo* in order to be developed, not a metaphysical and mysterious *liberum arbitrium*. A denial of "freedom of the will" in this metaphysical sense, and a praise of the power and freedom of the strong individual can be found in other writers, Spinoza, for example. But one may still wonder what meaning the moral pride and conscience hymned in this passage can possibly have if remorse has no meaning or validity. Nor is the kick for feeble windbags notably tender-minded. More radically, one must wonder whether the entire psychological complex known as the will to power can be separated from a drive to think well of oneself that presupposes the pressing reality of choice and the fear of bad choice, or the fear of being judged adversely by others.

Thus we have, in the final analysis, two positions. One is a praise of what can be called by no other name than moral pride, in which the will to power comes to its apogee as self-conscious self-mastery, an identification with a ruling "I," and a willingness for self-restraint because of confidence of victory. The other position, given in *Twilight* shortly after the denunciation of free will, is a pure, impersonal fatalism.

> What alone can be *our* doctrine? That no one *gives* man his qualities—neither God, nor society, nor his parents and ancestors, nor he himself.... No one is responsible for man's being there at all, for his being such-and-such, or for his being in these circumstances or in this environment. The fatality of his essence is not to be disentangled from the fatality of all that has been and will be....
>
> One is necessary, one is a piece of fatefulness, one belongs to the whole, one is in the whole; there is nothing which could judge, measure, compare, or sentence our being, for that would mean judging, measuring, comparing, or sentencing the whole. But there is nothing besides the whole. That nobody is held responsible any longer, that the mode of being may not be traced back to a *causa prima*, that the world does not form a unity either as a sensorium or as "spirit"—that alone is the great liberation; with this alone is the innocence of becoming restored. (T, "The Four Great Errors," 8)

Here Nietzsche's campaign against moralistic vengeance extends even to those who would blame God, as well as to the idea of human responsibility to God. There is nothing to blame because no one *intends* anything. All just is. But this redemption of the world makes nonsense of the will to power. The self as a locus of *Machtegfühl* has no meaning. There can be no glorying in one's strength and no kicks for windbags either, because both depend psychologically on an inner tension beset by the feeling that it could all be otherwise. One can say, therefore, that Nietzsche could define morality as internalized will to power because will to power was already seen in terms expressive of moralistic pride and moralistic insecurity. Alternatively, one could say that if Nietzsche wished to abolish moralistic insecurity and accusation, he should also have abolished the will to power.

5
The Critical Purpose of Nietzsche's
Philosophy of History

NIETZSCHE'S statements about the master and his morality in the *Genealogy* frequently appear normative, not just analytical and descriptive; and his abuse of the slave and his morality was often gross enough. But it would be an oversimplification of his purpose to regard the work as a straightforward praise of the former and condemnation of the latter. Without the Jew and the ascetic principle he embodied, Nietzsche declared, history would be altogether "too stupid a thing" (*G*, 1:7). He even called the bad conscience "a disease as pregnancy is a disease" (*G*, 2:19). Furthermore, at the very end of the work, Nietzsche credited the ascetic interpretation of existence with nothing less than saving mankind.

> Apart from the ascetic ideal, man, the human *animal*, had no meaning so far.... *This* is precisely what the ascetic ideal means: that something was *lacking*, that man was surrounded by a fearful *void*—he did not know how to justify, to account for, to affirm himself; he *suffered* from the problem of his meaning....
>
> Man, the bravest of animals and the one most accustomed to suffering, does *not* repudiate suffering as such; he *desires* it, he even seeks it out, provided he is shown a *meaning* for it, a *purpose* of suffering.... [A]*nd the ascetic ideal offered man a meaning!* It was the only meaning offered so far; any meaning is better than none at all.... In it, suffering was *interpreted* [as punishment and purification]; the tremendous void seemed to have been filled; the door was closed to any kind of suicidal nihilism. This interpretation—there is no doubt of it—brought fresh suffering with it, deeper, more inward, more poisonous, more life-destructive suffering: it placed all suffering under the perspective of *guilt*.
>
> But all this notwithstanding—man was *saved* thereby ... *the will itself was saved*.
>
> We can no longer conceal from ourselves *what* is expressed by all that willing which has taken its direction from the ascetic ideal: this hatred of

the human, even more of the animal, and more still of the material, this
horror of the senses, of reason itself, this fear of happiness and beauty,
this longing to get away from all appearance, change, becoming, death,
wishing, from longing itself—all this means—let us dare to grasp it—*a
will to nothingness*, an aversion to life, a rebellion against the most fundamental presuppositions of life; but it is and remains a *will!*... And ...
man would rather will *nothingness* than *not* will. (*G*, 3:28)

One may wonder whether man eternally seeks suffering as such if only he
can be shown its meaning, or whether, instead, he seeks meaning, even when
that meaning prescribes suffering. One would also like to know whether
Nietzsche really meant, as this passage clearly implies, that man in general
needs meaning, or only that man who has been taught by ascetics. The latter
maintains the dualism deeply embedded in the sharp dichotomy between
master and slave, whereas the former undercuts that dichotomy completely, reducing it to a relative matter of more and less, surely more defensible
but hard to square with much of Nietzsche's text. Yet, while these problems
are anything but minor, and never receive an adequate answer in his work,
the majestic close of the *Genealogy* certainly makes it difficult to read the
work as a pure denunciation of the slave and the ascetic principle, still less as
a pure commendation of masterful stupidity.

This becomes even clearer when we consider that Nietzsche closely
connected the ascetic principle with *philosophy*, and the *Genealogy* is not
intended as a polemic against philosophy at all, even if thinkers with a different, more absolutist conception of truth than Nietzsche possessed might
regard it as such. On the contrary, the *Genealogy* can be read as first and
foremost an attempt to liberate the philosopher from his own slavish self-
misunderstandings. This effort is reflected in Nietzsche's effort to show that
the philosopher is a powerful representative of will to power, one proceeding along a course dictated by his own imperious inner needs, not altruistic
virtue. (*G*, 3:7–8). It is reflected also in his questioning of an impersonal
truth, a slavish ideal before reality conceived as an overwhelming power, like
the master, fashioned, indeed, by the master; and in his contempt for the
scholars still fond of seeing themselves in this slavish light. Most clearly of
all, the effort to achieve a new self-understanding for the philosophic spirit is
reflected in his claim that that spirit had for ages used the ascetic ideal as a
kind of disguise, though one in which the philosopher himself believed, a
"result of the emergency conditions under which philosophy arose and sur-
vived at all." "To put it vividly: the *ascetic priest* provided until the most
modern times the repulsive and gloomy caterpillar form in which alone the
philosopher could live and creep about" (*G*, 3:10).

To deliver the philosopher as an individual from the pose of asceticism
might not strike everyone as being of "world-historical significance"; but

when it is realized that what is entailed in this enterprise is the deliverance of the concept of truth itself from slavery, then grandiose Hegelian terminology is no longer entirely inappropriate. There is, in fact, powerful evidence that Nietzsche envisioned a kind of progressivist interpretation of his own work, and approved of it. In a note from 1886, Nietzsche declared: "In my own way I attempt a justification [*Rechtfertigung*] of history" (*WP*, #63).[1] The *Genealogy* is far from being the only published work of Nietzsche's that demonstrates the relevance of this quotation. The tersest expression of a grand historical progression occurs in a famous, highly compressed section of *Twilight of the Idols*.

There, with a combination of wit, insight, and nonsense all his own, Nietzsche related the "history of an error." In the beginning, the philosopher *was* the true world. "'I, Plato, *am* the truth.'" Then, the true world retreated, but was still attainable for the pious sinner who repented. In other words, truth became "Christian" and *"female."* Then truth became still more withdrawn, "unattainable" but still a "consolation." This was the stage represented by Kant: "At bottom, the old sun, but seen through mist and skepticism." This was succeeded by a more resolute doubt, which no longer believed that an unattained truth could still obligate. ("The cockcrow of positivism.") The whole idea of the "'true' world" was then abolished ("Plato's embarrassed blush; pandemonium of all free spirits.") Finally, with the true world abolished, "What world has remained? The apparent one perhaps? But no! *With the true world we have also abolished the apparent one.*

"(Noon; moment of the briefest shadow; end of the longest error; high point of humanity; INCIPIT ZARATHUSTRA.)" (*T*, "How the true world finally became a fable.")

With the meaninglessness of the concept of the one true world, Zarathustra's truth, interpretation, comes into its own, not merely as the best available to man, but as all there is, truth being a function of will to power and perspectival in its *essence* (Cf. *G*, 3:12). Perspective is not one man's angle on a larger truth he does not know, nor the mere appearance of the world, with the implication that something lies behind what appears. Instead, reality is nothing but a multitude of conflicting interpretations. But Nietzsche clearly intended his own "perspective" to be very much a vision of the Whole, of the Whole as ever-contending parts. This perspective purports to possess a coercive, universal validity to the healthy, who have no need to slander the real world with the idea of a "truer" one beyond appearance.

In light of such a passage, Nietzsche could be interpreted, in spite of his own divergent but usually hostile evaluations of Hegel, as offering a philosophy of history of a semi-Hegelian sort, one which hinges upon the gradual unveiling of truth as expressed in philosophy and religion. To be sure, the epistemological states that Nietzsche sketched in his very compressed treatment only hint at the kind of dialectical necessity associated with Hegel's form of historical analysis. Nietzsche was more interested in wittily criticizing earlier stages and stating his own triumphant conclusion than in clearly showing how each stage presupposes the earlier one and the last presupposes them all. But he certainly was aware of the degree to which his own position was possible only as a dialectical negation of its antecedents. This is particularly true of his anti-Christianity. The complete moral freedom of post-Christian man brings innocence to a new level of completeness, for man's complete consciousness of innocence required the millennia of struggles with the Christian God and Christian morality. In one of his more famous assertions, moreover, Nietzsche contended that the difficult but liberating overthrow of both God and heteronomous morality presupposed a long preparation in intellectual honesty exacted by the God of Truth (*GS*, #357). By the same token, as we have seen, the alleged Christian negation of the world was intended to raise affirmation, like innocence and freedom, to an unprecedented level of exaltation and totality. A powerful strand of argument in Nietzsche, then, suggests the conclusion that, with the aid of the positive and above all the negative influence of Christianity, modern man has been able to reach a level of self-conscious freedom and innocence, and a will to an entirely *self*-supported affirmation of existence, which not merely surpasses anything attainable under the Christian dispensation, but also anything reached in Greece and Rome.

This view has considerable truth, and has not been set up simply as a straw man to be destroyed. But it must face many difficulties and, in the final analysis, must be sharply challenged. The difficulties can be stated in terms of Nietzsche's highly critical attitude toward modern man himself, his belief in the problematic openness of the future (which can lead man up or *down*), and his ferocious attacks on Christianity for its baneful historical effects, which were often delivered as if the baneful were alone what mattered. These denunciations are at least as representative of his late work as any retrospective blessing. And since Christianity was the principal means by which ancient strength, even if limited, was transformed into modern decadence, which might, but also might not, be overcome, it is best to begin the examination of what might be termed the regressive philosophy of history Nietzsche sometimes suggested with his conception of Christianity as an historical force.

From the very beginning Christianity had understood itself as an event within history as well as the revelation of timeless truths. As a revelation of timeless truths to men living in history, in fact, it presupposed the historical background of Jewish history and the history of mankind from Adam and Eve onward as understood and recorded in the Hebrew Bible. Certainly no interpreter of Christianity could overlook this Jewish background, and Nietzsche did not. But Christianity was also an event in another context, the context provided by the Roman Empire in which it developed; and while Christianity helped in countless ways to preserve the Roman legacy, it also did much to destroy or at least radically transform the Roman world. Consequently, attitudes toward Christianity's effect on the broad stage of human history can have a great deal to do with attitudes toward Rome.

Hegel, whose famous *Philosophy of History* Nietzsche had scorned in two of his earliest works,[2] illustrates this as clearly as Nietzsche, but with instructively opposed value judgments. However much Hegel admired Greece, his picture of Rome was very different. To be sure, the very nature of his method prompted him to point to the indispensable contribution of every major force in the past, including Rome; but Roman achievements were usually presented as effects of particularly odious faults. "To the constrained, non-spiritual, and unfeeling intelligence of the Roman world we owe the origin and the development of *positive law*" can serve as an example of the method.[3] Moreover, Hegel flayed the oppressiveness of the Roman Empire without mercy. This enabled him to greet Christianity as a valid protest against Rome, so that even the otherworldliness of Christianity, which, one could easily argue, was really no more to his taste than to Nietzsche's, could emerge as a valid protest against a world where despotism reigned.

Nietzsche wrote a note that reflects an attitude at least moderately akin to Hegel's with respect to Rome and, to a much lesser extent, toward Christianity. "The degeneration of the rulers and the ruling classes has been the cause of the greatest mischief in history! Without the Roman Caesars and Roman society, the insanity of Christianity would never have come to power.... When Nero and Caracalla sat up there, the paradox arose: 'the lowest man is worth more than that man up there!'" (*WP*, #874). There is much here in this note of 1884, if we leave aside the attribution of insanity to Christianity, which is reasonable. By recognizing the corruption of the Roman Empire and its power to provoke, Nietzsche also implicitly recognized that "mastery" is of many different kinds and degrees of legitimacy and resentment, correspondingly, cannot be uniformly unforgivable.

But the spirit and almost the letter of this passage were contradicted by the *Antichrist.*

> The Christian movement, as a European movement, has been from the start a collective movement of the dross and refuse elements of every kind (these want to get power through Christianity). It does *not* express the decline of a race, it is an aggregate of forms of decadence flocking together and seeking each other out from everywhere. It is *not*, as is supposed, the corruption of antiquity itself, of *noble* antiquity, that made Christianity possible. The scholarly idiocy which upholds such ideas even today cannot be contradicted harshly enough. At the very time when the sick, corrupt chandala strata in the whole *imperium* adopted Christianity, the

opposite type, nobility, was present in its most beautiful and mature form. (*A*, #51)

There is no need to think that Nietzsche had decided that Nero and Caracalla were great men after all (Cf. #58). What he was denying was the proposition that the Roman race was itself degenerating as a whole. But in order to bring the paroxysm of his resentment against Christianity to its height, he had to consign bad emperors and the entire structure and spirit that bred them to the realm of the unimportant, and to praise the positive harvest of Roman antiquity unreservedly, overlooking the immense *taedium vitae* accumulating under the increasingly barren yoke of Rome even among Romans themselves.[4] Imbued with this spirit, he lamented, "The whole labor of the ancient world *in vain*: I have no word to express my feelings about something so tremendous" (*A*, #59).

Nietzsche acknowledged that Christianity was one of a myriad of mystery cults flourishing in the Roman Empire; he knew also that the doctrine of eternal punishment was not an invention of a specifically Christian slavish hatred, or even Judaeo-Christian hatred, but had already been fought within the pagan world by Epicurus and Lucretius (*A*, #58). His entire point against Christianity, therefore, depends upon the belief that, notwithstanding the natural allies Christianity had found, it was still a disease within a predominantly healthy organism.

> And Epicurus would have won; every respectable spirit in the Roman Empire was an Epicurean. Then Paul appeared—Paul, the chandala hatred against Rome, against "the world," become flesh, become genius, the Jew, the *eternal* Wandering Jew par excellence. What he guessed was how one could use the little sectarian Christian movement apart from Judaism to kindle a "world fire"; how with the symbol of "God on the cross" one could unite all who lay at the bottom, all who were secretly rebellious, the whole inheritance of anarchistic agitation in the Empire, into a tremendous power. (*A*, 58)

Whatever one's attitude toward Christianity and Rome, this historical melodrama is vulgar in the extreme and ardently, unsurpassably, judgmental. Seldom has the devil himself been credited with such a power of subversion as Nietzsche bestowed on Paul, perhaps with the conviction that what Paul virtually alone had done he alone might undo. Alternatively, one could suggest that Nietzsche descended to vulgarity precisely in order to produce an effect of Pauline immensity.

The *Genealogy* had already suggested a kind of dialectical (if also quasibiological) contest between Roman health and Judaeo-Christian sickness across the centuries, and we can use that sketch to help finish the story. After the triumph of Christianity,

There was, to be sure, in the Renaissance an uncanny and glittering reawakening of the classical ideal, of the noble mode of evaluating all things; Rome itself ... stirred like one awakened from seeming death: but Judea immediately triumphed again, thanks to that thoroughly plebeian (German and English) *ressentiment* movement called the Reformation, and to that which was bound to arise from it, the restoration of the church....

With the French Revolution, Judea once again triumphed over the classical ideal, and this time in an even more profound and decisive sense: the last political noblesse in Europe, that of the *French* seventeenth and eighteenth century, collapsed, beneath the popular instincts of *ressentiment*—greater rejoicing, more uproarious enthusiasm had never been heard on earth. (*G*, 1:16)

With this we arrive at the present. Nietzsche's indictment of the modern age, as well as the slavish religion that produced it, as the last quotation should make clear, has an important political dimension. This topic will be treated in the next chapters. For now, the case for a regressive Nietzschean vision of history will concentrate on more general features of his onslaught on modernity. Much of his disgust with modern man found expression in an obsessively repeated denunciation of the taming and softening allegedly created by Christian influence. This theme, itself only a variant of Zarathustra's contempt for those without claws, was expressed, directly and indirectly, in all of Nietzsche's mature books, and in the *Genealogy* he indulged in contempt for modern weakness in each of its three essays. A single specimen will suffice.

[G]rant me from time to time—if there are divine goddesses in the realm beyond good and evil—grant me the sight, but *one* glance of something perfect, wholly achieved, happy, mighty, triumphant, something still capable of arousing fear! Of a man who justifies *man*, of a complementary and redeeming lucky hit on the part of man for the sake of which one may still *believe in man!*

For this is how things are: the diminution and leveling of European man constitutes *our* greatest danger, for the sight of him makes us weary.—We can see nothing today that wants to grow greater, we suspect that things will continue to go down, down, to become thinner, more good-natured, more prudent, more comfortable, more mediocre, more indifferent, more Chinese, more Christian—there is no doubt that man is getting "better" all the time. (*G*, 1:12)

Later in the work Nietzsche would make clearer that Christianity was, at the least, the principal cause of this weakening, for its entire method of "improving" man would consist in a manipulation of guilt-ridden emotion in a fashion that exhausts and emasculates (*G*, 3:21). In *Twilight of the Idols*, this point was repeated when Nietzsche charged Christianity with having hunted down the "most beautiful specimens of the 'blond beast'" (the famous phrase he had used in the *Genealogy*) and made them sick. "Physiologically speaking: in the struggle with beasts, to make them sick *may* be the only means for making them weak. This the church understood: it *ruined* man, it weakened him—but it claimed to have improved him" (*T*, "Improvers of Mankind," 2).

Yet, in a note from the same period, Nietzsche actually wrote that, for those "still savage and fateful," "Christianity is a cure, at least a means of taming (—under certain circumstances it serves to make sick: which *can be useful in breaking savagery and brutality*)" (*WP*, #236, emphasis added.) This remark, implying as it does that some measure of taming, even at the cost of making "sick," is better than no taming at all, by no means undercuts Nietzsche's conviction that refinement without loss of strength is the supreme desideratum, but has the advantage of being less morally ambiguous than nonsense about "beautiful specimens of the 'blond beast.'" One might surmise that, if Nietzsche published his denunciations of "taming" and left unpublished this note which reduces the force of them all, the reason was that he regarded the taming of man as complete insofar as it was desirable and merely denounced it to keep it from going any further. There is perhaps something, if not much, to be said for this view, which implies that Nietzsche took certain civilized standards of conduct for granted, and did not intend to undermine them.[5] At one point in *Twilight* itself, he referred briefly but with evident sarcasm to a reviewer who had "'understood'" him to desire to abolish "all decent feelings" (*T*, "What the Germans Lack," 37). Yet the penultimate section of the *Genealogy* predicted flatly: "morality will gradually *perish* now: this is the great spectacle in a hundred acts reserved for the next two centuries in Europe—the most terrible, most questionable, and perhaps also the most hopeful of all spectacles" (*G*, 3:27). Elsewhere, he denied that the modern European constituted any advance over Arabs and Corsicans, cited for their ferocity (*WP*: #90). Beyond doubt for the very late Nietzsche as for the Nietzsche of *Zarathustra*, refined strength was better than brutal strength. But his inability to think through the ideal of "the Roman Caesar with the soul of Christ" in any kind of detail left him a prey to constant shifts of mood, and the ideal of raw strength could surface in a fashion that served, however fleetingly, to cast doubt on all "civilizing" sublimation and even mental advance itself. Most intriguing in this regard was his contention, voiced long after his estrangement from Wagner, that the latter had created a *"very free"* man in his Siegfried (*BGE*, #256). Siegfried in the *Ring* is not especially cruel and has much that might be considered noble; but he is, even by the standards of operatic tenors, quite unusually stupid, a character who, most of the time, understands nothing of what goes on around him.[6] It would be harder to imagine an embodiment of an ideal more remote from a philosopher's, except by the law of attracting opposites.

As presented in his late works, the attack on modern man for being tame, weak, and sick (three different things, but tending to merge in Nietzsche's mind), scarcely constitutes even a line of thought. It is largely a vehicle for the expression of atrabilious feelings. But behind these denunciations stands a perception more subtle and worthwhile, the conviction that man is losing his capacity for lofty greatness of soul. This found its classic expression near the very beginning of *Zarathustra*, in his prophecy of the "last man."

> Alas, the time is coming when man will no longer give birth to a star. Alas, the time of the most despicable man is coming, he that is no longer able to despise himself. Behold, I show you the *last man*.
>
> "What is love? What is creation? What is longing? What is a star?" thus asks the last man, and he blinks.
>
> The earth has become small, and on it hops the last man, who makes everything small. His race is as ineradicable as the flea-beetle; the last man lives longest.
>
> "We have invented happiness," say the last men, and they blink. They have left the regions where it was hard to live, for one needs warmth. One still loves one's neighbor and rubs against him, for one needs warmth....
>
> One still works, for work is a form of entertainment. But one is careful lest the entertainment be too harrowing. One no longer becomes poor or rich: both require too much exertion. Who still wants to rule? Who obey? Both require too much exertion.
>
> No shepherd and one herd! Everybody wants the same, everybody is the same: whoever feels different goes voluntarily into a madhouse.
>
> "Formerly, all the world was mad," say the most refined, and they blink....
>
> One has one's little pleasure for the day and one's little pleasure for the night: but one has a regard for health. (*TSZ*, 1: "Prologue," 5)

It would be easy to maintain that there is nothing here that had not already been said with much more dignity, poise, and depth of analysis by Tocqueville in the second volume of *Democracy in America*, published in 1840, and with a vastly more civilized humor by Kierkegaard in his essay the *Present Age*, in 1846. But this is, nonetheless, one of the most celebrated passages in all of Nietzsche, and deservedly so. It gains in nobility by being offered as a prophecy rather than as pure indictment of the present, which tempers its otherwise intemperate hate, and elevates it to the status of a warning for the future rather than a personal attack on the living. The prophecy is vague, of course, but in a fruitfully stimulating rather than a simply nebulous fashion. Whether Nietzsche's thought as a whole, and his social thought in particular, succeeds in clarifying this vagueness and in showing a way of avoiding this subhuman condition without introducing cures more dehumanizing than the disease is a question to which this book gives a largely negative answer. But the vision of the "last man" at least offers a compelling reason to take Nietzsche's whole enterprise seriously, something that the fatuous yearning for "something still capable of arousing fear" certainly does not provide.

In light of this vision of the last man, we can say that Nietzsche's philosophy of history developed under a condition of anxiety about the human future, and developed in the form of a meditation about the past that sought to explain both the reasons for threatening degeneration and, in its more "progressive" aspects, the grounds for hope. At the least, it sought to provide a stimulus to action and thought designed to elevate the human future. In the "Preface" to the *Genealogy*, which announced Nietzsche's critical task, this positive aim is clearly implicit even when the accent seems focused on the negative. "What if a symptom of regression were inherent in the 'good,' likewise a danger ... through which the present was possibly *living at the expense of the future?* Perhaps more comfortably, less dangerously, but at the same time in a meaner style, more basely?—So that precisely morality would be to blame if the *highest power and splendor* actually possible to the type man was never in fact attained? So that precisely morality was the danger of dangers" (G, "Preface," 6). In his preceding book, *Beyond Good and Evil*, with its significant subtitle, *Prelude to a Philosophy of the Future*, Nietzsche had already questioned the worth of goodness, proclaimed the degeneration of man, the necessity of new evaluations, and his anxiety before a history that might yet miscarry. Simultaneously, he asserted the human need to take control over history, one of the most central and least emphasized aspects of his entire philosophy, with a pomposity as unsurpassable as it is, in its way, fitting.

> Where, then, must *we* reach with our hopes?
> Toward *new philosophers*; there is no choice; toward spirits strong and original enough to provide the stimuli for opposite valuations and to re-value and invert "eternal values"; toward forerunners, toward men of the future who in the present tie the knot and constraint that forces the will of millennia upon *new* tracks. To teach man the future of man as his *will* [cf. A, #3], as dependent on a human will, and to prepare great ventures and over-all attempts of discipline and cultivation by way of putting an end to that gruesome dominion of nonsense and accident that has so far been called "history"— ... It is the image of such leaders that *we* envisage: may I say this out loud, you free spirits? The conditions that one would have partly to create and partly to exploit for their genesis; ... a revaluation of values under whose new pressure and hammer a conscience would be steeled, a heart turned to bronze, in order to endure the weight of such responsibility; on the other hand, the necessity of such leaders, the frightening danger that they might fail to appear or that they might turn out badly or degenerate—these are *our* real worries and gloom—do you

know that, you free spirits?—these are the heavy distant thoughts and storms that pass over the sky of *our* life.

... [A]nyone who has the rare eye for the over-all danger that "man" himself *degenerates*; ... anyone who fathoms the calamity that lies concealed in the absurd guilelessness and blind confidence of "modern ideas" and even more in the whole Christian-European morality—suffers from an anxiety that is past all comparisons....

The *over-all degeneration of man* down to what today appears to the socialist dolts and flatheads as their "man of the future" ... is *possible*, there is no doubt of it. Anyone who has once thought through this possibility to the end, no longer knows any other nausea than other men—but perhaps also a new *task!*—(*BGE*, #203)

From the standpoint of both the ambition and the anxiety expressed here, which are perfectly complementary and underlie most of Nietzsche's late work as a whole (the pose of *amor fati* excepted), the apparent contradiction between condemning Christianity root and branch and claiming to be its grateful heir loses some of its force, just as the triumphalism of "I attempt in my own way a justification of history" loses some of its certainty. The present is a vantage point from which two basic possibilities for the future can be glimpsed, a decadence that will prevent man from reaching his highest splendor or a deliberate, willed reversal of decadence, which will carry man higher by virtue of the clarity gained in the struggle with Christianity and decadence themselves. This double possibility in turn throws a double light upon the past. Nor need one even say that this mode of interpretation reduces Nietzsche's works to the status of mere tracts for the times. There is no difficulty in conceiving them as collectively outlining a kind of eternal struggle, in the fashion of Augustine's *City of God*, but more truly eternal because without any hope of, or wish for, the intervention of God to introduce a final and fixed clarity into the situation. Nietzsche's own statements on the need to preserve Christianity in spite of everything, already noted, support such a reading.

In conceiving a philosophy of history with the present as a decisive crossroads, however, Nietzsche was less like Augustine, for whom man did not control history; less like Hegel, for whom history was, in its *essentials*, over; less like Marx, for whom final victory was guaranteed, than he was like Jean-Jacques Rousseau. I should like to pursue this comparison at moderate length. There can, I believe, be no better way either to summarize the weaknesses of the *Genealogy*, since Rousseau offered a countermyth of human origins perhaps no more, but certainly no less compelling, or to introduce Nietzsche's social thought proper, since inequality in some sense was its basic premise just as equality in some sense was Rousseau's.

The *Discourse on the Origins of Human Inequality*, like the *Genealogy*, was a kind of macropsychoanalysis of modern man, ferreting out the his-

torical causes of his neurosis. And, because of the ambiguous openness of
the present, Rousseau's work is ambiguous about man's past in a fashion
strikingly analogous to what we have observed in the case of Nietzsche.
The original preneurotic state could appear to be glorified as a rhetorical
foil highlighting the evils of man's present state. Yet the neurosis itself is
the precondition of a genuine self-elevation of the species. Thus, each author
lay himself open to a one-sided interpretation as an enthusiastic apostle of
progress or an apostle of a "return" to some paradise lost. (Nietzsche himself, typically, oversimplified Rousseau in just that latter way.)

What makes the comparison between Rousseau and Nietzsche so interesting, however, is that the basic opposition between them, which the above
similarities only set off, is so remarkably exact. To reduce the matter to brief
formulae: Rousseau saw the crisis of modern man as consisting in an ever-
deepening, ever more self-alienating competitiveness, which must be reversed, if possible (and Rousseau doubted that possibility) in the direction of
equality. Nietzsche saw it as consisting in an ever-deepening, more self-
alienating throttling of competitiveness, which must be reversed, not necessarily by some individualistic free-for-all, but in the direction of hierarchical
gradation.

Like Nietzsche himself, Rousseau was given to rather exaggerated formulations. One could easily oversimplify the contrast between the two by
citing Rousseau's dictum "All men are naturally lazy,"[7] taking it as the unequivocal expression of Rousseau's ideal without even troubling to find out
what he meant by laziness, and contrasting it with Nietzsche's vision of the
exceptional man as forever in need of obstacles and tasks. In order to avoid
such oversimplification while paying due recognition to the centrality of
this doctrine of natural laziness in Rousseau's thought, we might divide his
conception of the energy that contradicts laziness into several parts. The
first would entail the exertion to fill the simplest bodily needs. Because this
exertion could be very light in the favorable circumstances postulated by
Rousseau in what he took to be the nonsocial state of earliest humanity,
the concept of "natural needs," which Rousseau inherited from antiquity,
scarcely qualified laziness. In general, early man enjoyed repose punctuated
only by modest spurts of necessary exertion. The second form of energy was
the force that both untamed animals and men not already accustomed to
slavery could exert in defense of their freedom. This force could be great
indeed, leading even to death in self-defense or, in its socialized form, in
defense of the fatherland. But because this energy was defensive in character
rather than expansive or aggressive, it does not so much undermine the postulate of laziness as explain the sense in which Rousseau meant it. Man's
laziness, like that of untamed animals, is nothing more or less than the desire
for *autonomy*, the desire to follow a natural rhythm of desire that is purely
internal and easily satisfied by the majority of men, but that tolerates no

external constraint.

But man is not entirely the same as an animal that can do nothing but eat, procreate, and sleep. He has a capacity for "perfectibility," which is as open-ended as his mind when once stimulated by natural need and, far more, by social organization. The ambiguities of Rousseau's anthropology, and the ambivalence toward the human condition in his writings, center on this indeterminate faculty. On the one hand, Rousseau was far from blind to the glories of the moral, intellectual, and aesthetic splendors that man could attain in society. On the other hand, he was oppressed with the power of the social condition to alienate man from himself and to debase rather than elevate his nature by a competitive passion that was the product of socially induced *amour propre*, and resulted in the desire to find happiness only through others' esteem and, worse, at others' expense. Since the victory of a proper social organization that would guarantee freedom, permit a decent exercise of the genuinely ennobling human faculties, and encourage the avoidance of false desires and their increasingly destructive force was by no means assured, Rousseau's anxiety before history was also "past all comparisons."[8]

In describing the "origins of human inequality," Rousseau may be said to have attempted to provide a genealogy of the *master*, whom he did not take to be an original fact of "nature" but a socially derived one. If we return to Nietzsche, in light of this we must ask: what is *his* genealogy of the master? Strikingly, his account of the earliest facts about human society makes no mention of predatory violence at all, and is in a later section of the *Genealogy* than the fundamental discussion of masters and slaves. Instead, it offers an economic theory of the origin of comparisons and evaluations, both crucial to his conception of humanity and civilization. The "oldest and most primitive personal relationship," Nietzsche maintained, was that between "buyer and seller, creditor and debtor: it was here that one person first encountered another person, that one person first *measured himself* against another." It was in this economic activity of exchanging and determining prices that thinking and evaluating both developed, as did "human pride, the feeling of superiority in relation to other animals," which was itself both a part and a result of evaluating activity (*G*, 2:8).

It would be natural to wish to know who the *parents* of these original Yankees were, and whether Nietzsche would want us to conceive of their meeting as an exchange of favors. The issue is not entirely a laughing matter, for he purports to write the genealogy of morals, and one would think that such a topic would eventually produce some mention of the *family*. Astoundingly, it does not in Nietzsche's case. (This is all the more remarkable in a book that features the Jews so prominently, whose essence he had defined in *Zarathustra* in relation to the commandment: "honor thy father and thy mother" (*TSZ*, 1:15), a definition certainly open to question, but probably the most perceptive thing he ever said, positive, negative, or neutral, about the Jews). Furthermore, if man as a scrupulously evaluating animal emerged *prior* to the existence of genuine mastery, as appears to be the case in this account, then the claims for the master as the original fount of all concepts of value, a case he had made earlier, collapses. In the first essay of the *Genealogy*, Nietzsche maintained:

> The pathos of nobility and distance ... the protracted and domineering fundamental total feeling on the part of a higher ruling order in relation to a lower order, to a "below"—*that* is the origin of the antithesis of "good" and "bad." (The lordly right of giving names extends so far that one should allow oneself to conceive the origin of language itself as an expression of power on the part of rulers: they say "this *is* this and this," they seal every thing and event with a sound and, as it were, take possession of it.) (*G*, 1:2)

It is hard to know what to make of this astonishing parenthetical suggestion. That there is power and even a kind of metaphorical lordliness in human speech none will deny. But if there may be, as Nietzsche maintained, no society, "however low," which has no exchanges, there is certainly none that has no language, whereas there have been many in which the pathos of nobility is missing because there are no classes in the meaningful sense presupposed by this linguistic theory.

Let us, however, dismiss Nietzsche's hypothesis on language as a momentary, if revealing, excess.[9] What is not possible to dismiss is the larger argument out of which it grew. In the second essay of the *Genealogy*, the account of early society is economic and, indeed, the motives for joining it are unambiguously utilitarian: "one has bound and pledged oneself to the community with a view to injuries and hostile acts" (*G*, 2:9). Nietzsche's account of aristocratic morality, by contrast, explicitly denied a utilitarian component in their morality, and in the origin of the judgment "good"; for "it was 'the good' themselves, that is to say, the noble, powerful, high-stationed and high-minded, who felt and established themselves and their actions as good, that is, of the first rank, in contradistinction to all the low, low-minded, common and plebeian. It was out of this *pathos of distance* [Nietzsche's favorite phrase, repeated frequently] that they first seized the right to create values and to coin names for values: what had they to do with utility!" (*G*, 1:2). One might well argue that Nietzsche was clearly thinking here of a later stage of society than the primitive, prehistoric, economic community he speculated about in the second essay. This may well be true, although the hypothesis about language that soon follows the last quotation must make one unsure. Even apart from this uncertainty, however, the problem of the emergence of a horde of warriors in the first place and the development of an embryonic aristocratic ideology and self-identity is not solved. Hordes of rampaging warriors are not, so far as we know, an original fact of nature. They *developed*; and presumably they did so partly because of the utility, first of hunting animals, then of killing, robbing, and enslaving men. This utility, to be sure, was not felt by their victims, but it was certainly felt by the other members of their own horde, a utility that must have encouraged predatory behavior. One need have no faith in "utilitarianism" as the last word in either history or philosophical morality in order to concede that much.

An even more revealing instance of Nietzsche's will to overlook the depth of social influence in shaping the master is the following notorious passage, which has aroused so much righteous indignation that its manifest self-contradiction has, to my knowledge, been completely overlooked.

> Here there is one thing we shall be the last to deny: he who knows these "good men" [according to the masters' own evaluations] only as enemies knows only *evil enemies*, and the same men who are held so sternly in check *inter pares* by custom, respect, usage, gratitude, and even more by mutual suspicion and jealousy, and who on the other hand in their relations with one another show themselves so resourceful in consideration, self-control, delicacy, loyalty, pride, and friendship—once they go outside, where the strange, the *stranger* is found, they are not much better than uncaged beasts of prey. There they savor a freedom from all social constraints, they compensate themselves in the wilderness for the tension engendered by protracted confinement and enclosure within the peace of society, they go *back* to the innocent conscience of the beast of prey, as triumphant monsters who perhaps emerge from a disgusting procession of murder, arson, rape, and torture, exhilarated and undisturbed of soul, as if it were no more than a student's prank, convinced they have provided the poets with a lot more material for song and praise. One cannot fail to see at the bottom of all these noble races the beast of prey, the splendid *blond beast* prowling about avidly in search of spoil and victory; this hidden core needs to erupt from time to time, the animal has to get out again and go back to the wilderness: the Roman, Arabian, Germanic, Japanese nobility, the Homeric heroes, the Scandinavian Vikings—they all shared this need. (*G*, 1:11)

In this passage, the emphasis Nietzsche placed upon "*back*" may have owed something to the negative influence of Rousseau. Be this as it may, if men relapsing into animals *compensate* themselves for the tensions of society, how can it be assumed that the barbarism with which they refresh themselves is of the same kind as the animality they had left? And why assume that the tensions of society are those of peacefulness alone? It could just as easily be competitive pressures in peace that must be assuaged by making others suffer. This "relapse" into barbarism, in other words, can be viewed as the venting of frustration or an attempt to heighten one's social standing in relation to competitors within the group by successful conquest. In either event, these blond beasts (or Caesars and Pompeys) cannot be psychologically identified without more ado with primitive hunters in loose, nomadic societies. Finally, if one is convinced that, in behaving like a wildman, one has "provided the poets with a lot more material for song and praise," then the role of imitation, social example, and vanity cannot be denied without demonstrating the indemonstrable and, indeed, the highly improbable, proposition that such a conviction plays no part in determining the behavior. As a matter of fact, the "inspirational" value of poetry in "heroic ages" was very great, and not merely among the Greeks. But one may wonder how much the earliest hunters listened to poetry, and one can, consequently wonder whether the predatory activities of such hunters displayed a boundless will to power or a mere action from bodily need, followed by Rousseauist repose.

The purpose of the present discussion, and the purpose of bringing Rousseau into it, has not been to support any doctrine of "the natural goodness of man," about which Rousseau's views were much more complex than nonspecialists normally realize. It has been, instead, to show the importance of Nietzsche's ontology to his conception of the master, who is made to appear "natural" because of Nietzsche's undemonstrated conception of nature. In his late work, Nietzsche denounced morality as unnatural, and wrote that he sought a "return" and "ascent" to nature, in a stronger sense than Rousseau's (T, "Skirmishes," #48). Accordingly, one can say that Nietzsche's philosophy depends upon the "naturalness" of the desire to overcome obstacles and to "violate everything," even if the original forms of these desires can and should be sublimated; that it even depends upon the contention that hunger is derivative from a more basic drive and the rest of the ontological propositions of the Nachlass. By the same token, however, it would be equally plausible to maintain that the historical dogmas of the Genealogy constitute a kind of replacement for the missing ontological demonstration, one that seeks to establish the original, natural character of mastery by sleight of hand. One need not think that Nietzsche wanted a return to predatory behavior tant pur in order to recognize that his aim was to provide a stimulus for mastery in some sense. He aimed to erect a counterweight to the last man by this construction of a nature in which the history gains plausibility from the ontology, the ontology from the history, the "strong" in some dominating sense gain glorification from both, and the resentful are denounced, just as Rousseau aimed to denounce the tensions of competitive civilization as unnatural with the aid of his speculative reconstruction of social origins. In this dispute, neither, to repeat, is any less arbitrary than the other.

One of the gravest deficiencies of Kaufmann's reading of Nietzsche is that it depicts Nietzsche's thinking as rooted primarily in a strictly empirical psychology, shoving his ontological assumptions into the sidelines.[10] An empirical foundation for the primacy of the will to power, quite apart from the fact that it might not be possible at all, could not have the normative status Nietzsche obviously meant it to have, however free he considered the process of value-creation to be. Any empirical psychology can be countered with radically different kinds of evidence and its relevance to morality can always be questioned. There are warriors and nonwarriors, as Nietzsche knew well enough, and his task was to present the "warriors" (in a real or sublimated sense) as *higher representatives of being*. Furthermore, even if one takes a unitary view of human nature, which is possible provided one rises to a sufficiently high and empty level of abstraction, the question can still be asked: how did this nature originate? And even if the answer should lie, not in social conditions or history, but in the ontological limitations of human finitude, the insecurity guaranteed by death, for example, no normative status is achieved in this way either. (Hence Nietzsche's drive to depict finitude in a positive way, that its lust to overcome itself could be a norm of strength, not a reactive pathos.) In apparently endeavoring to rescue Nietzsche from the strictures of Anglo-Saxon positivism and Kantian criticism, (or from the enthusiastic metaphysical zeal of many of his modern French interpreters), Kaufmann verged upon reducing him to the sort of empirical investigators he scorned (even if he conceded their utility), whereas Nietzsche obviously thought of himself as a creator of values, one who shaped Being after his own heart, and sought power in the process.

> Science is flourishing today and her good conscience is written all over her face, while the level to which all modern philosophy has gradually sunk, this rest of philosophy today, invites mistrust and displeasure, if not mockery and pity. Philosophy reduced to "theory of knowledge," in fact no more than a timid epochism and doctrine of abstinence—a philosophy that never gets beyond the threshold and takes pains to *deny* itself the right to enter—that is philosophy in its last throes, an end, an agony, something inspiring pity. How could such a philosophy—*dominate!* (*BGE*, #204)

One need not believe with any seriousness that this desire for a dominating philosophy constituted any blanket invitation to mythmaking in Nietzsche's own eyes. But he had need of a supporting ontology. For, however paradoxical it may seem, the final and most important reason for troubling the reader with Rousseau in this discussion is that a very strong case can be made that Nietzsche really agreed with him about the centrality of society in forming the pathos of distance that Nietzsche, though not Rousseau, desired. Rousseau, we have seen, emphasized the importance of hierarchy and social competitiveness as historical variables. Nietzsche too, we shall see in the next chapter, stressed the role of social organization in producing, if not the germ, then the full development of the "psychology" of the will to power. If this stress is to avoid cutting the ground out from under Nietzsche's own feet, it must be supported by his ontology, by an insistence that a hierarchical society is the *natural* one and that the "pathos of distance" is entitled to the central place Nietzsche gives it.

It cannot, however, be natural in the strictest sense or its opposite would not be possible, and it *is* possible, as we have seen Nietzsche claim. In other words, in numbers is a strength that might overpower the more glorious strength of the few. In order to aid the endangered few, and maintain his own moral enthusiasm, Nietzsche will need all the vigor that only resentment can provide. The resentment of resentment will strengthen the few, and this reactive arrogance in the face of an apparently overwhelming threat will cap and crystallize aristocratic ideology and the will to power as nothing else could.

6
Foundations of Nietzschean Politics:
The Ideal of Inequality

"IN the age of *suffrage universel*, i.e., when everyone may sit in judgment on everyone and everything," runs a characteristic note from the *Will to Power*, "I feel impelled to reestablish *order of rank*" (#854). The doctrine of human inequality was one of the most basic axioms of Nietzsche's anthropology. More important, the *desirability* of inequality was perhaps the basic doctrine of his political philosophy. The ideal of what should be is even more important than the conviction about what is in defining Nietzsche's position, in spite of his hostility to "idealism" in the pejorative, "unrealistic" sense of the term, because the belief that people are unequal in native ability was and is widespread among convinced believers in democratic government. At the same time, other democrats could recognize *de facto* inequality of cultural or even moral attributes, but believe in a progressive elevation of the general level of humanity to the ranks once occupied exclusively by a few. Nietzsche, in contrast to the representatives of both of these forms of liberalism, did not believe in the desirability of political democracy or in the ideal of the eventual democratization of culture. This chapter will focus upon the reasons for his insistence upon "order of rank" (*Rangordnung*) and his very ambiguous ideal of the proper moral relationships between superiors and inferiors in the political order.

Why did Nietzsche make an ideal of inequality? All questions of race or genetic endowment aside, the most obvious support for the aristocratic principle among those whose interest was, like Nietzsche's, primarily in a cultural élite, was the purely material requirements of a leisure class. Inequality of wealth and even political power, in other words, could be defended as a way of ensuring that some people would have the time and resources to advance culture. There is certainly some reason to believe that this argument played a role in Nietzsche's thinking, but there is remarkably little evidence that points unambiguously in that direction. His general contention that a "high culture is a pyramid: it can stand only on a broad base" (*A*, #57) no doubt took material considerations related to the necessity of the division of labor into account; but Nietzsche did not stress this, and as we shall see shortly, the "broad base" is capable of a different construction, one on which he laid a much clearer emphasis. Furthermore, it is well to remind ourselves that Nietzsche wrote in a period when the Industrial Revolution was rapidly transforming the material condition of Europe and when education was being extended to ever-wider circles with equal rapidity. The prospect of a vast extension of the benefits of leisure and culture was no longer an idle Utopian fantasy.

The prospect of such an extension, to be sure, was limited by the possibility of radical inequality of natural endowment for cultural pursuits, and this unquestionably affected Nietzsche, who was enamored of the old tag *Pulchrum est paucorum hominum* (*A*, #57) (the beautiful is for the few). But since there was nothing in the belief in natural inequality that must necessarily lead anyone to oppose democratic government, we cannot rely upon the doctrine of natural inequality to provide the key to Nietzsche's hierarchicalism.

His belief in hierarchy would seem to have more to do with psychological considerations than with any other. By this, I do not mean his own psychology but his view of man as determined and defined by the concept of the will to power. A late note reads in its entirety: "What *I* fight against: that an exceptional type should make war on the rule—instead of grasping that the continued existence of the rule is the precondition for the value of the exception. For example, the ladies who, instead of feeling their abnormal thirst for scholarship as a distinction, want to disrupt the status of woman in general" (*WP*, #894). In other words, the continued existence of an ignorant mass is the essential precondition for the value of learning, among men, we must suppose, as much as among women.

This quotation is by no means unusual in the Nietzschean corpus. He gave the basic principle behind it repeated expression. "Absurd and contemptible form of idealism that would *not* have mediocrity *mediocre* and, instead of feeling a sense of triumph at a state of exceptionalness, becomes *indignant* over cowardice, falsity, pettiness, and wretchedness. *One should not desire these things to be different!* and should make the gulf *wider!*—" (*WP*, #891). That one could "desire these things to be different" without necessarily becoming "indignant" was something Nietzsche did not consider. Another example of this line of thought may be cited: "*The struggle with the canaille and the cattle.* If a certain taming and order is to be achieved, the chasm between [the] purified and reborn people and the remainder must be made as fearful as possible—.

"This chasm increases in the higher castes their self-regard, their faith in that which they represent—hence the chandala" (*WP*, #237). One can certainly argue that Nietzsche's emphasis upon this theme of comparative distinction may derive less from the wish to make the feeling of individual power an absolute end in itself than from the wish to exploit that feeling to strengthen the desire for excellence. There is some evidence, in addition to the last quotation, to support such an interpretation. "One would make a fit little boy stare if one asked him: 'Would you like to become virtuous?'—but he will open his eyes wide if asked: "Would you like to become stronger than your friends?'" (*WP*, #918). This is repulsive enough, and the passage has an accent of vulgarity rare in Nietzsche, even in his notes. But it suggests the idea of exploiting *Machtgefühl* in the interest of virtue, an idea made still more explicit by his stated desire to restore its "aristocratic magic" to virtue (*WP*, #317).

On the other hand, the abstract principle of comparison and the equally abstract notion of *Machtgefühl* are more deeply rooted in the philosophy of the will to power than any concrete value or form of virtue. The notorious vagueness of Nietzsche's positive ideals would seem to have much to do with his belief that by using purely comparative epithets he could actually say something very meaningful. But the opposite could as easily be maintained: that by referring as constantly as he did to what he called "the pathos of distance" and by using terms like *strong* and *weak*, which he once conceded were purely relative (*GS*, #118), he ran the risk of implying that the whole realm of human values, and every form of merit, are nothing but an optical illusion, with nothing of intrinsic worth anywhere. All positive values instead are dependent upon being seen next to something worse, and in turn capable of being annihilated by the reality or merely the thought of something better yet.

The premise of the quotations just presented is rooted in a common, all-too-common, sense. But these passages are nevertheless astonishing. They represent a betrayal of any genuine notion of aristocratic values perhaps without parallel in the history of serious and elevated thought. One might wonder whether, in writing them, Nietzsche was primarily moved by a desire born of desperation to shore up the truly valuable by any means at hand, or whether, instead, he was moved by a desire to degrade the aristocratic in the interests of showing the psychological truth inherent in the pettiest and most unworthy components of the doctrine of will to power. The former is most likely, but he actually accomplished the latter. This "accomplishment," moreover, not merely consigned the noble to the void of comparative nihilism, but also betrayed his aim of defending a concept of sturdily independent, "unalienated" individuality. A Rousseauist tirade on the corruption of thought and feeling in civilization could scarcely find better examples anywhere than in Nietzsche's assertion that "virtue ... does not suffer from the absence of virtue, but on the contrary regards this as the distancing relationship on the basis of which there is something to honor in virtue ..."

(*WP*, #317).

The most formidable obstacle to taking this line of thought as genuinely representative of Nietzsche's position when dealing with questions of value in a specifically *social* context appears in his manner of treating the "master" in the *Genealogy*. There, we recall, the master acted spontaneously out of the plenitude of his own strength and health of instinct. And Nietzsche had emphasized that, in contrast to the resentful, the "'well-born' *felt* themselves to be the 'happy'; they did not have to establish their happiness artificially by examining their enemies...." (*G*, 1:10). It would be a foolish and unfair pedantry that would confine this passage purely to its literal meaning and stress that inferiors need not be enemies. It would be much more to the point to observe that the "well-born" under discussion here are of a raw sort in Nietzsche's own view, and that what he says about them cannot be carelessly used to define his thought on the question of the best way to produce a highly sophisticated élite. His views on that question constitute, in fact, a combination of extolling the benefits of a domination based on conquest with a reliance upon the comparative principle among the established warrior class to produce a mature, self-conscious sense of superiority, which would then issue in ever-subtler spiritual manifestations.

The central text in all of Nietzsche's works for his views on the necessity of aristocracy will make this clear. It is the first aphorism from the chapter "What is Noble?" in *Beyond Good and Evil*. While the second paragraph only foreshadows the historical doctrine, already discussed, that Nietzsche was to propound in his next book, the *Genealogy*, the first remained the clearest argument on behalf of social stratification he ever wrote. Because of its immense importance, I quote the entire aphorism.

> Every enhancement of the type "man" has so far been the work of an aristocratic society—and it will be so again and again—a society that believes in the long ladder of an order of rank and differences in value between man and man, and that needs slavery in some sense or other. Without that *pathos of distance* which grows out of the ingrained difference between strata—when the ruling caste constantly looks afar and looks down upon subjects and instruments and just as constantly practices obedience and command, keeping down and keeping at a distance—that other, more mysterious pathos could not have grown up either—the craving for an ever new widening of distances within the soul itself, the development of ever higher, rarer, more remote, further-stretching, more comprehensive states—in brief, simply the enhancement of the type "man," the continual "self-overcoming of man," to use a moral formula in a supra-moral sense.
>
> To be sure, one should not yield to humanitarian illusions about the origins of aristocratic society (and thus of the presupposition of this enhancement of the type "man"): truth is hard. Let us admit to ourselves,

without trying to be considerate, how every higher culture on earth so far has *begun*. Human beings whose nature was still natural, barbarians in every terrible sense of the word, men of prey who were still in possession of unbroken strength of will and lust for power, hurled themselves upon weaker, more civilized, more peaceful races, perhaps traders or cattle raisers, or upon mellow old cultures whose last vitality was even then flaring up in splendid fireworks of spirit and corruption. In the beginning, the noble caste was always the barbarian caste: their predominance did not lie mainly in physical strength but in strength of soul—they were more *whole* human beings (which also means at every level, "more whole beasts"). (*BGE*, #257)

It should be clear from this passage that by "aristocratic society" Nietzsche did not mean a society that permits or encourages all and sundry to develop their talents to the utmost, but a society that is hierarchically and even repressively organized and that actively discourages any doctrine of the fundamental unity of mankind. Both the military origin of aristocratic classes emphasized here and the resulting psychological condition confirm this.

But, while there is an obvious connection between the depth of the feeling of distance and the possession of a privileged position arising from conquest, there is also, one would think, a difference between barbarian conquerors and their heirs, those free to develop those endless worlds of inward hierarchical feeling and aspiration which Nietzsche praised. He took pains in this aphorism not to present the heirs as effete epigoni. They have the power, as much psychological as political, to maintain continued repression, a power that distinguishes a "healthy" aristocracy capable of preserving its predominance from one that is not. But the enhancement of the type man for which Nietzsche looked to aristocratic society was, the first paragraph of the aphorism makes clear, primarily to be understood in spiritual terms. The "pathos of distance" is not a very convincing phrase for barbarian conquerors, and Nietzsche did not apply it to them, but to those later aristocrats whose power has become established and solidified and whose will to power has become rather more internalized.

Does this mean, then, that Nietzsche in effect presented the cultivated noble as similar to the slave in that both were products of a socially engineered internalization of will to power? There are, of course, obvious differences between the aristocratic and slavish condition. In the case of the slave, the internalization is imposed from without by the forcible action of others. In the case of the noble, the internalization appears to be the voluntary act of one who uses a passive foil for his own inward expansion. The former results in a depressive internalization Nietzsche disdained, the latter in a manic internalization he affirmed. All of this is true enough, and important. Nietzsche clearly wished to distinguish between free and unfree forms of self-discipline, and to praise the former rather than the undisciplined as such. Yet there are reasons not to let the matter rest there. What I termed, in interpretation of Nietzsche, the "voluntary act" of the one who feels distance does not simply proceed from his own *innate* strength and will to power, for in that case we would not be talking about a pathos of social distance but the act of overt aggression of the barbarian master as Nietzsche described it. And he would then have had no need to defend hierarchical social organization as a necessary *means* for the encouragement of this pathos and its spiritual fruits. "If you would do away with firm opposition and differences in rank," as a later note, entirely in accord with the aphorism just cited, has it, "you will also abolish all strong love, lofty attitudes, and the feeling of individuality" (*WP*, #936). The pathos of distance, therefore, is initially created at least in part by the effects on the psyche of a social position one does not make, but which helps to make oneself.

It is revealing that Nietzsche never says this directly, although he implied it unmistakably. In fact, he was engaged in a contradictory war on two fronts, one against resentful democrats whose mode of analysis emphasized the role of milieu[1] in producing great men, and the other for a social hierarchy needed to produce great men. The difficulties that this conflict posed for his social thought will be considered in greater detail later in this chapter. At present, one can note that it is even more revealing that Nietzsche never explicitly analyzed what really effects the sublimation of aristocratic will to power that he sought. There would be nothing necessarily reductive about such a discussion; and there would certainly be nothing in such a discussion that need prejudge the issue of whether the qualities of the aristocratic soul were worth preserving at the expense of repressive hierarchy or not. Yet Nietzsche evidently shied away from openly acknowledging what is surely one of the most important facts about the aristocrat: he is *seen*, and seen to be and *expected* to be superior. In other words, the crucial fact about the hereditary aristocrat is not that he seeks recognition as did his barbarian ancestors, according to the famous Hegelian "dialectic of the master and slave," which Nietzsche has been held to have wished to oppose,[2] but that he possesses recognition from birth and also a special incitement to live up to its demands. Nietzsche wished to present the noble's socially conditioned and even socially constrained act as a pure one, even if he also felt compelled to argue for a particular form of society by appealing to its effects. It is in this light that the following note, in which Nietzsche came as close as he ever came to acknowledging the importance of the visibility of the noble, should be read. "*What is noble?*—That one constantly has to play a part. That one seeks situations in which one has constant need of poses. That one leaves happiness to the great majority: happiness as peace of soul, virtue, comfort, Anglo-angelic shopkeeperdom à la Spencer" (*WP*, #944). One can reply to this, and in a spirit of nothing but gratitude for the sublime example presented by countless hereditary aristocrats through the ages, that the noble is simply not free to *seek* to pose. He *must* pose; and in countless situations, he must pose in a preordained way, to be properly dignified, conspicuously courageous, or self-advertisingly free, or else face grave social consequences. This emphatically does not mean, of course, that the nobleman, because of a socially derived inner security, cannot be magnificently capable of rising above any dependence on the esteem or judgment of others in particular concrete situations. The point is rather that the independence of soul that Nietzsche chose to present entirely as the effect of *looking down* in the aphorism from *Beyond Good and Evil* is in part the effect of *being looked up to*.

Taken by itself, this fact is neither good nor evil in the narrow sense of socially useful or useless respectively. But a nobleman who is above all an active leader of people, and concerned with the welfare, however inegalitarian, of the social organism of which he forms a part, might "pose" in a fashion that is in complete harmony with the moral expectations of his equals and inferiors alike. It was this moral unity between leaders and led that induced Edmund Burke, hardly a radical leveler, to stress the visibility of aristocratic existence with no pejorative connotations whatever in a majestic period that is here condensed considerably.

> To be bred in a place of estimation; to see nothing low and sordid from one's infancy; to be taught to respect one's self; to be habituated to the censorial inspection of the public eye; to look early to public opinion; to stand upon such elevated ground as to be enabled to take a large view ... of men and affairs in a large society; ... to be habituated in armies to command and to obey; to be taught to despise danger in pursuit of honour and duty; to be formed to the greatest degree of vigilance, foresight, and circumspection ... to be led to a guarded and regulated conduct ... to be employed as an administrator of law and justice ...—these are the circumstances of men, that form what I should call a *natural* aristocracy, without which there is no nation.[3]

It would be unjust to Burke, who knew how to stand alone, even if not always wisely, to think that what he was praising in this passage, for which there are many Nietzschean parallels, was conformity in any base sense of the term. The "public opinion" to which the noble looks in this mixture of sociology and idealization is not to be followed slavishly when it errs. Its importance is that it indicates that for Burke the "natural" aristocrat is part of a social body, in which he exhibits qualities admirable in themselves, but also "functional." Burke could stress the role of milieu and the psychological effects of inherited position without fearing that he was engaged in leveling or resentment, because he took for granted that the noble was and should be a part of society, rather than one whose pathos of distance threatened to remove him to a level of superiority in which he had nothing to do but congratulate himself upon his solitude.

Nietzsche, however, had a preternatural sensitivity to the fact that "function" and "utility" constituted a slippery slope which can end by destroying the difference between masters and slaves altogether. As a result, though he could frequently view the aristocracy specifically as a leadership class, as we shall see, he was also led to reaffirm the most brutal egocentricity of the noble as the criterion of health and resistence to "corruption," as the following should make clear.

> Corruption [is] the expression of a threatening anarchy among the instincts and of the fact that the foundation of the affects, which is called "life," has been shaken.... When, for example, an aristocracy, like that of France at the beginning of the Revolution, throws away its privileges with a sublime disgust and sacrifices itself to an extravagance of its own moral feelings, that is corruption; it was really only the last act of that centuries-old corruption which had led them to surrender ... their governmental prerogatives, demoting themselves to a mere *function* of the monarchy (finally even to a mere ornament and showpiece). The essential characteristic of a good and healthy aristocracy, however, is that it experiences itself *not* as a function (whether of a monarchy or the commonwealth) but as their *meaning* and justification—that it therefore accepts with a good conscience the sacrifice of untold human beings who, *for its sake*, must be reduced and lowered to incomplete human beings, to slaves, to instruments. Their faith simply has to be that society must *not* exist for society's sake but only as the foundation and scaffolding on which a choice type of being is able to raise itself to its higher task and to a higher state of *being*—. (*BGE*, #257)

That an aristocracy, especially one that originates in conquest, should regard itself as the purpose for which society exists has been, alas, often true enough. And there is no point in dwelling on the historical fact that the French nobility was largely *coerced* into surrendering its governmental privileges by the monarchy (to say nothing of the Revolution), although Nietzsche's contrary view is a revealing example of his illusory effort to present aristocracy as so dynamically powerful that it can give way only to its own inner decay. Far more important, however, is that the aristocrat who regards himself as the "meaning and justification" of a monarchy or commonwealth might be precisely the one who becomes a "mere ornament and showpiece" because he so disdains being a "mere *function*" that there is, in the absence of powerful spiritual impulses, little else for him to be.

The individual who is less concerned with his task and with an object of devotion outside himself than with developing himself as a specimen of self-enclosed perfection can be the perfection only of sublimated nihilism. In fact, this condition might be nothing but the internalization of the other's regard to such an extent that one takes this mode of self-relation as entirely one's own, and imagines that a perfect "autonomy" consists in doing only those things which advertise one's freedom from all moral or material concerns. There is certainly a form of resentment that seeks to degrade the exceptional into a mere function of the ordinary, which Nietzsche never forgot. But there is also a subtler form of "slavishness," one that wants to admire the high in its very self-enclosed vacuity, and this can conquer the high themselves. The proud man who confers value on himself is not necessarily nobler or less vain than the vain man who looks consciously to others for the self-confirmation that may follow a service done for them. He may, in truth, be sicker. Nietzsche never saw, or else chose to ignore, the degree to which the noble could be his own slave to his own very Nietzschean idea of mastery. He did not face the extraordinary dangers of the pathos of distance and the distortions it occasions, and the result was that his analysis of, and his case for, aristocratic existence remained radically uncritical and incomplete.

The heart of the problem was certainly not that Nietzsche wished to aid in the preservation of fox-hunting fops. He frequently made it clear, even in *Beyond Good and Evil*, that true nobility, in the absolute sense of the word, wants nothing so much as a task and an object of devotion. But his thinking on this point, as on so many others, was hopelessly abstract. (Notwithstanding the great vividness of his style, the claim can be made that Nietzsche was the most culpably abstract of all major thinkers, a claim that will become progressively more justified as we proceed.) In the present instance, he fled in terror from an abstract conception of the degradation of the great to a mere function (a degradation that has offended many more egalitarian thinkers as a characteristic problem of modern man in general), to an abstract egocentricity, ameliorated only by the sensible, if still abstract, belief that energy needs a *goal*. He could not, indeed, even hold firmly to that ameliorating principle, and occasionally allowed himself to depict the highest conceivable men as a race of "Epicurean gods," beings, in other words, of uncreative and limitless complacency (*KGA*, 7:3, p. 263; 7:1, p. 252).

For better and for worse, Nietzsche could not be faithful to an ideal of Epicurean divinity. It was, like many of his other images of redemptive innocence, too indistinguishable from weakness (immeasurably more so, one would think, than the life of Jesus). The will to power thrives only in society, and the pose of a serenely contented solitude is as unconvincing in Nietzsche's impersonal visions of perfection as in his personal glorification of himself. In the most explicit statement of his political ideal in all his works, Nietzsche attempted to strike a kind of balance between a concept of superiority beyond all contact with ordinary humanity and one immersed in such contact. Since, moreover, this ideal slightly qualifies the brutal self-centeredness of aristocracy presented in the aphorisms already quoted, which were written somewhat earlier, it must receive careful attention.

The passage concerned is in the *Antichrist*, where Nietzsche, attempting to make "Christianity look *contemptible*," sanctifies the laws of Manu (which, in his notes, he could criticize) and its *"order of castes"* as the correct depiction "of a *natural* order."

> The highest caste—I call them *the fewest*—being perfect, also has the privileges of the fewest: among them, to represent happiness, beauty, and graciousness on earth. Only to the most spiritual human beings is beauty permitted; among them alone is graciousness not weakness.... On the other hand, there is nothing that they may be conceded less than ugly manners or a pessimistic glance, an eye that makes ugly—or indignation at the total aspect of things. Indignation is the privilege of the chandalas; pessimism too.
>
> *"The world is perfect"*—thus says the instinct of the most spiritual, the Yes-saying instinct; "imperfection, whatever is beneath us, distance, the pathos of distance—even the chandala still belongs to this perfection." The most spiritual men, as the *strongest*, find their happiness where others would find their destruction: in the labyrinth, in hardness against themselves and others, in experiments; their joy is self-conquest; asceticism becomes in them nature, need, and instinct. Difficult tasks are a privilege to them; to play with burdens which crush others, a recreation. Knowledge—a form of asceticism. They are the most venerable kind of man; that does not preclude their being the most cheerful and the kindliest. They rule not because they want to but because they *are*; they are not free to be second.
>
> The *second*: they are the guardians of the law, those who see to order and security, the noble warriors, and above all the king as the highest formula of warrior, judge, and upholder of the law. The second are the executive arm of the most spiritual, that which is closest to them and belongs to them, that which does everything gross in the work of ruling for them—their retinue, their right hand, their best pupils.
>
> In all this ... there is nothing arbitrary, nothing contrived; whatever is *different* is contrived—contrived for the ruin of nature. The order of castes, the *order of rank*, merely formulates the highest law of life; the separation of the three types is necessary for the preservation of society, to make possible the higher and the highest types. The *inequality* of rights is the first condition for the existence of any rights at all....
>
> A high culture is a pyramid: it can stand only on a broad base; its first presupposition is a strong and soundly consolidated mediocrity. Handicraft, trade, agriculture, *science*, the greatest part of art, the whole quintessence of *professional* activity, to sum it up, is compatible only with a mediocre amount of ability and ambition; that sort of thing would be out of place among exceptions; the instinct here required would contradict both aristocratism and anarchism. To be a public utility, a wheel, a function, for that one must be destined by nature: it is *not* society, it is the

only kind of *happiness* of which the great majority are capable that makes intelligent machines of them. For the mediocre, to be mediocre is their happiness; mastery of one thing, specialization—a natural instinct.

It would be completely unworthy of a more profound spirit to consider mediocrity as such an objection. In fact, it is the very *first* necessity if there are to be exceptions: a high culture depends on it. When the exceptional human being treats the mediocre more tenderly than himself and his peers, this is not mere politeness of the heart—it is simply his *duty*. (A, #57)

One of the curious features of the presentation of this ideal is its partial suppression of the entire question of how this society comes into being. The suppression is only partial, because Nietzsche prefaced the passage by describing what the process of legal codification of Manu's type involves. It is the summary of a long experience and "experiment" undergone by a people and the reflection of an aspiration "to become perfect." This is achieved by the claim that the law, which is really based on experience, is a "revelation." The purpose of this "holy lie" (and the activity of holy lying was one which Nietzsche claimed in this work to approve when he approved its *purposes*)[4] is to push the conviction of the "right life" back away from "consciousness" (and, presumably, the risk of doubt, which may accompany consciousness) into "the perfect automation of instinct." In other words, when the right way is made into revealed law, it can replace doubt and experiment with the unthinking obedience of a second nature, a position entirely in harmony with Nietzsche's exaltation of the properly trained instinct over unreliable consciousness that he voiced earlier in the same work (A, #14).

But what we do not have, in spite of all this, which is by no means without its measure of intriguing insight, is a concrete description of how a society that is to obey this particular "natural" ideal gets formed, and it is precisely this lacuna that permits Nietzsche to idealize the relations between classes in the fashion he does. Instead of specifying that the priests and the warriors belong to a conquering group, a detail which was elsewhere so emphatically included, he is able to view each class as composed of those who belong, indeed, *wish* to be, exactly where they are. Consequently, the "base" of the "pyramid" is not *pressed* down into a function;[5] it is functional and limited entirely of its own genetic free will, as it were. By the same token, the upper classes perform functions for which *they* are fitted and do not need to be actively repressive. They rule because they are. Furthermore, they enjoy the security of an unchallenged position of superiority so that they can afford to be gracious and kindly without raising the question, so formidable for Nietzsche in other contexts, of whether their kindness stems from weakness or not. All of this is offered in a work that flays Christianity unmercifully for not "touching reality at any point."

Why did Nietzsche wish to resurrect this ideal, which, notwithstanding the effort "to make Christianity look contemptible," appears about as close to the Catholicism of the Middle Ages as to Manu, for the edification of modern Europe? The conclusion of the passage provides a clue:

> Whom do I hate most among the rabble of today? The socialist rabble, the chandala apostles, who undermine the instinct, the pleasure, the worker's sense of satisfaction with his small existence—who make him envious, who teach him revenge. The source of wrong is never unequal rights but the claim of "equal" rights.
> What is *bad?* But I have said this already: all that is born of weakness, of envy, of *revenge*. The anarchist and the Christian have the same origin.

Was it, then, simply to "hate" for the "socialist rabble of today" that we are indebted for this "gracious" if insufferably snobbish political ideal and for Nietzsche's temporary forgetfulness of the active conquest and ever-active repression usually needed, on his own view, to maintain an aristocratic class? Not entirely. Nietzsche's imagination was as powerfully attracted by images of harmonious, consummated power-in-repose as it was by the idea of a perpetually dynamic conquest of obstacles and of people. And, of course, in his presentation of the playful yet ascetic priest, securely on top of the pyramid and ruling without even wishing to rule, he endeavored once again to combine both the dynamic and the consummated. One must note, however, that in describing this position of the spiritual ruling class, he almost ignored the problem, which had so troubled Plato in the *Republic* and much of the Western tradition of political philosophy ever since, that those fittest to rule are those who genuinely do not wish to do so; and that consequently a position of active leadership must constitute a real sacrifice for those men of wisdom who feel compelled to accept it. The "natural order," therefore, is one which demands an "unnatural" renunciation on the part of the very beings who are most excellent, a renunciation that could certainly be demanded on Christian premises but not on Nietzsche's.[6] His attempt to solve this problem by stipulating that the king and warrior class will take care of the grimy details of governance was clearly inadequate. Nietzsche was somewhat troubled, on a personal basis, by the potential psychological incompatibility between will to power in a concrete political sense and the philosopher's contemplative eros, a point to which it will be necessary to return in a later chapter. In the passage now under discussion, it is clear that he simply indulged in a blithe fantasy of universal harmony, a veritable *harmonie pré-établie*.

Yet even the "harmony" is not consistently maintained, as far as the relations between classes were concerned. "Indignation is the privilege of the chandalas; pessimism too," and the "most spiritual," who say "the world is perfect," regard the chandala as belonging "to this perfection." It is difficult to see this as anything but confirmation that in Nietzsche's world, even the world of his dreams, someone must always suffer. Without the indignation of the chandala, the satisfaction the priest obtained would be imperfect. This is an echo, more restrained but scarcely very appealing, of Nietzsche's suggestion, already quoted, that the most superior man might well be the one who caused all others to perish from envy, which dates from about the same time, but which was confined to his notes. Furthermore, if "the separation of the three types is necessary for the preservation of society, to make possible the higher and highest types," we see that the social ideal is not the highest welfare of the whole, but the possibility of the highest individual. This is a position identical with that of *Beyond Good and Evil*, where the ruthlessness of the upper class was stressed and justified on precisely such a premise. The kindliness here attributed to the ascetic rulers thus threatens to be without any moral content, one which simply means that those in a position of unchallenged superiority can afford some tenderness, that form of tenderness which helps keep the mediocre where they belong. To point this out, of course, is not to deny that any form of kindliness is better that none.

Nietzsche himself could not afford to be so kindly. Where the ascetic priest of his ideal finds the indignation of the chandala exactly what it should be, he himself must "hate" the "socialist rabble, the chandala apostles." The measure of this contrast, Nietzsche presumably meant us to infer, unless we are to believe he was oblivious of it (which is highly unlikely), is the measure of the distance between the only natural order and the reality of Nietzsche's Europe. The cause of this contrast is, apparently, purely and simply the subterranean hate of socialist agitators and their allies, anarchists and Christians.

The situation of Europe, therefore, is in flux, destroying the graciousness possible for a stably hierarchical society. Yet the problem could not be entirely due to the socialist rabble, however much they had two millennia of Christianity supposedly on their side. In *Twilight of the Idols*, written not long before the *Antichrist*, Nietzsche essentially conceded his awareness of this.

> *The labor question.* The stupidity—at bottom, the degeneration of instinct, which is today the cause of *all* stupidities—is that there is a labor question at all. Certain things one does not question; that is the first imperative of instinct. I simply cannot see what one proposes to do with the European worker now that one has made a question of him. He is far too well off not to ask for more and more, not to ask immodestly. In the end, he has numbers on his side. The hope is gone forever that a modest and self-sufficient kind of man, a Chinese type, might here develop as a class: and there would have been reason in that, it would almost have been a necessity. But what was done? Everything to nip in the bud even the preconditions for this: the instincts by virtue of which the worker becomes possible as a class, possible in his own eyes, have been destroyed

through and through with the most irresponsible thoughtlessness. The worker was qualified for military service, granted the right to organize and to vote: is it any wonder that the worker today experiences his own existence as distressing—morally speaking, as an injustice? But what is *wanted*? I ask once more. If one wants an end, one must also want the means: if one wants slaves, then one is a fool if one educates them to be masters. (*T*, "Skirmishes," #40)

The degeneration of instinct here is no doubt the same as the "corruption" that induced the French aristocracy to surrender its privileges, a degeneration of the ruling classes themselves. In a note from 1884, Nietzsche had already lamented: "How the aristocratic world increasingly bleeds itself and makes itself weaker! Because of the nobility of its instincts it throws away its privileges and because of the refinement of its hyper-culture it takes an interest in the people, the weak, the poor, the poetry of the petty, etc." (*WP*, #938). This effusion, one must note, quoted in its entirety, was written at the height of the power of Bismarck, whom Nietzsche cordially, if not *entirely* uniformly, detested, the subtlest bulwark of aristocratic power since Metternich, perhaps of the whole nineteenth century.

Nietzsche's position was clearly awkward in the extreme. It is not easy to maintain contempt for both extremes when one is oneself anything but a man of the middle. If the upper classes are suffering an acute degeneration of instinct, then they no longer can rule because they "are." If the lower classes can have their subservient instincts ruined by being "qualified for military service" and by being "granted the right to organize and to vote," then the "instincts" in question must have been rather unstable to begin with, the product of art more than nature. And if both of these conditions obtain, Nietzsche was surely in no position to blame the entire destruction of the "natural order" upon the socialist rabble.

Nevertheless, at times he did precisely that.[7] It is important to expand upon the moral character, not merely of Nietzsche's mode of condemning the socialists and democrats, but his general tendency to use the notion of resentment as a sweeping indictment of every ideology, religious or overtly political, that has supported the concept of the brotherhood of man and the idea of equality in any sense of the term whatever. One should not, of course, overlook the reality of the poison of resentment. The desire to pull down whatever is up simply because it *is* up, to make the happy unhappy simply because they *are* happy, to deprive some rather than to aid others have certainly been realities in human history, and all constitute (to put the matter in deliberately moralistic terms) vices to be on guard against, like any other. Other writers, who have had no more use for sheer resentment, as just defined, than Nietzsche, have balanced their condemnations with a realization that the unjustifiability of resentment has nothing to do with the justifiability of everything that may provoke it, which Nietzsche did very rarely, and that concern for the welfare of all cannot be invariably equated with the simple hatred of the few, which he scarcely did at all. What is regrettable (to use no sharper term) in the imbalance of Nietzsche's position is that it encourages a self-righteous defense of *any* kind of privilege and inequality by the very act of condemning resentment of them, and gives a good conscience in the process to aggression, aggrandizement, and hatred. It is this which makes his resentment of resentment a truly serious matter, and which gives moral point to the charge, often made without sufficient concreteness, that Nietzsche exhibited what he purported to condemn by his very manner of condemning it. If a man is to be condemned for resenting me no matter what I do, then I am in mortal danger of tempting myself to do my worst, and of regarding his ensuing resentment as proof that my worst was not bad enough. In Nietzsche's Imperial Germany, people were not wanting who regarded every sign of hostility to their bumptious Reich as indicative of nothing but the contemptible envy of foreigners. I am far from wishing to suggest that Nietzschean psychology had any appreciable influence on this state of affairs (or even that he would have approved of it.) The provocative line of insult discussed here was too obvious to have awaited the promulgation of the will to power before being employed. Indulgence in the gratuitous attack on the envy of others seems to have been a veritable cliché of conceit in, for example, Nietzsche's beloved Renaissance,[8] but is made no lovelier by such august examples. Moreover, even when the resentment of resentment is as directly provoked by social insurgency as the original resentment may have been provoked by egregious injustice and hardship, whatever is foul in resentment still clings to the resentment of resentment, constituting an invitation to acts of hate and vindictiveness far transcending measures necessitated simply for the maintenance of order.

Nietzsche never displayed the slightest awareness of these dangers. (His demand that the superior treat the inferior "more tenderly than himself" hardly constitutes evidence of such awareness, particularly in its context.) In fact, Zarathustra himself reveals this process of corruption by the resentment of resentment perfectly.

> Thus I speak to you in a parable—you who make souls whirl, you preachers of *equality*. To me you are tarantulas, and secretly vengeful. But I shall bring your secrets to light; therefore I laugh in your faces with my laughter of the heights. Therefore I tear at your webs, that your rage may lure you out of your lie-holes and your revenge may leap out from behind your word justice. For *that man be delivered from revenge*, that is for me the bridge to the highest hope, and a rainbow after long storms. (*TSZ*, 2:7)

This last sentence, which certainly expresses a noble ideal, if with intolerable artificiality of style, easily lends itself to being quoted in isolation to prove the sublime morality of Nietzschean immoralism. But in context it is far from being unambiguously edifying. The section as a whole is entitled "On the Tarantulas," *not* "On Deliverance from Revenge"; and under such a rubric, the deliverance from revenge looks more like an excuse for an attack on the tarantulas, the teachers of equality, than anything else. The object of the onslaught on the secret vengefulness of the preachers of equality is to bring this vengefulness into the open. But enough wanton and self-righteous aggression will bring out vengefulness from almost anyone. In the meantime, the attacker enjoys what in other contexts Nietzsche sneeringly called the "affect" of impotent power if he is weak, or proceeds to visit vengeance upon the secretly vengeful if he is strong.

Nietzsche was perhaps right in his implicit contention in the *Genealogy* that the cruelty of a ruling class is frequently not cruel in a malicious way, but that such a class exploits with a "clear conscience" by the simple device of not considering the objects of its exploitation to be fully human. Righteous indignation on the part of rulers is more likely to be the result of the perception of a truly alarming threat, in other words, the result of weakness or the fear of weakness. In Nietzsche's own case, this perception is obvious enough (though he hardly belonged to a ruling class) and some of his remarks have the character of a conservative's panic.

Socialism represented the extreme against which Nietzsche fought, but his resentment of resentment was too sweeping to require the extreme in order to be activated. "Liberalism" in politics and moral philosophy fared no better because Nietzsche almost invariably presented any kind of moral or political universalism as an insistence upon uniformity and an attack on any form of exception. Typical of this is his claim that Kantian ethics, in which the principle of univerality reached a degree of clarity never previously attained in moral philosophy, demands that all people behave like machines (*T*, "Skirmishes," #29), a misrepresentation of surpassing grossness even by the standards of Nietzschean polemics. Nietzsche paid no attention to the obvious fact that for Kant the universality criterion was one which insisted that the abstract maxim implied in any concrete action, its basic moral tendency, should be universally valid, but that the permissible specific content was one which of necessity could and should vary enormously. The principle, for example, to develop one's legitimate individual talents to the fullest, to which Kant subscribed, obviously did not mean for him (or anyone else) that it is the duty of everyone to set libretti by Da Ponte to music or tell the story of King Lear in verse and five acts. Nor, equally obviously, did it mean that, because such activities are not incumbent on all, they may be undertaken by none.

Similarly, in the excesses of his resentment of resentment, Nietzsche overlooked the degree to which the categorical imperative, like the Golden Rule, of which it was an intended clarification, was simply an elementary check upon the infringement of the legitimate rights of the other, who possesses his own positive goals, and presupposes no norm of uniformity at all. This is especially clear in the negative form of the Golden Rule used by Rabbi Hillel and Confucius (i.e., "Do not do to others what you would not have them do to you"), but is clear enough in the positive formulation as well. To the degree that Nietzsche recognized this aspect of the principles of universality and equality, it was only to stress the element of unjust leveling down supposedly incorporated within them rather than to endorse the element of protection against being victimized.

> Here the concept of the "equal value of men before God" is extraordinarily harmful; one forbade actions and attitudes that were in themselves among the prerogatives of the strongly constituted—as if they were in themselves unworthy of men. One brought the entire tendency of the strong into disrepute when one erected the protective measures of the weakest (those who were weakest also when confronting themselves) as a norm of value.
>
> Confusion went so far that one branded the very virtuosi of life (whose autonomy offered the sharpest antithesis to the vicious and unbridled) [condemned, vaguely, earlier in the note⁹] with the most opprobrious names. Even now one believes that one must disapprove of a Cesare Borgia; that is simply laughable. (*WP*, #871)

Regardless of the degree of Nietzsche's enthusiasm for Cesare Borgia, regardless also of the character of Borgia's life, both controversial matters, this passage is typical of the imbalance of a position that tended to see the threat *to* the strong as far more important than the threat *from* the strong, an imbalance that abstract condemnations of "the vicious and unbridled" do exceedingly little to correct. Nietzsche was aware of some of the paradox here, but this awareness did not stop him from allowing his imagination to run away with him, and from discerning the essence of nihilism in the opposition of the weak majority to the strong few.

> *Anti-Darwin.*—What surprises me most when I survey the broad destinies of man is that I always see before me the opposite of that which Darwin and his school see or *want* to see today: selection in favor of the stronger, better-constituted, and the progress of the species. Precisely the opposite is palpable: the elimination of the lucky strokes, the uselessness of the more highly developed types, the inevitable dominion of the average, even the *sub-average* types ... the strongest and most fortunate are weak when opposed by organized herd instincts, by the timidity of the weak, by the vast majority....
>
> Strange though it may sound, one always has to defend the strong

against the weak; the fortunate against the unfortunate; the healthy against those degenerating and afflicted with hereditary taints.…

I rebel against the translation of reality into a morality: therefore I abhor Christianity with a deadly hatred, because it created sublime words and gestures to throw over a horrible reality the cloak of justice, virtue, and divinity—. (*WP*, #685)

Christianity, castigated in the works Nietzsche published at the same period as this was written for being anti-natural and unreal, here emerges as the quintessential expression of reality from which it is apparently necessary to flee, and erect a counter "ideal". It is interesting to note that Georg Brandes, one of Nietzsche's few distinguished admirers before the latter's breakdown, mildly reproved him for fulminating against the "earthquake" of the French Revolution, and received the reply from Nietzsche conceding his folly, but confessing his inability to refrain from "Quixotic" crusades.[10] The clear implication of this is that Nietzsche believed his own moral crusades were at worst Quixotic (and he loved Don Quixote more than *Don Quixote*) whereas everyone else's were resentful. Yet he was capable of expressing his resentment of resentment in unmistakably personal form, claiming that "out of the *ressentiment* of the masses [Christianity] forged its chief weapon against *us*, against all that is noble, gay, high-minded on earth. 'Immortality' conceded to every Peter and Paul has so far been the greatest, the most malignant, attempt to assassinate *noble* humanity" (*A*, 43). Had it been Nietzsche's intention to provide a graphic illustration of how easily feelings of resentment get out of hand, he could scarcely have done so more neatly.

The sole reason for emphasizing Nietzsche's resentment of resentment as strongly as is done here, and with such excruciating quotations, is to make explicit the stress that distorted his thought. This author has no quarrel with anyone who sought to claim that the uncritical endorsement of aristocratic ruthlessness to which he fiercely subscribed, especially in *Beyond Good and Evil*, of which we must endure further examples later, did not represent the "real" Friedrich Nietzsche, any more than the gloating recommended by Tertullian over the agony of the damned represents the essence of Christianity. But the Nietzsche we actually have in his writings is one whose resentment simply prevented him from attaining a balanced moral position. This, it seems to me, is about as close to the "fact" of the matter as one can come without engaging in the wholesale rewriting of Nietzsche in the interests of presenting his moral philosophy as he might possibly have wished it to be rather than as he actually made it.

It would be natural to conclude from Nietzsche's resentment of resentment that he should be classified as a "conservative." There are, however, a number of reasons to reject the notion of a conservative Nietzsche. For one thing, he clearly believed that the old order, which in his time was an unstable combination of old monarchical and aristocratic elements and novel democratic ones, was dying. This realism was no doubt what lay behind Zarathustra's question: "What do princes matter now?" (*TSZ*, 3:12, 12). The question may not express a pure contentment (although Zarathustra, in the same section, indulged in some delightful wit at the expense of courtiers), but Nietzsche evidently perceived that hereditary power had lost much of its natural connection to the real sources of power in the modern world and, at the same time, had ceased to have a vital creative function. This is, however, speculative, for Nietzsche's vagueness about the concrete realities of his day constitutes an insuperable barrier to certainty. His advice in *Twilight of the Idols*, in a section entitled "Whispered to the Conservatives" ("Skirmishes," #43), helps very little in giving precision to his thought; for he merely asserted, in the most general terms, that man cannot walk backward, and that a return to a past morality is impossible. Whether he had in mind primarily a Christian morality or a specifically feudal one is unclear. But at least the section is evidence that militates against any politically conservative construction of his thought.

Second, Nietzsche's entire philosophy emphasized creativity and emphasized, as well, what he took to be the interdependence of creation and destruction (*TSZ*, 2:12). Such an attitude is at variance with the very essence of conservative traditionalism, whether political, philosophical, or religious.[11] It is, of course, also at variance with the ideal (and ideally stable) tripartite order of the *Antichrist* as well. The end result is that Nietzsche's thinking points both to a praise of radical change and to the advantages of the slow ripening of cultures and peoples. He never resolved this conflict, but it is perhaps reasonable to stress creative innovation as most characteristic of his total position. The aspiration to control history, which has been mentioned in the last chapter, is certainly in accord with such a stress.

Finally, there is Nietzsche's faith, however mixed with anxiety, that the continuation of modern decadence, even in its leveling aspects, will beget or at least permit its own reversal and the creation of a new aristocracy. Men must put an end to the absurdly accidental character of history; but it is perhaps the confusions of modernity which will eventually permit that. "The dwarfing of man must for a long time count as the only goal; because a broad foundation has first to be created so that a stronger species of man can stand upon it" (*WP*, #890). This theme is treated more fully in another note, also from Nietzsche's last period.

> *The strong of the future.*—That which partly necessity, partly chance has achieved here and there, the conditions for the production of a stronger type, we are now able to comprehend and consciously *will*: we are able to create the conditions under which such an elevation is possible....
> Such a task would have to be posed the more it was grasped to what

extent the contemporary form of society was being so powerfully transformed that at some future time it would be unable to exist for its own
sake alone, but only as a tool in the hands of a stronger race.

The increasing dwarfing of man is precisely the driving force that brings
to mind the breeding of a stronger race—a race that would be excessive
precisely where the dwarfed species was weak and growing weaker (in
will, responsibility, self-assurance, ability to posit goals for oneself)....

As soon as it is established, this homogenizing species requires a justification: it lies in serving a higher sovereign species that stands upon the former and can raise itself to its task only by doing this. Not merely a master
race whose sole task is to rule, but a race with its own sphere of life, with
an excess of strength for beauty, bravery, culture, manners to the highest
peak of the spirit; an affirming race that may grant itself every great
luxury—strong enough to have no need of the virtue-imperative, rich
enough to have no need of thrift and pedantry, beyond good and evil; a
hothouse for strange and choice plants. (WP, #898)

The desire to control history in the most thorough and radical way (as
opposed to the piecemeal way that is presupposed by all human action)
could evidently produce in Nietzsche, at times, the same kind of wondrous
faith that has been found frequently among many Marxists. But from a
pragmatic standpoint, the faith in dialectical reversals and the interdependence of antitheses appears rather confusing. There seems to be a great deal
of doubt about whether one's cause can best be served by directly promoting
it or by promoting its opposite. It should be clear, if we take these quotations together with ones previously cited against the socialists and against
the indulgence of the worker, that Nietzsche himself could not make up his
mind on this question.

The tendency of these passages, however vague, might be held to point to
a kind of natural, painless development, an emerging meritocracy or even
plutocracy that might be acceptable to, even welcomed by, the dwarfed and
drifting masses. But this is unlikely. Nietzsche never explicitly abandoned
the insistence upon the importance of conquest to establish the requisite
pathos of distance proclaimed in *Beyond Good and Evil*; and one should
point out in all honesty the reasonableness of that insistence from such a
perspective. If one really wants a pathos of distance above all, with a certain
condescending graciousness as a desirable but superadded *refinement*, then
surely the conquest of one group by another is a better way to achieve it than
public service examinations or the gradual emergence of a dominating plutocracy whose members might never quite transcend a certain democratic
residue. In the light of this consideration, regardless of whether Nietzsche
had conquest in mind in the last quotation, one is justified in singling out the
following, still later, note as especially representative, even definitive, of his
views on this issue.

Overall view of the future European: the most intelligent slave animals, very industrious, fundamentally very modest, inquisitive to excess, multifarious, pampered, weak of will—a cosmopolitan chaos of affects and intelligence. How could a stronger species raise itself out of him? A species with *classical* taste? Classical taste: this means will to simplification, strengthening, to visible happiness, to the terrible, the courage of psychological nakedness.... To fight upward out of that chaos to this form—requires a compulsion: one must be faced with the choice of perishing or prevailing. A dominating race can grow up only out of terrible and violent beginnings. Problem: where are the *barbarians* of the twentieth century? Obviously, they will come into view and consolidate themselves only after tremendous socialist crises—they will be the elements capable of the greatest severity toward themselves and able to guarantee the most enduring will. (*WP*, #868)

We have a somewhat better idea than Nietzsche of where the barbarians of the twentieth century were. One need not argue that they would have been much to his taste. But, as this quotation makes perfectly clear, he always aspired to take the long view. Besides, it should be equally clear that one cannot pick and choose one's barbarians. One must make do with what one gets.

7
Nietzsche and the Barbarians of the Twentieth Century

LITTLE research has been done, to my knowledge, which permits any comprehensive attempt to assess the influence of Nietzsche upon the members of the Nazi party and their more enthusiastic supporters.[1] This is no doubt regrettable, but the actual influence of a thinker is frequently impossible to measure precisely in any case, especially when the doctrines concerned are general in character rather than highly specific. Anyone whose thinking is affected by the formula $E=mc^2$ works under the influence of Einstein even if, as is probable, someone else might have eventually arrived at the same formula had Einstein never lived. But general ideas such as most of those contributing to Nazi and fascist ideology (the term *fascist* is more comprehensive than *Nazi*, and will be used here occasionally to refer to both German Nazism and Italian fascism) had many sources and were spontaneously generated many times; hence the causal role of any particular individual is always open to grave question. In the case of as complex and contradictory a figure as Nietzsche, these difficulties are all the greater, because he affected so many different kinds of people in such different ways. If many Germans of impeccably anti-Nazi credentials were readers and admirers of Nietzsche, then examples of Nazi Nietzscheans would prove nothing very clear. The causal problem is merely pushed back a step, leading us to ask why some readers were particularly open to Nietzschean suggestion of one kind and others of radically divergent kinds.

No conceivable amount of research will entitle scholars to move beyond a vague, indeterminate manner of speech in dealing with Nietzsche's "responsibility" for Nazism. It is understandable, therefore, even apart from the paucity of research of the kind in question, that the issue of Nietzsche's relation to the Nazi movement has been discussed primarily in terms of the resemblance or lack of resemblance between Nietzsche's views and the Nazis' deeds. This is as it should be, and that procedure will be followed here. Let me say in advance, to avoid any misunderstanding about the purpose and purport of this discussion, that it is as easy for me to imagine Nietzsche's joining the Nazi Party as would be his joining the Salvation Army. But his writings had much more to offer the budding twentieth-century barbarian than one could possibly gather from the most important secondary literature about him, and the horrors of this century will always remain mysterious enough without hiding the darker side of the Nietzschean contribution to the *Zeitgeist* out of which they emerged. Accordingly, I shall treat a number of topics here concerning which Nietzschean apologetics have been misleading and overly simple. Since the topics overlap to a considerable extent, the subheadings are somewhat artificial, but express the main focus of each section. They are: The State; Napoleon and War; The Jews; and Pity, Suffering, and the Elimination of the Weak.

The State

Nietzsche castigated the state bitterly in a famous passage from *Thus Spoke Zarathustra* entitled "The New Idol."

> Somewhere there are still peoples and herds, but not where we live, my brothers: here there are states. State? What is that? Well then, open your ears to me for now I shall speak to you about the death of peoples.
>
> State is the name of the coldest of cold monsters. Coldly it tells lies too; and this lie crawls out of its mouth: "I, the State, am the people." That is a lie! It was creators who created peoples and hung a faith and a love over them: thus they served life.
>
> It is annihilators who set traps for the many and call them "state": they hang a sword and a hundred appetites over them....
>
> All-too-many are born: for the superfluous the state was invented....
>
> ...Alas, to you too, you great souls, it whispers its dark lies. Alas, it detects the rich hearts which like to squander themselves.... With heroes and honorable men it would surround itself, the new idol! It likes to bask in the sunshine of good consciences—the cold monster!...
>
> Behold the superfluous! They steal the works of the inventors and the treasures of the sages for themselves; "education" they call their theft— and everything turns to sickness and misfortune for them....
>
> Behold the superfluous! They gather riches and become poorer with them. They want power and first the lever of power, much money—the impotent paupers!...
>
> Escape from the bad smell! Escape from the idolatry of the superfluous!
>
> Escape from the bad smell! Escape from the steam of these human sacrifices!
>
> The earth is free even now for great souls. There are still many empty seats for the lonesome and the twosome, fanned by the fragrance of silent seas....
>
> Only where the state ends, there begins the human being who is not

superfluous....
    Where the state *ends*—look there, my brothers! Do you not see it, the
rainbow and the bridges of the overman? (*TSZ*, 1:11)

Such a sweeping and one-sided polemic against a necessity of civilized
human life would not normally, in spite of its undeniable measure of insight, have greatly enhanced the reputation of its author. But because the
fascists exalted the state as such, Nietzsche's attacks on the state are not
merely less offensive; they seem to prove that he condemned fascism in advance. Such a reading is understandable but misleading. In the first place,
many of the things about which Nietzsche complained here are so deeply
embedded within modern life (and even premodern life) as a whole, like
organized education and the quest for wealth, that the relevance of his
attacks to any particular form of government, or *degree* of exaltation of the
state, is questionable. Second and more important, to debunk the concept of
the state in favor of the concept of the people is to attack a word beloved by
Nazis in favor of one much more beloved by them. The endorsement of a
radical individualism presented in the last lines raises a particularly crucial
problem in light of this. One can read it as reflecting an absolute and timeless
ideal of individual greatness or as an ideal that is to be distinctly understood
as a *faute de mieux*, one that is forced on the great man given the conditions
of modernity. In both cases it suggests an irresponsibility from which bad
government benefits.[2] But, in the case of an absolute reading of Zarathustra's
advice, the Nazi effort to recreate a people would be considered pointless
from the standpoint of the higher men, while the alternative reading would
see Nietzschean individualism as something he himself found unsatisfactory.
This is a problem to which it will be necessary to return. For the present, it
suffices to observe the ambiguity and to note that there is no respect in
which Nietzsche mirrors the tensions of the modern "intellectual" more
clearly than in precisely this ambiguity.
    There is another, less well-known, discussion of individualism and its re-
lation to modern society to be found in Nietzsche, one of the most insightful
passages on a social theme in all his works. In the last book of the *Gay
Science*, which, unlike the earlier ones, was written after *Zarathustra*, he
considered "*How things will become ever more 'artistic' in Europe.*" He
wrote that, even in "our time of transition," when social pressures were
loosening, most men do not choose their role, but have it chosen for them,
and eventually confound themselves *with* their role, forgetting how many
other roles they might have been able to play. In the Middle Ages, "men
believed with rigid confidence, even with piety, in their predestination" for
their calling, and hence "classes, guilds, and hereditary trade privileges managed to erect those *monsters of social pyramids* [emphasis added] that distinguish the Middle Ages and to whose credit one can adduce at least one thing:

durability (and duration is a first-rate value on earth)." On the other hand, there have been "really democratic" ages like Athens in the Periclean Age, America in the modern age, and, increasingly, modern Europe as well, when the "individual becomes convinced that he can do just about everything and *can manage almost any role*, and everybody experiments with himself, improvises, makes new experiments, enjoys his experiments; and all nature ceases and becomes art."

With the aid of this faith, Nietzsche continued, there occurred among the Greeks "a rather odd metamorphosis that does not merit imitation in all respects: *They really became actors....* [and] what I fear, what is so palpable that today one could grasp it with one's hands, if one felt like grasping it, is that we modern men are even now pretty far along on this same road; and whenever a human being begins to discover how he is playing a role and how he *can* be an actor, he *becomes* an actor." (This was no compliment from Nietzsche's mouth.[3])

> With this a new human flora and fauna emerged that could never have grown in more solid and limited ages.... It is thus that the maddest and most interesting ages of history always emerge, when the "actors," *all* kinds of actors become the real masters. As this happens, another human type is disadvantaged more and more and finally made impossible; above all, the great "architects": the strength to build becomes paralyzed; the courage to make plans that encompass the distant future is discouraged; those with a genius for organization become scarce: who would still dare to undertake projects that would require thousands of years for their completion? For what is dying out is the fundamental faith that would enable us to calculate, to promise, to anticipate the future in plans of such scope, and to sacrifice the future to them—namely, the faith that man has value and meaning only insofar as he is *a stone in a great edifice*; and to that end he must be *solid* first of all, a "stone"—and above all not an actor!
>
> ... What will not be built any more henceforth, and *cannot* be built any more, is—a society in the old sense of that word; to build that, everything is lacking, above all the material. *All of us are no longer material for a society*; this is a truth for which the time has come. It is a matter of indifference to me that at present the most myopic, perhaps most honest, but at any rate noisiest type that we have today, our good socialists, believe, hope, dream, and above all shout and write almost the opposite. Even now one reads their slogan for the future "free society" on all tables and walls. Free society? Yes, yes! But surely you know, gentlemen, what is required for building that? Wooden iron! (*GS*, #356)

The suggestiveness of this passage is extraordinary. To reduce its purpose to the anti-socialist polemic at the end would, I think, be unwarranted. Even that polemic is, by Nietzsche's standards, rather mild and certainly good-humored. The spirit of the passage as a whole is more one of rather detached observation and analysis than invective. But one must also note a certain ambiguity in the implied value judgments, an ambiguity that could easily be transformed into pure denigration with the aid of other sections of Nietzsche's works, some of which, like his later discourse on the only "natural" society, we have already encountered. Nietzsche's admiration for "great 'architects,'" who require human stones, and for "the strength to build," and for "the courage to make plans that encompass the distant future" is evident even in this passage, while in later works and notes it becomes only stronger and more brutally expressed. *Twilight of the Idols* flatly identifies the "decrease in the power to organize, that is, to separate, tear open clefts, subordinate and super-ordinate" with the "decline of life" ("Skirmishes," #37).

Nietzsche's hostility to the German *Reich*, the new empire of unified Germany proclaimed in 1871, certainly did not abate in the years after *Zarathustra*, with its "New Idol," was written. Sometimes he expressed this hostility in terms which pitted the cause of philosophy directly against that of "power," to the decided detriment of the latter, as occurs in *Twilight* itself. "One pays heavily for coming to power: power *makes stupid*. The Germans— once they were called the people of thinkers: do they think at all today?" ("What the Germans Lack," 1). One who takes this passage together with "The New Idol" might easily find his mind moving effortlessly to a view of Nietzsche as an exponent, however qualified, of a kind of liberalism. How erroneous this would be can be gauged from another of Nietzsche's attacks on the *Reich* in the very same work.

Critique of modernity. Our institutions are no good any more: on that there is universal agreement. However, it is not their fault but ours. Once we have lost all the instincts out of which institutions grow, we lose institutions altogether because we are no longer good for them. Democracy has ever been the form of decline in organizing power.... I [have] already characterized modern democracy, together with its hybrids such as the "German *Reich*," as the form of decline of the state. In order that there may be institutions, there must be a kind of will, instinct, or imperative, which is anti-liberal to the point of malice: the will to tradition, to authority, to responsibility for centuries to come, to the solidarity of chains of generations, forward and backward *ad infinitum*. When this will is present, something like the *imperium Romanum* is founded; or like Russia, the *only* power today which has endurance, which can wait, which can still promise something—Russia, the concept that suggests the opposite of the wretched European nervousness and system of small states, which has entered a critical phase with the founding of the German *Reich*.

The whole of the West no longer possesses the instincts out of which institutions grow, out of which a *future* grows: perhaps nothing antagonizes its "modern spirit" so much. One lives for the day, one lives very fast, one lives very irresponsibly: precisely this is called "freedom." (*T.*, "Skirmishes," #39)

The *Reich* is not too much of a *state*, or even too much of an idol. It is too democratic, too pleasure-loving, not illiberal enough, and enough is "to the point of malice." It is not *Russian* enough! But let it be emphasized instead that for Nietzsche the *Reich* was not sufficiently Roman. His admiration for Rome has already been remarked. Here it need only be stressed that the "state" as Westerners have come to know it derives in very large part from Roman sources, which Nietzsche certainly knew, and that hostility to the state as such on the one hand and enthusiasm for that Roman organizational genius which Nietzsche so often extolled on the other are completely antithetical. Enthusiasm for the ancient Roman example was central, of course, to Nazism, to say nothing of Italian fascism. If "power *makes stupid*," Rome was stupid.[4]

Yet the contrast between liberal hedonism and the *imperium Romanum* is itself too simple. In the section immediately prior to the "critique of modernity" quoted above, Nietzsche contrasted the bovine contentment that flourishes under secure liberal institutions with the strenuous and ennobling effects of the war *for* such institutions, adding:

> The highest type of free men should be sought where the highest resistance is constantly overcome: five steps from tyranny, close to the threshold of the danger of servitude. This is true psychologically if by "tyrants" are meant inexorable and fearful instincts that provoke the maximum of authority and discipline against themselves; most beautiful type: Julius Caesar....
>
> Those large hothouses for the strong—for the strongest kind of human being that has so far been known—the aristocratic commonwealths of the type of Rome or Venice, understood freedom exactly in the sense in which I understand it: as something one has or does *not* have, something one *wants*, something one *conquers*. (*T.*, "Skirmishes," #38)

Nietzsche doubtless knew, and presumably expected his readers to know, that the aristocratic Roman commonwealth which produced the "beautiful type" of Julius Caesar was itself a hybrid republic combining oligarchic and popular elements declining into anarchy and being pushed into it by such figures as Caesar himself. The best freedom, the freedom that flourishes "five steps from tyranny," is here that of a competitive tension among oligarchs that maintains them at a perpetual state of maximum alert and the need for an energetic *conquest* of freedom. But Nietzsche also presumably knew that it had been a commonplace of political thought for millennia, and historically confirmed time and again, that such conditions of oligarchical tension are so unstable as to be incapable of enduring long. They provoke a reaction in which the chaos or near-chaos is resolved by some Caesar or Napoleon. The oligarchy becomes a tyranny; the Roman Republic becomes the Roman Empire.

Now, since, as we have seen, the Roman Empire is praised in the very next section and since, as we saw earlier, the supposed destruction of that Empire by Christianity is denounced in Nietzsche's next book, the *Antichrist*, (a book that also erects the ideal of a stable, tripartite, pyramidal regime, monstrous pyramids having been denounced in the *Gay Science*,) what have we? Praise of long-enduring empires in which hedonism flourishes (and Nietzsche's absurd fondness for Petronius should be mentioned in this context[5]); denunciation of liberal regimes because hedonism flourishes; praise of oligarchic strife, because warrior instincts are kept on the alert; denunciation of the *Reich* because power makes stupid and undermines thought; praise of apolitical individualism because the state is an idol; praise of a class society in which the wise rule.

The reader must make of this bewildering farrago of affirmations and negations what he can and what he will. I suggest, with the utmost tentativeness, the following reconstruction, one which does *not* unify *all* this material, but that takes some of it and, with the aid of other material, offers a unity that is at least historically suggestive, and at least as accurate a reflection of the relevant Nietzschean sources as any other.

The small man can be no better than a stone, but in modern times he is not capable of being even that, while the great architects who would shape and "justify" him are missing because the decline of vitality and the ability to obey have reduced all men to "actors." If, however, as we "*must*," "go forward—step by step further into decadence" (*T*, "Skirmishes," #43), armed with Nietzschean wisdom, the great men who can create new values and hang a new faith and love over an increasingly chaotic, despairing tribe of actors may appear. Then even liberalism could be "justified" in the total scheme of things, like the nihilism confronted by Nietzsche's own philosophizing, as the preparation for a new Roman edifice for millennia, the confusion of liberalism begetting an antithesis made possible by the freedom of the confusion itself. This confusion permits and even necessitates radical creativity rather than subservient traditionalism.

On any reconstruction of his thought, Nietzsche's hostility to the state cannot be used to imply a condemnation of fascists in advance. The vague abstractions he employed in criticizing liberal society and in outlining the ideal could all be claimed by fascists for their own criticisms and their own ideals, although they certainly had to pick and choose their texts carefully, precisely like any one else. To say this is not to deny, but rather to affirm, the extraordinary "sensitivity" with which Nietzsche registered all of those spiritual forces and fears of weakness that exploded in the decades following his death, as the next section will also show.

Napoleon and War

The position deservedly occupied by Adolf Hitler as the modern Prince of Darkness does not depend, of course, exclusively upon his subversion of democracy in Germany or his death camps. It also depends upon his wars of conquest. Nothing, perhaps, is more closely identified with Nazism than war. Furthermore, since there is no closer analogue to Hitler considered as a relentless warmonger than Napoleon, Nietzsche's comments on both war and Napoleon are of obvious relevance in any effort to ascertain the relation between his teachings and National Socialism. Before examining them, however, a few cautionary words are advisable in fairness to *all* parties concerned.

First, the belief that war plays a precious role in building character and "purifying" morals in its death-defying discipline and insistence upon rising above the "petty comforts" of bourgeois civilization was an extremely common one throughout Europe and America throughout Nietzsche's life and beyond it, until the havoc of the Great War shook the faith. It can be found, moreover, on the left as well as the right of the political spectrum.[6] In some ways, indeed, the very advance of bourgeois comfort gave the apology for war a more insistent moral urgency than it possessed earlier even at the hands of glorifying poets. Furthermore, the dangers of the Atomic Age should not entail that we treat this entire line of thought with automatic and absolutely unmitigated contempt. Even a pacifist might admire the willingness to be killed, if not to kill, for a good cause.

Second, while opinions about Napoleon differ greatly and perhaps always will, and while no total judgment, still less a comprehensive presentation, of him will be attempted here, it is reasonable to say that the atrocities which stain his record (apart from the wars themselves) are almost as nothing in comparison to Hitler's. No favorable view of Napoleon, even as a conqueror, should be taken to imply by itself that the same judge would have a favorable view of Hitler.

Third and finally, however, the identification of war with the very essence of Hitlerism is a mistake, if an understandable one. The Second World War endured for half the life of the Third Reich, but war was for Hitler a means toward a new world order and not *simply* an end in itself.[7] One can regard Hitler's intended order as fully as repulsive as the war that was meant to bring it about. But that does not change the fact that war was for him a means, and that his end certainly included a new civilization, which was supposed to bear *cultural* fruit. This is not to praise Hitler's exceedingly meager learning or to exaggerate the depth of his culture. It is simply to observe, as one of his most illustrious emigré opponents, Thomas Mann, well knew and subsequent writers have too often forgotten, that Hitler was very much an aesthete, like many of his supporters. No emphasis upon

Nietzsche's cultural values, therefore, means anything, when taken by itself, about the relationship between his doctrines and those of Nazism.

Nietzsche's numerous if never very extensive comments on Napoleon are almost always favorable, and frequently extravagantly so. A few of the exceptions, largely confined to his notes, should be dealt with first before discussing the grounds of his admiration, for they were written before most of his encomia. In a fragmentary note of 1884, Nietzsche referred to those who give a *"false* picture" of powerful men, supported by armies and officials, even geniuses "without inner consummation" (*ohne innere Vollendung*) like Frederick the Great and Napoleon, who give rise to the question "For what?" (*Wozu?*) (*KGA*, 7:2, p. 79). One might like to know what sort of *innere Vollendung* a Napoleon of all people could be expected to attain. Later, in a completely uncritical spirit, Nietzsche would say that Napoleon justified the mess of the French Revolution (*WP*, #877; cf. *G*, 1:16). So far from giving rise to the question "For what?", he was expressly proclaimed as a supreme end in himself, the requirement of *innere Vollendung* having been dropped or simply forgotten. (That Nietzsche came to think Napoleon had attainted it is unlikely in the extreme.)

In the early 1880s Nietzsche specifically addressed the problem of Napoleon's ruthlessness, and provided remarkable divergence of judgment. "Such men as Napoleon," he wrote in 1883, "must come again and again and confirm the belief in the autocracy of the individual: but he himself was corrupted by the means he *had to* employ and lost *noblesse* of character. If he had had to prevail among a different kind of man he could have employed other means; and it would thus not seem to be a necessity for a *Caesar* to become bad" (*WP*, #1026). This is a rather absurd specimen of sentimentality from a writer who prided himself on his realism as much as did Nietzsche. Who and what decided the means Napoleon *"had to"* employ, the men around him or the goals he himself chose to pursue? This note is certainly indisputable evidence that Nietzsche could be squeamish, even if his manner of expressing it is singularly dubious. On the other hand, still another note from approximately the same period specifically and unambiguously praised Napoleon's ruthlessness (*KGA*, 7:2, p. 44). The contrast of sentimentality and ruthlessness indicates a conflict in Nietzsche that was perhaps never entirely resolved, whether on Napoleon or anything else.

But it is nevertheless true that he suppressed all traces of this ambivalence in his last works. The only comment in which it appears to survive occurs in the *Genealogy*, where Nietzsche referred to "Napoleon ... the most isolated and late-born man there has ever been, and in him the problem of the *noble ideal as such* made flesh [appeared]—one might well ponder *what* kind of problem it is: Napoleon, this synthesis of the *inhuman* and *superhuman*" (*G*, 1:16). Walter Kaufmann quoted the last words of this quotation as evidence that Nietzsche was "evidently not charmed by Napoleon's inhuman qualities";[8] but this is a curiously enlightening misreading. The context of the passage is entirely favorable to Napoleon. Even more important, it was one of Nietzsche's most basic points, both in the *Genealogy* and during the period when he was capable of being fitfully repelled by Napoleon's ruthlessness, that the strong man must be precisely a synthesis of the human and inhuman.[9] "Man is beast and superbeast, the higher man is inhuman and superhuman: these belong together" (*WP*, #1027). "*Napoleon*: insight that the higher and the terrible man necessarily belong together. The 'man' reinstated; the woman again accorded her due tribute of contempt and fear. 'Totality' as health and highest activity; the straight line, the grand style in action rediscovered; the most powerful instinct, that of life itself, the lust to rule, affirmed" (*WP*, #1017). Both of these notes are from the year the *Genealogy* was completed, and display no discomfort with "Napoleon's inhuman qualities."

Nietzsche admired Napoleon as a splendid specimen of individual power, political and even military.[10] He even went as far as to dub him the "*ens realissimum*" (most real being, a traditional term for God) (*T*, "Skirmishes," #49). But he also praised him as one of those profound spirits who anticipated the need for Europe's unity. In this spirit he berated the Germans repeatedly for their Wars of Liberation against Napoleon. In one of the climactic onslaughts on the Germans in his autobiography, Nietzsche declared that

> when on the bridge between two centuries of decadence, a *force majeure* of genius and will become visible, strong enough to create a unity out of Europe, a political and *economic* unity for the sake of a world government—the Germans with their "Wars of Liberation" did Europe out of the meaning, the miracle of meaning in the existence of Napoleon; hence they have on their conscience all that followed, that is with us today—this most *anti-cultural* sickness and unreason there is, nationalism, this *névrose nationale* with which Europe is sick, this perpetuation of European particularism, of *petty* politics: they have deprived Europe itself of its meaning, of its reason—they have driven it into a dead-end street. (*EH*, "Case of Wagner," #2)

There can be no question that this passage is genuinely representative. Nietzsche frequently and almost entirely consistently denounced the nationalism of his time and of his own nation in particular in the bitterest way. There is no point in the whole arsenal of Nietzschean apologetics in relation to the Nazis that is any sounder, perhaps none as sound, as this one.

Yet Nietzsche's thought on Napoleon and European unity is nevertheless deeply puzzling in a number of respects. Napoleon did play a major role in the rise of German nationalism, not merely by provoking a reaction, but also, more positively, in simplifying the German political map by eliminating large numbers of small principalities, in the process making subsequent German unification that much easier. He also, of course, established, for a short period, a kind of European unity, spreading the ideals of French egalitarianism and thus paving the way for the century of social unrest that followed and that Nietzsche deplored.[11] But Napoleon rode the crest of *French* nationalism, and greatly intensified the nationalist fervor of practically all European countries. (As we shall see shortly, Nietzsche, amazingly enough, realized this latter point clearly.) Furthermore, while the French nationalism of the Empire was vastly more tolerant and generous-spirited, as well as immeasurably less racist, than the German nationalism that found expression in Hitler, there is no reason to believe, and Nietzsche never attempted to present any reason to believe, that the French domination of Europe would have done anything whatever very positive for European culture. Perhaps the damage to culture, including France's own, from a long-lived Napoleonic unity of Europe would have been immeasurable. Napoleon believed, not in education for its own sake, "but in education for the service of the state," as one of his most authoritative and impartial biographers has written.[12] His idea for addressing the complaint that his France produced no great literature was to say that the Home Minister "ought to set about getting some decent stuff written."[13] Even apart from such considerations, however, Nietzsche's double standard with respect to Napoleonic France on the one hand and the German *Reich* on the other was complete.

Napoleon was, first and foremost, a maker of war; and Nietzsche's praise of him expressly included the warlike element, and his role in reawakening the warrior spirit in Europe. Nietzsche could even praise the violent nationalism created by Napoleon as a kind of historical stage to be traversed before European unity. The following aphorism from the *Gay Science* reveals all of this clearly.

> *Our faith that Europe will become more virile.*—We owe it to Napoleon (and not by any means to the French Revolution, which aimed at the "brotherhood" of nations and a blooming universal exchange of hearts) that we now confront a succession of a few warlike centuries that have no parallel in history; in short, that we have entered *the classical age of war*, of scientific and at the same time popular war on the largest scale.... All coming centuries will look back on it with envy and awe for its perfection. For the national movement out of which this war glory is growing is only the counter-shock against Napoleon and would not exist except for Napoleon. He should receive credit some day for the fact that in Europe the *man* has again become master over the businessman and the philistine.... [Napoleon] brought back again a whole slab of antiquity, perhaps even the decisive piece, the piece of granite. And who knows whether this slab of antiquity might not finally become master again over the national movement, and whether it must not become the heir and continuator of

Napoleon in an *affirmative* sense; for what he wanted was one unified Europe, as is known—as *mistress of the earth*. (*GS*, #362)

The ultimate aim of a unified Europe, if an imperialistic one, was obviously more precious to Nietzsche, even here, than nationalism. But the same nationalism is recognized for its part in resurrecting *men* where there had once been only businessmen and philistines, and praised for that reason. There is nothing even in Hegel, sometimes taken to be much worse than Nietzsche in this respect, that hymns nationalistic war so rapturously as this.[14] (One must grant that the expression of rapture was not exactly Hegel's stylistic forte.)

Nietzsche was not, however, always so rapturous about war at all. In some moods he lamented the petty dynastic wars of Europe (*KGA*, 8:3, p. 451); and, in a more unequivocally humane spirit, he attacked wasting the strength of men by treating it as cannon-fodder, calling it "madness" (*Wahnsinn*) (*Ibid.*, p. 457). He bemoaned the militarism in the very sound of the German language as it was declaimed under the Empire (*GS*, #104). More important, as Kaufmann noted, his praise of war frequently was praise of war in a very sublimated sense, meant to extol the intrepid courage of the seekers of truth and the campaigners in the realm of the spirit. Yet one should not make too much of this "sublimation," for the separation between wars of the spirit and actual war was anything but sharp in his own mind. "I welcome all signs that a more virile, warlike age is about to begin, which will restore honor to courage above all. For this age shall prepare the way for one yet higher ... the age that will carry heroism into the search for knowledge and that will *wage wars* for the sake of ideas and their consequences" (*GS*, #283). Zarathustra's famous "You say it is the good cause that hallows even war? I say unto you: it is the good war that hallows any cause" (*TSZ*, 1:10) certainly does not exclude war in a very unsublimated sense, and this declaration is the absolutely *classic* statement of bellicose nihilism in the literature of the world. Other passages do not permit any ambiguity about which kind of war is meant at all. "One must learn from war: (1) to associate death with the interests for which one fights—that makes *us* venerable; (2) one must learn to sacrifice *many* and to take one's cause seriously enough not to spare men; (3) rigid discipline, and to permit oneself force and cunning in war" (*WP*, #982). It is this second point which is so dangerous, so Hitlerian, in its brutality. Granting, what I have already demonstrated, that this kind of brutality was balanced by assertions in a very different spirit, Nietzsche's insistence on hardness was one of the most repeated of all his *Leitmotiven*. How much, in the final analysis, can one "sublimate" hardness and war? The greater the emphasis on hardness, the more peace becomes inevitably stigmatized as that which does not permit the highest virtue (in the original Roman sense of the term). The more one praises the spirit as warlike, the more one encourages ideological wars, the most terrible of all. And, indeed, a note from the period of the *Antichrist*, which Nietzsche perhaps rejected, declares that a truth shows itself by what it costs, and asks how philosophy can show its superiority to "God," "Fatherland," and "Freedom," except by requiring the sacrifice of even *"greater* hecatombs" than those ideas (*KGA*, 8:3, pp. 412–13).

One truth, in any case, should emerge clearly. One cannot speak of either understanding or misunderstanding Nietzsche on the subject of war. His own impulses were so divided on this issue as to produce a confusion of attitudes out of which one can pull whatever one wants. The passages in favor of war are more numerous than those unequivocally against it. Moreover, in an age that saw many glorifiers of war, Nietzsche was, to the best of my knowledge, the only one who specifically admired war as a school teaching one how to sacrifice *others*. Perhaps in that respect he was more consistent than the idealists who referred to war only as a school of self-sacrifice.

On the other hand, although several notes from his final active year are bellicose, one must note that his final pronouncement on the subject of war was in a different spirit, if also, to be sure, more than tinged with the signs of oncoming madness. In a paragraph he intended for the end of *Ecce Homo*, but decided to omit, he wrote: "If we could dispense with wars, so much the better. I can imagine more profitable uses for the twelve billion now paid annually for the armed peace we have in Europe; there are other means of winning respect for physiology than field hospitals.—Good; *very* good even: since the old God is abolished, I am prepared to *rule the world*—."[15]

The Jews and Racism

Even in his youthful letters, Nietzsche's unfavorable references to the Jews were fairly mild and conventional in tone. Moreover, in his mature published writings, as Kaufmann and many others have noted, general comments on the Jews are sometimes highly complimentary, especially where the Hebrew Bible was concerned. Far more important, he opposed the anti-Semitism of his day openly and consistently. Writing in *Beyond Good and Evil* of the modern Jew's desire for assimilation, he advised that "this bent and impulse ... should be noted well and *accommodated*: to that end it might be useful and fair to expel the anti-Semitic screamers from the country. Accommodated with all caution, with selection; approximately as the English nobility does" (*BGE*, #251). This is hardly the classic statement of liberal tolerance, but it is, of course, even farther removed from Nazi or proto-Nazi declarations on the subject. Similarly, when his sister became engaged to a prominent anti-Semitic agitator, Nietzsche's reaction was bitter. "Your association with an anti-Semitic chief expresses a foreignness to my whole way of life.... It is a matter of honor with me to be absolutely clean and unequivocal in relation to anti-Semitism, namely, *opposed* to it, as I am in my writings."[16] Nietzsche's relation to his sister was complex, and one can hardly be certain he would have welcomed her marriage to anyone. But it is still reasonable to take this evidence (and there is more of the kind) as a definitive statement of his opposition to anti-Semitic agitation.

All the more remarkable, therefore, are some passages in the *Genealogy*, written slightly before the letter quoted above, and the *Antichrist*, written after it. I shall discuss only two long passages, one from each work.

> Did Israel not attain the ultimate goal of its sublime vengefulness precisely through the bypath of this "Redeemer," this ostensible opponent and dis- integrator of Israel? Was it not part of the secret black art of truly *grand* politics of revenge, of a farseeing, subterranean, slowly advancing, and premeditated revenge, that Israel must itself deny the real instrument of its revenge before all the world as a mortal enemy and nail it to the cross, so that "all the world," namely all the opponents of Israel, could unhesi- tatingly swallow just this bait? And could spiritual subtlety imagine any *more dangerous* bait than this? Anything to equal the enticing, intoxicat- ing, overwhelming, and undermining power of that symbol of the "holy cross," that ghastly paradox of a "God on the cross," that mystery of an unimaginable ultimate cruelty and self-crucifixion of God *for the salva- tion of man?*
>
> What is certain, at least, is that *sub hoc signo* Israel, with its vengefulness and revaluation of all values, has hitherto triumphed again and again over all other ideals, over all *nobler* ideals. (G, 1:8)

Three comments should be made about this passage. First, the phrase *"nobler* ideals" is unquestionably normative, not "sociological." That does not contradict the claim in the same work that without the Jews history would be "altogether too stupid a thing." The ideal of the future would incorporate something descended from Jewish spirituality within a masterful aristocracy. On the other hand, the defining essence of this synthesis will certainly be non-Jewish and even anti-Jewish, since what is quintessentially Jewish is the passion of the negative and vengefulness against life.

Second, the "ghastly paradox of a 'God on the cross'" was ghastly to the Jews, whose tradition had not prepared them for a Messiah whose victory would be to suffer humiliating death. It is almost inconceivable that Nietzsche did not know as much.

Third, the background of this notion of a "secret black art of truly *grand* politics" is not without interest. The Christian Church had always claimed, on the basis of some Pauline texts, that the rejection of Jesus by the Jews was part of God's plan for the preliminary salvation of the Gentiles and fore- ordained. Such rejection signified Jewish "carnality," as Pascal, whom

Nietzsche read, put it.[17] This gave a particular meaning to the Jews in the Christian interpretation of God's grand politics: they were made to suffer, but allowed to endure, that they might, in both their suffering and their endurance, be an eternal sign that Jesus *was* the Messiah. Is it fair to assume that Nietzsche was fully conscious of this when he ascribed, in effect, the Christian interpretation of God's plot against the Jews to the "premeditated" plotting of the Jews? Perhaps not. But he certainly knew something of what their "premeditated revenge" had cost them and was continuing to cost them. As for the subsequent history of this notion of grandiose Jewish plots, we know it all too well. Nietzsche presented his own version, complete with the wallowing in verbosity that later, rather less literate masters of the German language were to employ in their own.

Let us move on to the *Antichrist*.

The Jews are the strangest people in world history because, confronted with the question whether to be or not to be, they chose, with a perfectly uncanny deliberateness, to be *at any price*: this price was the radical *falsification* of all nature, all naturalness, all reality, of the whole inner world as well as the outer. They defined themselves sharply *against* all the conditions under which a people had hitherto been able to live, been *allowed* to live; out of themselves they created a counter-concept to *natural* conditions: they turned religion, cult, morality, history, psychology, one after the other, into an incurable *contradiction to their natural values*. We encounter this same phenomenon once again and in immeasurably enlarged proportions, yet merely as a copy: the Christian church cannot make the slightest claim to originality when compared with the "holy people." That precisely is why the Jews are the *most catastrophic* people of world history: by their aftereffect they have made mankind so thoroughly false that even today the Christian can feel anti-Jewish without realizing that he himself is *the ultimate Jewish consequence.* ...

Psychologically considered, the Jewish people are a people endowed with the toughest vital energy, who, placed in impossible circumstances, voluntarily and out of the most profound prudence of self-preservation, take sides with all the instincts of decadence—*not* as mastered by them, but because they divined a power in those instincts with which one could prevail against "the world." The Jews are the antithesis of all decadents: they have had to *represent* decadents to the point of illusion; with a *non plus ultra* of histrionic genius they have known how to place themselves at the head of all movements of decadence (as the Christianity of *Paul*), in order to create something out of them which is stronger than any *Yes-saying* party of life. Decadence is only a *means* for the type of man who demands power in Judaism and Christianity, the *priestly* type: this type of man has a life interest in making mankind *sick* and in so twisting the concepts of good and evil, true and false, as to imperil life and slander the world. (*A*, #24)

Once again we are back in a world infected with the most grandiose and the most *harmful* Jewish plots. The statement that the Jews chose to be at any price is of particular interest in light of the entire series of mammoth and ferocious Jewish rebellions against Rome in the time of early Christianity, revolts which almost led to the extermination of the Jewish people. It is impossible to believe that Nietzsche knew nothing of them. This point has a twofold interest. One of his notes, probably roughly contemporaneous with the above, reads "It is quite in order that we possess no religion of oppressed Aryan races, for that is a contradiction: a master race is either on top or it is destroyed" (*WP*, #145).[18] This enthusiasm for the Aryan as such is quite untypical of Nietzsche, but it must be cited in connection with the diatribe against the Jews for the possible clue it offers to what was in his mind in writing it. To this one should add that Nietzsche was living in a world in which it was already being claimed that the Maccabees must have been Aryans; they were too valorous to be Jews.[19]

As we have seen earlier in this chapter, to possess "histrionic genius" was, for Nietzsche, a form of corruption more than anything else. And to claim that the Jews had adopted degenerate ideals without being a prey to them is to magnify the strength as well as the unscrupulousness of Jewish power, an impression heightened in the most extravagant way by saying that "the Jews are the *most catastrophic* people of world history."

Why should an opponent of anti-Semitism (sneers at anti-Semites are in both books) give such material to the objects of his scorn? I have given some reason above to rule out Nietzsche's famous and vastly overrated "intellectual integrity" as an answer deserving respect. One can argue, more plausibly, that much of the anti-Semitism of which he had knowledge was Christian or, at least, pseudo-Christian, and the emphasis upon the Jewishness of Christianity could consequently be seen as an attempt to undercut a favorite anti-Semitic theme, the radical divergence between the Jews on the one hand and Christians on the other.[20] That there is some truth in this is likely. That there is much in it is highly unlikely. To present the Jewish rejection of Christianity as a Jewish plot to corrupt mankind with the aim of protecting Jews against Christian anti-Semites is, to say no more, a far-fetched miscalculation. Equally important, the anti-Christian anti-Semitism of the Nazis had roots in Nietzsche's own time and Nietzsche himself was indisputably aware of it. Eugen Dühring, referred to with utter contempt in the *Genealogy*, was an anti-Christian anti-Semite, as were others in the 1870s and 1880s. That Nietzsche's writings had some effect in intensifying precisely this kind of anti-Semitism because of the very vehemence of their anti-Christian polemics is a thesis that scarcely admits of doubt,[21] and it would be well, for the sake of the historical record, for this to be more openly acknowledged than is usual.

To insist upon this, however, is not to imply that Nietzsche meant the

Jews any harm. A brief note, written before Nietzsche's opposition to anti-Semitism became decided, advises taking their money from the Jews and giving them "another direction" (*KGA*, 7:1, p. 366). Such a remark is a fitting revelation of the absurdity of Nietzsche's efforts at the control of history. But such fragments are exceedingly few and tentative in comparison with his open denunciation of anti-Semites. Moreover, he was opposed to racism in general, and not merely in its anti-Semitic form. To be sure, his writings offer sweeping, usually negative, characterizations of races, sexes, and nationalities, almost all of them in the most execrable taste. He believed in the Lamarckian doctrine of the "inheritance of acquired characteristics," and this doctrine underpinned his aristocraticism while occasionally producing an affection for the word *blood* as an explanatory term, one with social and racial overtones (*WP*, #942, e.g.). He could speak of "pride of race" as something desirable. All of this serves well enough to show that nothing resembling the moral principles dominant in the modern opposition to racism was important to him. But it does not alter the fact that he regarded racism as absurd, and could not even make up his mind whether "purity" of race was desirable (because it suggested unity of "instincts") or undesirable because mixtures, even the confusion of instincts, might be fruitful.

Pity, Suffering, and the Elimination of the Weak

In many of his works Nietzsche vehemently criticized pity, and this criticism is closely connected to the most brutal features of his thought. But on this as on so many topics in his moral philosophy, Nietzsche's points vary greatly in their reasonableness, and it is important at least to be fair to his grounds for questioning pity, even if there need be no pretense to admiration or even modest respect for his more important conclusions.

Pity is, like any emotion, capable of great variation in intensity, and most of Nietzsche's more justifiable criticisms reflect a concern with its almost infinite expansibility. In a late note he demanded that compassion "must be habitually sifted by reason; otherwise it is just as dangerous as any other affect" (*WP*, #928). The *Gay Science* had, rather more concretely, observed that life continuously offers an infinite number of "decent and praiseworthy ways of losing [one's] *own way* ..." in order to help others (*GS*, #338). The entire passage is obviously intensely personal, even explicitly defensive. Were it to be taken as suggesting a "universal law," it would be open to grave question. There are doubtless those who, without either talent or a genuine devotion to a spiritual concern, invent their "own way" as nothing but a means of escape from some legitimate duty. But it is not necessary, in spite of some of his phraseology in the aphorism as a whole, to suppose that Nietzsche meant to imply a universal law here or anywhere else; and it was perfectly reasonably to observe, in effect, that an unchecked religion of pity could prevent many of the most important individual accomplishments that have enriched all mankind.

At its most extensive level of development, the "religion of pity" becomes the belief that all that is, is pitiable. Nietzsche's respect for pity was bound to be one of the principal casualties of his conversion from Schopenhauer and his estrangement from Wagner, whose *Ring*, he charged, was ruined by Schopenhauer's influence.[22] "Schopenhauer was consistent enough," he declared in the *Antichrist*; "pity negates life and renders it *more deserving of negation.*"

> Christianity is called the religion of *pity*. Pity stands opposed to the tonic emotions which heighten our vitality: it has a depressing effect. We are deprived of strength when we feel pity. That loss of strength which suffering as such inflicts on life is still further increased and multiplied by pity. Pity makes suffering contagious... That is the first consideration, but there is a more important one.
>
> Suppose we measure pity by the value of the reactions it usually produces; then its perilous nature appears in an even brighter light. Quite in general, pity crosses the law of development, which is the law of *selection*. It preserves what is ripe for destruction; it defends those who have been disinherited and condemned by life. (*A, #7*)

If pity is so dangerous when enshrined at the center of a philosophy of pessimism (as Schopenhauer, more than Christianity, had certainly done), and dangerous, as well, for reducing men *to* a philosophy of pessimism, it should at least be possible for it to be less dangerous when it is only a facet of a basically affirmative character and outlook. Nietzsche had conceded this, in a limited way, in an earlier work.

> A man who says, "I like this, I take this for my own and want to protect it and defend it against anybody"; a man who is able to manage something, to carry out a resolution, to remain faithful to a thought, to hold a woman, to punish and prostrate one who presumed too much; a man who has his wrath and his sword and to whom the weak, the suffering, the hard pressed, and the animals, too, like to come and belong by nature, in short a man who is by nature a *master*—when such a man has pity, well, *this* pity has value. But what good is the pity of those who suffer. Or those who, worse, *preach* pity.
>
> Almost everywhere in Europe today we find a pathological sensitivity ... to pain; also a repulsive incontinence in lamentation, an increase in tenderness that would use religion and philosophical bric-a-brac to deck itself out as something higher—there is a veritable cult of suffering. The *unmanliness* of what is baptized as "pity" in the circles of such enthusiasts is, I should think, what always meets the eye first. (*BGE, #293*)

There is surely something verging on the reasonable here, as well as something more than verging on the embarrassing. The pity of the "strong," even if one might prefer to define strength in different ways than is done here, may well be of greater worth than that of the "weak" because the former are not in search of someone worse off than they in order to feel powerful. The preachers of pity, too, might be an unwholesome lot because at bottom they might wish, not to get something done for the pitiable, but to indulge in a certain kind of feeling (an objection that, to be sure, might also be lodged against those who preach hardness). But the value of pity cannot depend solely upon the quality of the one who feels it and acts upon it. That value must also be partially dependent upon the value of the compassionate action itself, which, according to the *Antichrist*, can be nonexistent. If it is good to give a starving man a meal, some of this goodness remains even if the provider in question does not hold his woman. And if it is good to "*let* the foreground law of thousandfold failure and ruin prevail," as Nietzsche had proclaimed earlier in *Beyond Good and Evil* itself (#62), then this charity is bad, even if the provider does hold his woman.

It is at this point that we arrive at the heart of the problem which compassion in general and in Nietzsche's philosophy in particular presents: what is and should be the relationship between pity and beneficent *action*, and how desirable are the very actions that pity promotes?

The importance of pity, considered specifically as an emotion and not as a shorthand designation for kindly action, dates largely from the eighteenth century. This importance in the Enlightenment was due to pity's character as a "natural" inducement to beneficent action, one that does not depend upon divine revelation or rationalistic moral imperatives, both of which were becoming dubious for many Enlightenment thinkers.[23] Because of this relation between pity and action, it should go without saying that pity was not praised purely as an emotion to be relished for its own sake by serious moralists, or to any degree that might undermine action. Though praised as a mode of feeling, it was intended to be a feeling that led irresistibly to action. (Few thinkers realized how false this assumption could prove to be.) There are three corollaries to this. First, in moral systems that enjoined kindliness, consideration, and helpfulness while prohibiting cruelty, but did so without dwelling on pity *per se*, some capacity for pity was generally presupposed, but did not need to be stressed when the corresponding action was stressed. Second, when the emotion of pity was actually condemned, whether simply because it was an emotion (and hence a "weakness," as with Spinoza and Kant), or because it might have no active consequences (in which case it was condemned even by Rousseau), it did not follow that beneficent action was condemned. As a consequence, when Nietzsche, in a very uncharacteristic appeal to the authority of previous moralists for rhetorical support, named Plato, Spinoza, La Rochefoucauld, and Kant as typical of a premodern contempt for pity (*G*, Preface, 5), the real moral doctrines of these writers were left completely unaffected and largely unillumined by this remark. This is not to argue that they all enjoined every form of compassionate action, but simply that their disapprobation of pity says nothing about what they did or did not enjoin. The same point cannot be made so unreservedly for Nietzsche, as some depressing evidence has already made clear.

It is probable that pity is most meaningfully conducive to moral action when set within a basically affirmative view of life, as was the case with Rousseau and the Enlightenment in general, and as was not the case with Schopenhauer, because only when supported by such affirmation would the amelioration of suffering it was intended to promote appear worthwhile, as opposed to appearing as a meaningless ripple on a vast sea of suffering. Nietzsche's mode of affirmation, however, challenged the desirability of compassionate action on two fronts. They were incompatible with one another, yet equally brutalizing in their effects. On the one hand, he repeatedly stressed the advantages of suffering for the strong, and castigated all those optimistic progressives who would endeavor to abolish it. On the other hand, he condemned pity for preserving sufferers who should perish instead of remaining around to depress the healthy. The "healthy," therefore, are those who can triumph over suffering. They are also such delicate flowers that they must be kept even from the sight of suffering. Thus Nietzsche condemned pity for multiplying suffering and for threatening to end it, and sought the enhancement of life by the increase of suffering and by its decrease. Let me expand upon these points and their practical corollaries, in which Nietzsche's moral philosophy reaches the climax of its brutality and of its incoherence.

You want, if possible—and there is no more insane "if possible"—*to abolish suffering*. And we? It really seems that *we* would rather have it higher and worse than ever. Well-being as you understand it—that is no goal, that seems to us an *end*, a state that soon makes man ridiculous and contemptible—that makes his destruction *desirable*.

The discipline of suffering, of *great* suffering—do you not know that only *this* discipline has created all enhancements of man so far? That tension of the soul in unhappiness which cultivates its strength ..., its inventiveness and courage in enduring ... and exploiting suffering, and whatever has been granted to it of profundity, secret, mask, spirit, cunning, greatness—was it not granted to it through suffering, through the discipline of great suffering? In man *creature* and *creator* are united: in man there is material, fragment, excess, clay, dirt, nonsense, chaos; but in man there is also creator, form-giver, hammer hardness, spectator divinity, and seventh day: do you understand this contrast? (*BEG*, #226)

One may wonder, in response to this question, whether Nietzsche's philosophy is simply Calvinism shorn of redemption. What is clearer, however, are those more mundane but crucial questions which this passage does not put, let alone answer. Exactly what forms of suffering are desirable, and how will the controllers of history proceed to intensify them? It is precisely on issues such as pity and suffering that the typical abstractness of Nietzsche's philosophical method is truly disastrous, and becomes simply harangue without method and without thought. Nietzsche could not be troubled to distinguish between the dark night of the soul and the bubonic plague; and the absence of such distinctions is not made any less absurd, given the sweeping character of his ode to suffering, in the light of the indubitable truth that much good can come out of suffering, as theologians, in particular, have emphasized for millennia. But the theologians had never seen man as the controller of history, and had often sought to maintain exactly that submissiveness to Providence which Nietzsche regarded with limitless contempt.

In spite of the alleged benefits of suffering, Nietzsche feared its depressing effects sufficiently to desire to segregate the sick from the healthy, presumably in some more drastic way, and with greater latitude in the designation of the "sick," than standard medical practice followed as a matter of course. The demand that "the healthy should be *segregated* from the sick, guarded even from the sight of the sick" (*G*, 3:14) was made in a context that assailed that form of resentment and revenge by which the sick make the healthy feel guilty about their own happiness as something "disgraceful" when there is so much misery. But any such neat dichotomy between sickness and health as the passage as a whole implies is scarcely sustainable on the premises of Nietzsche's own thought. Zarathustra had defined man as a disease on the skin of the earth (*TSZ*, 2:18), and the *Genealogy* itself had maintained that man's susceptibility to sickness, presumably in some psychological sense, was intimately related to his courage and creativity (*G*, 3:13). Nietzsche's own resentment of resentment, as well as his own morbidity, are what is doubtless responsible for the intrusion into his work of such risible absurdities as this segregation plan.

Unfortunately, Nietzsche suggested more drastic action as well. "The weak and the failures shall perish: first principle of *our* love of man. And they shall even be given every possible assistance" (*A*, #2). The insertion of this quotation into the typical book on Nietzsche that deals with moral subjects at all written since the Second World War would suffice to blow it completely apart. There is nothing whatever in the context of this imperative that palliates it. Nor can it be regarded as a transient effect indicating Nietzsche's oncoming madness, for notes written much earlier anticipate it clearly. "*Vernichtung der Missrathenen—dazu muss man sich von der bisherigen Moral emancipiren.*" ("The annihilation of the misbegotten—for that one must emancipate himself from the previous morality") (*KGA*, 7:2, p. 71).

This was written in 1884. Many other notes, though mostly from the period of the *Antichrist* itself, are to the same effect,[24] though one should add that Nietzsche occasionally advocated preserving the weak because of their utility, if for that reason alone (*WP*, #895).

Only once, however, did Nietzsche discuss what can only be termed mass murder in anything approaching a detailed way, and that discussion was ambiguous in the extreme. In *Twilight of the Idols*, he dealt with Manu's legislation as an example of an attempt to breed a particular kind of race.

> How wretched is the New Testament compared to Manu, how foul it smells!
>
> Yet this organization too found it necessary to be *terrible*.... [I]t had no other means for keeping [the member of the lower class] from being dangerous, for making him weak, than to make him *sick*.... Perhaps there is nothing that contradicts our feeling more than *these* protective measures of Indian morality....
>
> The success of such sanitary police measures was inevitable: murderous epidemics, ghastly venereal diseases....
>
> These regulations are instructive enough: here we encounter for once *Aryan* humanity, quite pure, quite primordial—we learn that the concept of "pure blood" is the opposite of a harmless concept. On the other hand, it becomes clear in which people the hatred, the chandala hatred, against this "humaneness" has eternalized itself.... Seen in this perspective, the Gospels represent a document of prime importance.... Christianity, sprung from Jewish roots and comprehensible only as a growth on this soil, represents the countermovement to any morality of breeding, of race, of privilege: it is the *anti-Aryan* religion par excellence. Christianity, the revaluation of all Aryan values, the victory of chandala values, the gospel preached to the poor and base, the general revolt of all the downtrodden, the wretched, the failures, the less favored, against "race": the undying chandala hatred as the *religion of love*. (*T*, "'Improvers,'" #3–4)

The ambiguities here are endless. That Nietzsche did not endorse Aryan supremacy as such can be gathered, if not from the passage itself, then from his generally negative attitude toward Aryan racism. On the other hand, "breeding" and "privilege" certainly stood high in his esteem. Yet the manufactured quality of the suffering provoked by Manu's legislation would not seem to involve a very selective method for social or racial improvement. The passage as a whole is probably critical and, though again one must say "probably," reflects an attempt to discountenance the racists. Yet it could be read the other way. The modern feeling he referred to, which is revolted by this aspect of Manu, was most likely his own, but in the general context of his writings, with their laments about modern softness, one cannot be sure. At the least, it must be observed that Nietzsche was so consumed by his resentment of resentment as to pour much more contempt on Christianity than on the horrors of Manu's legislation.

Furthermore, whatever Nietzsche thought about this aspect of the laws of Manu, for whom, in general, he was so perversely enthusiastic, it must be said that he repeatedly condemned Christianity because it "preserved too much of *what ought to perish*" and, in the process, helped to *"worsen the European race"* (*BGE*, #62). This claim, closely resembling statements from the *Antichrist* encountered before, is from *Beyond Good and Evil*. Nietzsche saw fit to make the identical point in almost literally the final words of *Ecce Homo*, his last offering to mankind. As so often with Nietzsche, repetition of ideas not worth stating once does nothing to improve, amplify, or even clarify them. It is exceedingly difficult even to guess at what types of persons were unfortunately preserved by the effects of Christianity, on his view. Was it those who were psychologically tormented but found enough comfort in Christianity to keep them from suicide?[25] Or the impoverished failures (or victims) physically preserved by organized Christian charity? Since, as we have seen, Nietzsche did not normally have faith in "natural selection" as a force favoring the stronger over the weaker, there would seem to be reason not to read these passages as specimens of Social Darwinism. But one cannot be sure that Nietzsche did not simply forget that opposition when he wrote these attacks on Christianity for corrupting the process of selection.

There is, however, reason to believe that Nietzsche objected to the Judaeo-Christian tradition, not merely for keeping alive those who might otherwise have perished from their weakness and failure, but also for preventing the active sacrifice of individuals by this or that great man for some distant purpose. In a late note he wrote that "through Christianity, the individual has become so important, so absolute, that he could no longer be sacrificed" (*WP*, #246). One must wonder, given how much sacrificing of mankind has occurred in Christian countries across the centuries, exactly what novelties of horror Nietzsche hoped would follow in the wake of his polemics, designed as they were to divide history in two. No answer to these and similar questions is possible on the basis of the texts.

The question of the sense in which Nietzsche can be said to have meant the most horrific aspects of his doctrine will be considered in the next chapter. But those aspects can no more be regarded as extraneous to his philosophy than anything else therein. Anyone who, taking a hint from Zarathustra (*TSZ*, 4:13), writes in general terms about the misunderstanding and misuse of Nietzsche by the Nazis or anyone else, as is done constantly, must explain how precisely the passages quoted in this section, and others quoted earlier of similar moral content, are to be properly understood and properly used. The lurid passages collected here do not suffice in any way to define the thought of Friedrich Nietzsche. *But without them, Nietzsche's thought cannot be accurately defined.*

Conclusion

The relation between Nietzsche's writings and Nazi ideology is obviously very mixed. On some issues, Nietzschean apologetics has served a very useful purpose. On the other hand, the tendency to emphasize the occasional Nazi misquotations and quotations out of context has only obscured the evident fact that a large number of passages can be culled from Nietzsche without any alteration or violence to their immediate context which could serve Nazi purposes to perfection. Whether one regards the balance of Nietzsche's writings, especially on politically and socially related themes, as inclining in a pro- or anti-Nazi direction must depend on how one defines the essence of Nazism. Insofar as that essence should be understood in terms of German racism and active anti-Semitism, then Nietzsche must be regarded as an anti-Nazi. Insofar as it should be understood in a looser way, as an assault on the morality of the "weak" on behalf of the drastic subordination of the many to the few, regardless of how, specifically, the many and the few are to be defined, one would be justified in a different judgment. This is all the truer if one substitutes the broader term *fascist* for the narrower term *Nazi*.

Furthermore, the frequently ruthless character of Nietzsche's inegalitarianism deprives his opposition to racism of much of its relevance as far as the general moral characterization of his political philosophy goes, and perhaps also as far as his historical impact is concerned. The division of mankind into groups, those unworthy of existence and those who are worthy because of intrinsic superiority or utility to their superiors, constitutes a major feature of Nietzsche's thought, and it constitutes the heart of what is most deplorable in Nazism as well. In comparison to this general doctrine, the difference between Nietzsche's and the Nazis' views about the most suitable candidates for annihilation is a colossal irrelevance. There is, I trust, no need to expatiate upon this point. What is remarkable is that it should have to be made at all. By stressing Nietzsche's opposition to anti-Semitism, Nietzschean apologists have normally ignored the broader doctrine of *Vernichtung der Missrathenen* as of no account.

Nietzsche traced the European idea of equality to Christianity. This is an oversimplification, since more than a hint of that idea can be found in pre-Christian Stoicism and at least a hint in the classical doctrine of the Golden Age.[26] But there can be no denying the importance, on an abstract metaphysical level, of the Christian teaching of "equality before God," which he found so offensive and threatening. On the level of concrete political teaching, however, the mainstream of Christian teaching, at least through Luther, was resolutely opposed to "leveling" of any kind, and usually counseled passive obedience. More important, the transformation of the notion of "equality before God" into a political doctrine of equality and a moral doctrine of universalistic ethics was by no means conceptually dependent upon retaining theistic assumptions. Equality before the law, equality of opportunity, and equal rights of political participation could be and were defended on grounds that had nothing to do with such assumptions, but instead were defended on the basis of a variety of beliefs ranging from a minimum of rationality in all men to less "idealistic" considerations about social order and the best way to maintain it. It would, therefore, be a mistake to claim that, if one concedes the validity of Nietzsche's attack on specifically Christian doctrines, one must also concede that Nietzsche succeeded in placing the burden of proof for equality on those who uphold it. On the contrary, the burden of proof lies equally upon egalitarians and inegalitarians alike, that is, on anyone who claims to know the order that *should obtain*. Furthermore, since Nietzsche never claimed that might makes right, but feared such a doctrine, as we have seen, he was deprived of that easy way out, and it was all the more necessary for him to provide the cogent foundation for his politics, something he never did nor even attempted. The advantages of the "pathos of distance" constitute nothing of the sort without some reason, apart from force, for everyone, the oppressed included, to agree to it. But the more that pathos was stressed, the more brutal it was in constant danger of becoming; as a result any rationale for Nietzsche's order in the minds of its victims vanished correspondingly.

The arbitrariness of Nietzsche's procedure found its perfect expression in a rare paragraph in praise of religion in *Beyond Good and Evil*.

> To ordinary human beings, finally—the vast majority who exist for service and the general advantage, and who *may* exist only for that—religion gives an inestimable contentment with their situation and type, manifold peace of the heart, an ennobling of obedience, one further happiness and sorrow with their peers and something transfiguring and beautifying, something of a justification for the whole everyday character, the whole lowliness, the whole half-brutish poverty of their souls. Religion and religious significance spread the splendor of the sun over such ever-toiling human beings and make their own sight tolerable to them. Religion has the same effect which an Epicurean philosophy has on sufferers of a higher rank: it is refreshing, refining, makes, as it were, the most of suffering, and in the end even sanctifies and justifies. Perhaps nothing in Christianity or Buddhism is as venerable as their art of teaching even the lowliest how to place themselves through piety in an illusory order of things and thus to maintain their contentment with the real order, in which their life is hard enough—and precisely this hardness is necessary. (*BGE*, #61)

This is a remarkable passage in many ways, not the least being its curious mixture of affection and contempt, which it would probably be erroneous to read as simply a repellant condescension. But two other points are of more concern here. The very need in the lowly to be made tolerable in their own sight, their very capacity for "something transfiguring and beautifying," could easily be taken to mean that there must be something right with the doctrine of equality, not because everyone's need for self-respect and capacity for transfiguration is equal to everyone else's, but because the presence of any such need and capacity makes an individual an "end in himself," not one of so many cattle and sheep. This, of course, might be denied; but no more easily than the proposition that the many "*may* exist only" "for service and the general advantage." In a book that pays particular attention to the ungrounded assumptions of philosophers, this dogmatism is all the more striking, and characterizes Nietzsche's inegalitarianism in general.[27]

A further problem of a more practical nature arises if we ask how Nietzsche proposed to maintain, let alone increase, such inequality as remained, especially given the vehemence of his assault on Christianity. He may have explicitly expected, of course, that Christianity would survive his assault, and that he was writing for the few. But the coexistence of faith and faithlessness requires considerably more delicacy on the part of the faithless than was provided by his example. If, in fact, this example were meant to be taken as a norm for the "free spirits," then permanent coexistence would be seriously threatened and social order with it, not because the faithful cannot tolerate the faithless, but because orgies of recrimination may be utterly uncontrollable.

Only once did Nietzsche point in a serious way to a kind of treatment of the "masses" that seemed designed to make them willing members of a new order by appealing for the elevation of their dignity and welfare. He declared that workers should be made to feel like soldiers, with an honorarium, but not with pay; and that there should be no relation between payment and performance. Rather, individuals should be so placed that each can do the highest task of which he is capable (*WP*, #76). It is unnecessary and unfair to be much alarmed by the military element in this proposal. The intention was clearly nothing more ominous than to place the contribution of the worker on a positive, rather than a negative, footing. The notion of the honorarium was to dignify labor as positively fulfilling, rather than as a mere means to staying alive. But how did Nietzsche propose to implement this idea, which has more in common with socialism than Nietzsche perhaps realized? In any case, while anyone is free to believe that these suggestions constituted Nietzsche's deeply cherished conviction, this benign note was followed shortly thereafter by *Twilight of the Idols*, whose contemptuous reference to the excessively good treatment meted out to the modern worker has already been quoted.

Nietzsche's political thought must be pronounced a failure, not merely

because it usually violates the most cherished liberal and humanitarian senti-
ments, but also because it is fragmentary in the extreme. One can concede
with alacrity that it points only ambiguously and dubiously toward Nazism.
One must add that it scarcely points at all.

But does that very truth not mean that Nietzsche was in his philosophic
and temperamental essence *apolitical*? In what sense can he be said really to
have meant these forays into politics and the egregious brutality to which
he often gave expression? The next chapter will attempt to deal with these
questions.

8

Nietzsche and Nietzscheanism

In *Ecce Homo* Nietzsche referred to himself as "the last *anti-political German*" (*EH*, 1:3). The sense in which he meant this is by no means clear. But it can certainly be said that he did not participate in politics or political movements; he was spiritually and physically almost a man without a country in his last years; and he probably did not follow daily political developments in any detail or with great interest.

But does that mean that his *thought* should or even could be read anti-politically? In a note of 1885 for the projected *Will to Power*, Nietzsche wrote:

> A book for *thinking*, nothing else: it belongs to those for whom thinking is a delight, nothing else—
> That it is written in German is untimely, to say the least: I wish I had written it in French so that it might not appear to be a confirmation of the aspirations of the German *Reich*.
> The Germans of today are no thinkers any longer: something else delights and impresses them.
> The will to power as a principle might be intelligible to them.
> It is precisely among the Germans today that people think less than anywhere else. But who knows? In two generations one will no longer require the sacrifice involved in any nationalistic squandering of power and in becoming stupid. (*WP*, Intro., xxii–xxiii)

This is, on the face of it, very precious evidence for Nietzschean apologetics. It appears to do much more than dissociate Nietzsche from German nationalism, which it certainly does; it also seems to render possible a quick, unanalytical, blessedly blanket disclaimer against the validity of using Nietzsche's thought to direct events. Instead, it proclaims a philosophic innocence amounting to a philosophic innocuousness.

But does this line of exculpation not rest on a sheer absurdity? There may be such a thing as a book for thinking and nothing else, but even if Nietzsche

149

had attached this note to every volume he published, instead of not publishing it at all, it would still be difficult to comprehend the meaning such a disclaimer was supposed to have. If a man writes that the "weak and the failures shall perish.... And they shall even be given every possible assistance," it does not matter whether he founds a party or even reads newspapers. He has, one may think, entered the realm of political discourse, where there is no such thing as "thinking and nothing else," but only thinking that wants to be taken seriously, thinking, in other words, that is supposed to *mean* something, and thinking that does not. The intended meaning, of course, need not be revolutionary. It can concern the futility of politics or the irrationality of Utopian expectations; but such a meaning is not for thinking and nothing else any more than was the thinking of Marx or Hitler. And a writer who wished to put an end to the reign of accident in history could scarcely have believed in the futility of politics.

Furthermore, Nietzsche explicitly protested, in a note later than the above quotation, against any severing of the life of thought from that of action (*WP*, #458). The interpreter faced with the apparent contradiction between this protest on the one hand and the claim of thinking and nothing else on the other is not at liberty to choose what he personally prefers to regard as representative of the real meaning of Nietzsche's work. On the contrary, in dealing with this or any other contradiction, the method must surely be to ask which view is more in accord with the philosophy as a whole, insofar as that philosophy can be discerned beneath the contradictions, and insofar as the subject under discussion is integral to it. In the present case, there can be little doubt. Nietzsche's entire philosophy, in spite of its status *as* a philosophy, a way of *looking* at the world, was predicated on an inveterate and fierce hostility to any form of bifurcation of human life, any relic of a duality between one world and another, between inner and outer, between body and soul. "Thinking and nothing else" presupposes just such a dualism, a veritable scholasticism and worse than scholasticism of knowledge. How can thinking and nothing else *dominate*? The central position of cultural values in Nietzsche's axiology has never been in doubt in this book; but such centrality does not presuppose, and does not even make very intelligible, any doctrine of "thinking and nothing else."

But did Nietzsche really wish to dominate? An intriguing note from 1883 reads, in its entirety: "To rule? Impose my type on others? Ghastly! Is my happiness not precisely the sight of many who are *different*? Problem" (*KGA*, 7:1, p. 555). There is much that should be said against using this quotation from the *Nachlass* as a serious reinforcement of "thinking and nothing else." For one thing, too much in the published writings is inconsistent with it. In addition to the ideal of the tripartite society already examined, there is Zarathustra's explicit affirmation of rule: "The lust to rule— but who would call it *lust* when what is high longs downward for power?

Verily, there is nothing diseased or lustful in such longing and condescending. That the lonely heights should not remain lonely and self-sufficient eternally; that the mountain should descend to the valley ...—oh, who were to find the right name for such longing? 'Giftgiving virtue'—thus Zarathustra once named the unnamable" (*TSZ*, 3:10).

There is, however, an even more obvious problem, and that lies in Nietzsche's word *problem* itself. Surely this is embarrassing for the whole theory of sublimation if that theory is to be understood as involving a complete *internalization* of the will to power to the point of the innocently innocuous. If Nietzsche understood will to power to rise naturally to such a point, or meant to affrm it whether it were natural or not; if he saw his own reluctance to impose his ideal on any one else as following from or even merely consistent with his philosophy of power, then this "problem" would not exist at all.

Does this not mean that we are faced with two very different issues, the question of Nietzsche's philosophy and the question of his personality? To maintain this is by no means to commit oneself to the absurd proposition that Nietzsche's personality had no influence on his philosophy, which he would have been the first to deny. What it does mean is that the relation between the two is complex, and that his philosophy, even with all its contradictions, may have been an imperfect and, in some ways, an inverted expression of his personality.

Much of what I have termed Nietzschean apologetics, which should be distinguished from works on Nietzsche that resolutely avoid his moral philosophy altogether, derives its plausibility from the implicit conviction that Nietzsche did not mean much that he wrote, that it is legitimate to choose his noblest pronouncements as definitively representative of his thought because one can no more imagine Nietzsche actually countenancing the elimination of the weak in his name than one can imagine Marx as pope. It is in this light that we should understand the affection that Nietzsche has inspired, an affection that induced Albert Camus to write shortly after the Second World War, "We shall never finish making reparation for the injustice done to him."[1] This affection by people of unquestioned humanity in word as well as deed is not simply the result of the value of Nietzsche's insights on nonmoral subjects, but the result of what surely is perceived as a curious irreality in his brutality, even his snobbishness. Thomas Mann expressed this perception when he referred to his own sense of "tragic pity for [Nietzsche's] overburdened soul," one born for "noble friendships," not the solitude he endured, "a mind by origin profoundly respectful, shaped to revere pious traditions; and just such a mind fate chose to drag by the hair, as it were, into a posture of wild and drunken truculence.... This mind was compelled to violate its own nature, to become the mouthpiece and advocate of blatant brute force, of the callous conscience, of Evil itself."[2] There is

much that one can quarrel with here, of course; the question-begging character of "fate," although it was a word Nietzsche loved, and the degree to
which Nietzsche ever really espoused the callous conscience, at least when
he was not praising "what is noble"![3] But in its depiction of a mind at war
with itself, and frequently induced to give most vivid expression to its worst
half, Mann's claims have a value which the present writer would be the last
to deny.

Even writers who are far from willing to acknowledge the degree of
brutality in Nietzsche's works that Mann conceded, and who maintain with
fervor that those works contain a consistent philosophy, not the revelations
of a moral schizophrenic, will sometimes hint at a psychological ingredient
in Nietzsche that occasionally distorted the character of his writing. Thus
Kaufmann wrote that Nietzsche was preoccupied with weakness in his philosophy because he feared it in himself.[4] R. J. Hollingdale observed, similarly, that the megalomania frequently found in Nietzsche's letters, in which he
predicts that one day people will swear by his name, must be regarded as
"wild over-compensations of an ailing and half-blind man."[5]

The problem with these statements is certainly not that they attempt to
replace righteous indignation with "understanding." Nor is it that they beg
psychological questions they do not answer. It should be possible to make
psychological observations on Nietzsche without attempting a psycholanal-
ysis, as this writer intends to do. The problem is rather: how do we interpret
Nietzsche's *philosophy* in the light of this psychological issue? When Hollingdale maintains that the "*hubris*" of Nietzsche's letters and their over-
compensations "must not be confused with his *philosophy*," one must ask
how such a statement can be justified. Nietzsche's megalomania was hardly
confined to his letters, notes, and spoken pronouncements to his sister. It is
embedded in *Ecce Homo* directly, and only slightly less directly in his entire
philosophy of power and the feeling of power. Is it not unavoidable, in light
of this, that we see his megalomania, even if it was fitful and by no means
without mitigation in his writings, to say nothing of his well-mannered personal life, as offering a key to how he himself understood his philosophic
enterprise, at least in part, namely, as a proof of and means to *Machtgefühl*?
And when Kaufmann says that Nietzsche feared weakness in himself, do we
simply use this remark to pass over the more outrageous elements of his
philosophy, or to question whether that philosophy might not be saturated,
root and branch, with just this fear?

It is at this point that we might briefly consider a work on Nietzsche that
is not at all "psychologically" conceived, but is instead perhaps the most
successful systematization of his contradictions, from a purely philosophic
standpoint, ever attempted: Wolfgang Müller-Lauter's *Nietzsche: His Philosophy of Contradiction and the Contradictions of His Philosophy*. Müller-
Lauter discerned two ideals in Nietzsche which were not and could not be

adequately unified, given the manner in which Nietzsche conceived them: the ideal of the "strongest" man and the ideal of the "wisest" man. This thesis does not depend upon regarding wisdom or the capacity for it as weakness. It depends rather on the view that the wise man cannot display strength of particular kinds, kinds which Nietzsche could never relegate to the domain of the unimportant. The wise man is committed to an understanding of others, to "the sight of many who are *different*." This entails, not the understanding of others as a tool for manipulation, but as an end in itself, a complete penetration of the "perspective" of the other, which serves to multiply the perspectives of the wise man himself, increasing his wisdom. This culminates in *appreciation*, love, the recognition that all that is is divine, which found its supreme expression in the eternal recurrence when conceived, not as an inducement to create the most desirable of futures, but as universal benediction. The wise man, as Müller-Lauter notes, recognizes contradictions. Such recognition is inherent in his whole enterprise of multiplying perspectives that are inherently at odds. But he brings these contradictions *into* himself, as different perspectives demanding to be understood.[6]

The *strong* man, by contrast, does not internalize contradictions at all, but embodies particular convictions, on behalf of which he acts combatively against others. The strong man demonstrates strength by refusing to internalize conflict, by confronting his obstacle in open opposition. The wise man may demonstrate strength of a kind by internalizing conflict, but when this process is carried to the limits of the ideal of a perfectly *comprehensive* wisdom, he cannot appear strong in the strong man's sense; he becomes "incapable of life" because of the very breadth of his wisdom and the justice he discerns in each perspective.[7]

It is obviously possible to harmonize this philosophical depiction of Nietzsche's dualism with the psychological view of his need for overcompensation. His understanding of the philosopher in terms of a radical strength-weakness clearly produced a need to conceive the philosopher in terms of power. This could be done only by a philosophy that frequently abandoned internalized innocence in favor of a reexternalization of power, a depiction of the philosopher as strong *over* others and strong enough to embrace the value of this kind of power as exhibited by nobles determined to maintain their position.

There is a double gain in introducing these psychological considerations. One is to make more explicit the tension in Nietzsche and in his conception of himself that led, however fitfully, to evil; but the other is of a different character, to lend some substance to the apologetic intuition that Nietzsche was not capable of real harm, did not, in other words, "mean" his worst thoughts. Taken together, these points, if sound, would entail a kind of "exculpation" of Nietzsche's person but *not* his philosophy.

If we take Nietzsche's fear of weakness seriously, without attempting to discern its ultimate "cause," then we can say, in the spirit of Kaufmann's view, that he projected his inward enemies, his fear of weakness, outward, externalized them in a sense, by objectifying them in his thought as the "weak," the "sick," the "resentful," and so forth. Much of his philosophy of internalization, which analyzed related forms of externalization, was, as I hope to show shortly, based more on his understanding of himself than he admitted, perhaps even to himself. But, precisely because he was internalized, because he was a philosopher rather than a man of strength, he did not, paradoxically, really externalize them at all, but kept them within. He had need of obstacles and enemies, but enemies in *idea*, not in reality. This process of internalization is reflected, not merely in what Nietzsche himself says about the philosopher and the ascetic priest, with a confusing and un-resolved tension between admiration and contempt, but in his mode of comprehending those who are neither philosophers nor ascetic priests. In *Human, All-Too Human*, he twice observed that those who attack and hurt others do so, not in order to hurt as such, but in order to become conscious of their own strength (#103, #317). This foreshadows the analysis of the master later given, as we have seen, in the *Genealogy*, where cruelty is less the aim than the mere means to *Machtgefühl*. It may be an *indispensable* means, to be sure, since only by producing some demonstrable effect on the other can one be certain of strength, but the self-reflexivity of the aim carries with it the possibility of greater internalization and sublimation.

To see this, it will help to consider Nietzsche's own code as a "warrior." "I am warlike by nature," he felt obliged to tell us, "Attacking is one of my instincts.

> Being *able* to be an enemy, *being* an enemy—perhaps that presupposes a strong nature; in any case, it belongs to every strong nature. It needs objects of resistance; hence it *looks for* what resists: the aggressive pathos belongs just as necessarily to strength as vengefulness and rancor belong to weakness....
>
> The strength of those who attack can be measured in a way by the opposition they require: every growth is indicated by the search for a mighty opponent—or problem; for a warlike philosopher challenges problems, too, to single combat. The task is *not* simply to master what happens to resist, but what requires us to stake all our strength, suppleness, and fighting skill—opponents that are our *equals*.

The self-inflation of these remarks needs no comment; neither does their conformity with Nietzsche's most basic psychological and ontological pre-suppositions in the doctrine of the will to power. Equally worthy of note, however, and more interesting, are the implications of the specific principles that follow this gross preface:

My practice of war can be summed up in four propositions. First: I only attack causes that are victorious; I may even wait until they become victorious.

Second: I only attack causes against which I would not find allies, so that I stand alone—so that I compromise myself alone.—...

Third: I never attack persons; I merely avail myself of the person as of a strong magnifying glass that allows one to make visible a general but creeping and elusive calamity. Thus I attacked David Strauss—more precisely, the *success* of a senile book with the "cultured" in Germany....

Fourth: I only attack things when every personal quarrel is excluded, when any background of bad experiences is lacking. (*EH*, 1:7)

What is of interest here is not the intrinsic merits of this code, nor whether Nietzsche entirely followed it, though one can remark in passing that the distinction in the third proposition could well seem academic to the person actually attacked.[8] More worthy of note is that such a code, if consistently followed, would seem to guarantee failure. René Girard has noted that "this chivalrous behavior is in keeping with the demands of the mystique, no doubt. But it can also be described as a feverish enterprise of self-destruction, especially in a man who attaches as much importance to victory as Nietzsche does. What the mystique adds up to, really, is a Herculean and systematic effort to bring about its own metamorphosis into *ressentiment*."[9] This is insightful and, given both the importance of victory in Nietzsche's doctrine and the quantity of resentment in his writings, it is fair. But it is also an oversimplification. For there is a paradox in a code of noble conduct that guarantees failure: one can say that to fail, inevitably, to conquer is to succeed equally inevitably. The condition of this success, of course, is that one seeks, not actual victory over the external obstacle, but internal self-confirmation through having fought the good fight. If *Ecce Homo* sometimes succeeds in conveying a convincing euphoria in spite of the lack of recognition and "success" from which Nietzsche continued to suffer, part of the reason surely lies in that very internalization which enabled him to engage in combat of just this kind, the kind he *could not lose*.

Nietzsche's conviction that it was a mark of nobility not to despise one's enemies may be regarded as a step towards not having any enemies at all, in the sense of those over whom one *must* triumph or lose self-respect. The enemy becomes only a necessary foil for the internal confirmation of the internal self. But this process cannot go all the way to the abolition of the need for enemies of any kind. *Machtgefühl* requires an obstacle, even if it does not require actually doing anyone any harm. Seen in this way, the "thinking and nothing else" excuse is not quite so fatuous as I first made it appear. Nietzsche could at times write the vilest things without meaning them. But what he could not do, in spite of his protestations to the contrary, was preserve the dignity of his opponent. The very ferocity of his attacks was his guarantee that he was fighting a real war, a reality guaranteed by the *despicability* of his enemies, especially Christianity and the Germans, which permitted him to compensate in vividness of feeling for the unreality, the pure internality, of his combat. The result was the combination of resentment and self-glorification, hatred and benediction that characterizes his thought and over which he had an ever-decreasing control, marring the euphoric poses of *Ecce Homo* with attacks on the Germans transparently rooted in his own frustrations.

The internalization that can almost, if not quite, dispense with the other as enemy is paralleled by the internalization that can almost dispense with the other as an object of love. " 'Joy in the Thing' people say," runs an aphorism from *Human, All-Too Human*, "but in reality it is joy in itself by means of the thing" (#501).[10] Much later he was to offer a very similar dictum. "In the end one loves one's desire and not the thing desired" (*BGE*, #175). Whether Nietzsche's own feeling in holding this view was one of triumph, disillusionment, or both, the lines are quintessential acts of Nietzschean unmasking. As such, they subtly foreshadow his claim in the *Genealogy* that Judaeo-Christian love is really the product of hate. The line from *Human, All-Too Human* purports to say what a free, unforced individual really wants from an object or person to whom he is positively related. The claim of the *Genealogy* purports to say what a forcibly internalized individual wants from another to whom he is negatively related, but lacks the courage to admit the negativity of the relation. Both taken together mean that there is scarcely such a thing as a positive relation between people at all, but merely different ways of using people for the enhancement of the feeling of self. More important, however, is that this very "insight" presupposes internalization. Just as the "unsublimated" opponent wants victory, so, surely, the uninternalized lover cannot separate his desire from what he desires. We need not assume Nietzsche had no sense of this. On the contrary, his awareness of precisely this consideration was a fundamental reason why he feared, as well as identified with, philosophy as an ascetic triumph over "life." To become convinced that one desires only one's desire is a step toward disengaging oneself from any concrete desire, just as the conviction that one has morality only in order to demonstrate strength is a step toward having no morality.

Perhaps the most intriguing way, however, in which Nietzsche revealed the character and extent of his own internalization was his treatment of Jesus and its extraordinary, if incomplete, parallels with his presentation of himself, parallels which, to the best of my knowledge, have not been noticed.[11] Nietzsche, we recall, had described Jesus as weak, a designation I termed "arbitrary." So it is when considered simply on the evidence of the New Testament. But the arbitrariness becomes more intelligible, if no more defensible, in light of evidence he gave about himself in his autobiography.

Ecce Homo was meant, of course, in its very title to express an ironic inversion of Christianity. In keeping with this inversion, the book ends with tirades identical in meaning with some of those in the *Antichrist*. But the irony of the title and the all-too unironic tirades do not obviate the possibility that Nietzsche could show the basis for his comparative friendliness toward Jesus in the same work.

> Freedom from *ressentiment*, enlightenment about *ressentiment*—who knows how much I am ultimately indebted ... to my protracted sickness! ... If anything at all must be adduced against being sick and being weak [!], it is that man's remedial instinct, his *fighting instinct* wears out. One cannot get rid of anything, one cannot get over anything, one cannot repel anything—everything hurts. Men and things obtrude too closely....
>
> Against all this the sick person has only one great remedy: I call it *Russian fatalism*, that fatalism without revolt which is exemplified by a Russian soldier who, finding a campaign too strenuous, finally lies down in the snow. No longer to accept anything at all ...—to cease reacting altogether....
>
> Because one would use oneself up too quickly if one reacted in *any* way, one does not react at all any more: this is the logic. Nothing burns one up faster than the affects of *ressentiment*. Anger, pathological vulnerability, impotent lust for revenge ...—no reaction could be more disadvantageous for the exhausted.... *Ressentiment* is what is forbidden *par excellence* for the sick—it is their specific evil—unfortunately also their most natural inclination.
>
> This was comprehended by that profound physiologist, the Buddha. His "religion" should rather be called a kind of *hygiene*, lest it be confused with such pitiable phenomena as Christianity: its effectiveness was made conditional on the victory over *ressentiment*. (*EH*, 1:6)

That Nietzsche refers here to the Buddha and not to Christ should deceive no one, even if we cannot categorically rule out the possibility that Nietzsche deceived himself or at least intended to deceive others. The psychology of the weakness that triumphs over resentment aided by nothing but hygienic astuteness is essentially identical with the characterization of the similar triumph by Jesus as presented in the *Antichrist*.

> *The instinctive hatred of reality*: a consequence of an extreme capacity for suffering and excitement which no longer wants any contact at all because it feels every contact too deeply.
> *The instinctive exclusion of any antipathy, any hostility, any boundaries or divisions in man's feelings*: ...
> These are the two *physiological realities* on which, out of which, the doctrine of redemption grew.... The fear of pain, even of infinitely minute pain—that can end in no other way than in a *religion of love*. (*A*, #30)

Nietzsche "knew" that Jesus was weak because he translated the love of Jesus into the terms suitable to the effects of the weakness he observed in himself.[12] Whether Nietzsche as a psychologist *ever* understood anyone but himself is a larger question into which we need not enter.

As if this similarity were not striking enough, Nietzsche's description of himself shares other traits with his characterization of Jesus, though they merely embellish and confirm the analysis of the purifying effects of sickness given above. In the *Antichrist* he insisted vehemently, against Renan, that Jesus was not a "hero." "[I]f anything is unevangelical it is the concept of the hero. Just the opposite of all wrestling, of all feeling-oneself-in-a-struggle, has here become instinct: the incapacity for resistance becomes morality here ... blessedness in peace, in gentleness, in not *being able* to be an enemy" (*A*, #29). Similarly, Nietzsche protested against "any attempt to introduce the fanatic into the Redeemer type.... The 'glad tidings' are precisely that there are no longer any opposites; the kingdom of heaven belongs to the *children*; the faith which finds expression here is not a faith attained through struggle—... it is, as it were, an infantilism that has receded into the spiritual" (*A*, #32).

If we return to *Ecce Homo* we find: "I cannot remember that I ever tried hard—no trace of *struggle* can be demonstrated in my life; I am the opposite of a heroic nature" (*EH*, 2:9). "It is no fanatic that speaks here..." (*EH*, Preface,4). "[I]n vain would one seek for a trait of fanaticism in my character" (*EH*, 2:10).

The ferocious vehemence of the *Antichrist* (when Jesus was not the subject) and the euphoria of *Ecce Homo* both belong to Nietzsche's final creative year, and the completion of the latter was soon followed by Nietzsche's collapse. In the first days after that collapse, he dashed off a few notes to friends in which he signed himself, alternately, "the Crucified" and "Dionysus," the Greek god whom he had made into the supreme symbol of his affirmation of life in all of its destructiveness and suffering. *Ecce Homo* had ended "Have I been understood?—*Dionysus vesus the Crucified.*—" This final cry designed for public consumption was Nietzsche's last effort at a truly *decisive* clarification, the most radical either/or. Yet the difficulty of taking it entirely seriously is made only greater, not merely by the fact that he signed himself "the Crucified" only a few weeks later, but by the contents of the brief message itself: "Sing me a new song: the world is transfigured and all the heavens are full of joy."[13]

This only confirms what the *Antichrist* itself makes clear enough, that Christ was joyous, that the difference between him and Dionysus does not lie in the abstraction "joy," still less in some distinction between joy without suffering and joy in spite of suffering. For while Nietzsche emphasized Christ's sensitivity to suffering, he also wrote that Christ's death could only have been intended by him as "exemplary" (*A*, #40), a demonstration of the possibility of suffering and dying without resentment, without loss of joy, because it is always possible, even *in extremis*, to withdraw into infantile bliss.

It is at this point that the relation between Nietzsche and Christ as conceived by Nietzsche becomes most interesting. For if we return once again to *Ecce Homo* in order to discover how Nietzsche rose above resentment apart from the "Russian fatalism" taught to him by sickness, we find an astonishing answer, one that perhaps he partly intended, partly did not intend, to give us: *he withdrew.*

> In all these matters—in the choice of nutrition, of place, of climate, of recreation—an instinct of self-preservation issues its commandments ... as *self-defense*. Not to see many things, not to hear many things, not to permit many things to come close—first imperative of prudence, first proof that one is no mere accident but a necessity. The usual word for this instinct of self-defense is *taste*. It commands us not only to say No when Yes would be "selfless" but also to say *No as rarely as possible*. To detach oneself, to separate oneself from anything that would make it necessary to keep saying No.... Warding off, not letting things come close, involves an expenditure—let nobody deceive himself about this—energy *wasted* on negative ends. Merely through the constant need to ward off, one can become weak enough to be unable to defend oneself any longer. (*EH*, 2:8)

The withdrawal described here is given in very general terms, without any unambiguous declaration that withdrawal from other people is particularly crucial. But somewhat earlier, Nietzsche had emphasized just that. "[E]xtreme cleanliness in relation to me is the presupposition of my existence ... I constantly swim and bathe and splash, as it were, in water—in some perfectly transparent and resplendent element. Hence my association with people imposes no mean test on my patience: my humanity does *not* consist in feeling with men how they are, but in *enduring* that I feel with them....

"But I need *solitude*—which is to say, recovery, return to myself, the breath of a free, light, playful air" (*EH*, 1:8).

Nietzsche presented his withdrawal into solitude, which had become virtually total by the time *Ecce Homo* was written, entirely in terms of his own strength, the loftiness of his tastes, a sensible appreciation of the wastefulness of fruitless reactivity, and the magnitude of his intellectual task, which would make such waste particularly absurd. One need not quarrel too much with this. One might even admire his refusal to give way to self-pity. Nor need such admiration be stopped in its tracks by the obvious fact that public self-pity would have shamed Nietzsche beyond endurance, and had to be reserved for his letters, where it is certainly to be found. But one must also note that what he appears to have wished to present as the "light air" of *his* solitude is the light air of solitude as such. If there is, no doubt, a kind of weakness that cannot bear solitude, there is also no denying that in solitude we are free from much, very much. Nor does the *mauvaise foi* of Nietzsche's self-analysis stop there. He believed that his need for solitude was the result of his perception of what people were like; he never entertained the suspicion that the character of that perception itself might have been the creation of his own morbid fears.

Nietzsche, of course, balanced all of these revelations of withdrawal and sickness with self-descriptions of an altogether different character. We have already encountered his advertisement of himself as "warlike by nature." More important, in the present context, is material with which he sought to avoid any possible misunderstanding about the reality of his strength and the genuine character of his triumph over resentment that could result from his remarks about his sickness. Thus Nietzsche insisted that he was healthy at bottom, decadent only "as an angle, as a specialty." "A typically morbid being cannot become healthy, much less make itself healthy. For a typically healthy person, conversely, being sick can even become an energetic *stimulus* for life.... This, in fact, is how that long period of sickness appears to me *now*.... I tasted all good and even little things, as others cannot easily taste them—I turned my will to health, to *life*, into a philosophy" (*EH*, 1:2). His philosophy was, in other words, a means of cure; but it was not solely that, for it proceeded from a genuine degree of health that both guaranteed the depth of the philosophy and made the cure possible. It is certainly true that so creative a cure presupposes that one is far from that kind of morbid illness which enables one only to crawl toward death. But the same measure of health can presumably be claimed by energetic and creative believers of all kinds.

Equally important to the confirmation of his image as essentially healthy was Nietzsche's belief that his transcendence of resentment was not fundamentally born of his sickness. Rather, while he avoided resentment in sickness out of prudent insight, when he was not sick he instead rose above it. "Born of weakness, *ressentiment* is most harmful for the weak themselves. Conversely, given a rich nature, it is a *superfluous* feeling; mastering this feeling is virtually what proves riches" (*EH*, 1:6). It was this claim and all of its implications, presumably, that enabled Nietzsche to maintain his attitude of condescension toward Jesus, who never mastered anything, according to his account; who was not rich in "internal opposition" and able to surmount the contrasts within himself; who could only retreat.

Yet Nietzsche knew that the philosopher could easily be charged with weakness, if not weakness of every kind, as a remarkable passage, one appropriately emphasized by Müller-Lauter, shows.

> But some day, in a stronger age than this decaying, self-doubting present, he must yet come to us, the *redeeming* man of great love and contempt,

the creative spirit whose compelling strength will not let him rest in any
aloofness or any beyond, whose isolation is misunderstood by the people
as if it were flight *from* reality—while it is only his absorption, immer-
sion, penetration *into* reality, so that, when he one day emerges again into
the light, he may bring home the *redemption* of this reality: its redemption
from the curse that the hitherto reigning ideal has laid upon it. (*G*, 2:24)

The philosopher, in short, must synthesize Caesar and Christ. He is too
easily capable of being merely Christ. That Nietzsche thought he, or rather
Zarathustra, embodied this ideal is at least likely (Cf. *G*, 2:25). But there is
no need to insist on this. What is certain is that the Nietzsche who recognized how the philosopher could appear, how he often *was*; who insisted so
vehemently that gentleness could not be admired when unsupported by
claws; who could condescend to the infantilism of Jesus, had to show us his
claws and make his withdrawal into solitude appear as a *reculer pour mieux
sauter*, a phase preparatory to the end of the reign of accident in history. The
"riches" of his nature could hardly be taken for granted otherwise. The
coincidentia oppositorum between self-sufficient plenitude and self-sufficient
emptiness, between God and the stone, everything and nothing, could not
be allowed to permit any confusion about who and what Nietzsche was,
precisely because he himself had continuously identified God with nothing
and philosophic transcendence with nihilism, as if there could be no doubt
about the validity of these equations.

Once Nietzsche had availed himself of a symbol which, like those he most
often attacked, could be mistaken for designating a fulfillment too weak for
respect, not too strong for words. The very first of Zarathustra's speeches is
on "the three metamorphoses of the spirit." The first metamorphosis was
into the form of a camel, wanting to be "well loaded," that it could "exult in
[its] strength." Only by measuring up to an external burden could it prove
itself strong. The spirit then became a lion, which slew the great dragon
"'Thou shalt,'" the dragon that declared that all "value has long been created, and I am all created value." The power of the lion clears the way. But
the lion is not the way. It must become something else, a *child*.

> But say, my brothers, what can the child do that even the lion could not
> do? Why must the preying lion still become a child? The child is inno-
> cence and forgetting, a new beginning, a game, a self-propelled wheel, a
> first movement, a sacred "Yes." For the game of creation, my brothers, a
> sacred "Yes" is needed: spirit now wills his own will, and he who had
> been lost to the world now conquers his own world. (*TSZ*, 1:1)

The problem here is that this child could just as easily be regarded as weak as
well as strong, strong as well as weak. The power to set one's own goals can
be a flight from, not a transcendence of, the burden that the camel assumed in

bearing an externally imposed burden. Nor does the child's self-absorption presuppose the strength of the lion; he merely inherits the freedom won by the lion. It is astonishing that the apotheosis of the child follows very shortly after the excoriation of the "last man." A Nietzschean malice could make very merry with the idea of the last child.

But so what? Who compels us to speak with Nietzschean malice? We can, surely, be gracious instead, and take this as proof positive that Nietzsche's ideal was innocence and forgetting. Certainly the image of the child is indeed innocent as Nietzsche presented it here, a fact that deserves emphasis. There might seem to be no need to take vengeance on Nietzsche's ascription of infantilism to Jesus by doubting that he himself had any right to the symbolism of the child.

The point, however, is not that he had *no* right to this symbolism, but that he had a most incomplete one, given other elements of his philosophy and other parts of *Zarathustra* itself. Nietzsche's ideal of the child, however commendable, is simply incompatible with his far less commendable insistence that the higher man possess claws, and that it be known that he does; for the child's claws are so withdrawn that one must take it on faith that they exist at all. More important, Nietzsche evidently believed more in the importance of showing claws than in the ideal of the innocent child, as is demonstrated by his determination to show claws in his work. "I am by far the most terrible human being that has existed so far," he felt constrained to declare in *Ecce Homo*, so that the character and quality of his freedom from resentment not be misunderstood and his "riches" be denied. "This does not preclude the possibility that I shall be the most beneficial. I know the pleasure in destroying to a degree that accords with my powers to destroy—..." (*EH*, 4:2). The possibility, however, that he will be the most beneficial even in his destructiveness is presumably dependent on the merits of his opposing what takes the side of the weak, in other words, "all that ought to perish..." (4:8).

"Whoever is dissatisfied with himself is continually ready for revenge, and we others will be his victims...." The reader will recall that Nietzsche had once written this. (In fact, not once but twice.) Precisely because he could transcend the phenomenon of "overcompensation" by seeing it for what it is, one can scarcely reduce him to overcompensation. But there is strikingly little evidence that Nietzsche ever turned his psychological gaze inward, and he once repudiated the idea very explicitly (*WP*, #426). As a result, his philosophy points both beyond and *to* overcompensation, to acting from power and acting for it. This ambiguity would be far less serious as far as the moral character of his doctrines are concerned if the demands of *Machtgefühl* were adequately checked by a clear recognition of the other as constituting a check on the variety of ways in which the feeling of power should be obtained. But Nietzsche's internalization, the source of his insight and of his innocence, prevented this. The other must not interfere with the plenary freedom of the imagination's visions of power. Every ounce of graciousness must proceed from what one is, not from what the other is. The strength to see value in the other, and to insist that the value one sees proceeds from the other himself, and is not placed there by the value-"creating" strength of the one who sees, may or may not be the highest strength. But it was one Nietzsche did not have; and if it be possible to maintain a consistently humane ethical attitude without it or its equivalent, his writings do not reveal this possibility. Thus Zarathustra's "gift-giving virtue" is continuously in danger of turning into the drive for power of those who do not wish to give, but who rule and impose "form" upon others solely because they wish to rule, "to feel" their "*power* over a people" (*WP*, #964).

Considered as "apologetics," the psychological explorations of this chapter may be more offensive than indignation. While they stand very much within the tradition of Kaufmann's remark that Nietzsche feared weakness in himself, the consequence of expatiating upon this point as opposed to mentioning it in an offhand manner is to risk making Nietzsche look ridiculous, one who either lacked the courage of his philosophy to the degree that he did not mean to dominate, let alone destroy, anyone, or lacked integrity in his life because he wrote as if he did. To this it is necessary to reply that there is much in Nietzsche that can only be regarded with indignation insofar as it was genuinely intended to have grievous consequences, or contempt in danger of sliding into pity insofar as it was merely a device for his own feeling of power.

A more serious problem, however, is the advisability of inserting any discussion of Nietzsche's psychology into the discussion of his philosophy, an insertion which will offend the sense, less of Nietzsche's dignity than of philosophy's. Indignation, some may feel, would be preferable to a shift from "objective" verities or falsities to subjectivities of any kind, even those which, like those dealt with here, are not "reductive" the way psychological considerations deriving from a system like that of Freud, for example, which is alien to Nietzsche's own doctrines, would be. But to this an obvious answer presents itself. That Nietzsche was a philosopher, concerned with being, is certainly true. But he revolted against a mode of philosophizing that constituted, to use a phrase of his own, only "shadows of God" (*GS*, #109). He did not endeavor to replace philosophy with psychology; but a psychological emphasis was embedded in his entire manner of conceiving of philosophy and, still more, in the central doctrine of the will to power itself. This will is a doctrine of being, but also a doctrine of beings. Without psychology, that is, for Nietzsche, the centrality of *Machtgefühl* and its demands, there would be no philosophy and no philosophers. Since Nietzsche did not hesitate to write that "the philosopher ... affirms *his* existence and *only* his existence, and this perhaps to the point at which he is not far from harboring the impious wish: *pereat mundus, fiat philosophia, fiat philo-sophus, fiam!*" (*G*, 3:7),[14] it will not do to seek to shield Nietzsche and his philosophy with concepts of the purity of philosophy.[15].

Yet the emphasis in this chapter on Nietzsche's person, on Nietzsche as the author of *Ecce Homo*, the builder of his own Bayreuth,[16] is no way to end a study of Nietzsche; for he was quite right to associate his name with something much greater than his feeling of power (even if that association enhanced his feeling of power), a moment of crisis in the history of the mind. The present chapter was intended, quite frankly, as a kind of emetic, de-signed to purge Nietzsche, this writer, and his readers from the "barbarians of the twentieth century." In the following and concluding chapter, *Macht-gefühl* and Nietzsche's personality will continue to be important. The cen-tral issue, however, will be something no less "objective" than his effort to put the higher man in the place of reverence once occupied by God.

9

The Shadow of God

ONE reason for the breadth of Nietzsche's appeal has surely been that both opponents of asceticism and opponents of hedonism can derive almost equal comfort from his works. On the one hand, Nietzsche attacked Christian guilt-feeling and everything, or almost everything, descended from it. On the other hand, he despised modern bourgeois, or as he put it, "English," notions of happiness to such a degree that he praised suffering and a sense of responsibility that assumed almost cosmic proportions. The centrality of religion is presupposed in each of these facets of his thought.

The critique of Nietzsche need not depend on religious assumptions, and by giving a central place to theology in the remainder of this concluding chapter, which I have deliberately refrained from giving it earlier in this study, I emphatically do not wish to invite misunderstanding on this point. But the will to power is at bottom, I believe, (and I am scarcely the first to do so,) an attempt to recapture an intensity of feeling and purpose that religion had once given to humanity, which the last men, who cannot give birth to a star, threaten to extinguish altogether, and which liberal humanism, even if it zealously seeks to forestall the triumph of the last man (which was certainly not, of course, Nietzsche's view), cannot entirely replace. For this reason it is necessary to examine Nietzsche's atheism with the aim of discovering whether or not it was this atheism, at least in its dogmatic radicality, that offers the clue both to what the theory of the will to power was supposed to accomplish, and to the reasons for its failure. In this examination, special attention will be devoted to the theme of what I shall call Nietzsche's reclamation project, his specific desire to reclaim for man what had once been bestowed upon God, a theme which runs throughout the various discussions that follow.

Nietzsche never attempted a logical refutation of the possibility of God's existence. He does not appear to have thought it attainable. What he substituted was a genetic reduction of faith, which was clearly intended to have the effect of a refutation by suspicion. *"Historical refutation as the definitive refutation.*—In former times, one sought to prove that there is no God—today one indicates how the belief that there is a God could *arise* and how this belief acquired its weight and importance: a counter-proof that there is no God thereby becomes superfluous" (*D,* #95). That Nietzsche himself had rather varying ideas of how this belief could arise does not help to clarify this statement, but this consideration does not present a counter-argument either. Nietzsche's implication is that belief in God is traceable to human *needs.* Even if these needs are various, a belief that arises from need and has no other compelling justification becomes suspect. A refutation by suspicion might not have a very devastating effect, however, on those not already predisposed to be ashamed of their religions needs or not already beyond feeling their urgency.

For it cannot be emphasized too strongly that a "healthy" will to power as presented by Nietzsche does not *want* God. God is an "objection to existence" (*EH,* 2:3), an infringement of its freedom, and a lure to "nothingness" beyond the tangibilities of reality. In line with these convictions, Nietzsche posed in *Ecce Homo* as one who had always been an atheist, as an atheist by "instinct" (*EH,* 2:1). I say "posed" because we know that it was untrue, that Nietzsche was fairly pious well into his teens, and that later his unfaith caused him pain, at least occasionally. The claim of instinctive atheism is very seldom quoted by his admiring interpreters, not because Nietzsche often lamented his lack of faith, but because he made much of intellectual honesty, and this virtue scarcely means anything if it costs nothing.

> At every step one has to wrestle for truth; one has had to surrender for it almost everything to which the heart, to which our love, our trust in life, cling otherwise. That requires greatness of soul: service of truth is the hardest service. What does it mean, after all, to have *integrity* in matters of the spirit? That one is severe against one's heart, that one despises "beautiful sentiments," that one makes every Yes and No a matter of conscience. Faith makes blessed: consequently it lies. (*A,* #50)

Nietzsche knew that the "will to truth" was itself a vestige of a moralism he sought in all other respects to transcend. But it never seems to have occurred to him that self-inflation with the aid of moral pomposity was no more inherently ridiculous or canting than these trumpets and drums on the subject of intellectual honesty. Praising virtue performed "unconsciously, without noise, without pomp, with that modesty and concealed goodness which forbids the mouth solemn words and virtue formulas," he added with considerable and commendable insight that "morality as a pose—offends our taste today" (*BGE,* #216). But not entirely, it would appear, when intellectual honesty was involved. To be fair, one note actually declares: " 'it is immoral to believe in God'—but precisely this seems to us the best justification of such faith" (*WP*, #1015). This, however, is truly exceptional, even if it can be squared with an attitude toward truth Nietzsche sometimes voiced, one that completely renounced any "ascetic" truthfulness.

One might assert with some plausibility and much nastiness that the self-contradictory self-glorification of claiming to be an atheist by instinct and claiming the philosophic virtue of self-overcoming in the service of truth is only to be expected from Nietzsche, who could not pass up one form of glory simply because it conflicted with another to which he was equally devoted. There is surely some truth in this, but it is not the whole truth. Nietzsche had to present the most developed will to power as atheistic by will and instinct because otherwise the unlimited, absolute affirmation that had once been bestowed on God *would no longer be possible anymore*, and his philosophy would consequently descend to the level of a *faute de mieux*. One does not dominate with a *faute de mieux*. One is not exultant with it either. And where there is no exultation, the last man awaits. Yet he also could not, much of the time, forget the pain of atheism because he knew that God was not merely a reflection of either human weakness, human self-contempt, or the desire for vengeance.

"We know it well," he wrote in the *Gay Science*, "the world in which we live is ungodly, immoral, 'inhuman'; we have interpreted it far too long in a false and mendacious way, in accordance with the wishes of our reverence, which is to say, according to our *needs*. For man is a reverent animal" (*GS*, #346). Can this capacity to revere, this *need* to revere, be understood simply as a weakness? A remarkable passage in *Zarathustra*, the "Night Song," provides, not an answer, but at least an amplification of the problem.

> Night has come; now all fountains speak more loudly. And my soul too is a fountain.
> Night has come; only now all the songs of lovers awaken. And my soul too is the song of a lover.
> Something unstilled, unstillable is within me; it wants to be voiced. A craving for love is within me; it speaks the language of love.
> Light am I; ah, that I were night! But this is my loneliness that I am girt with light. Ah, that I were dark and nocturnal! How I would suck at the breasts of light! And even you would I bless, you little sparkling stars and glowworms up there, and be overjoyed with your gifts of light.
> But I live in my own light; I drink back into myself the flames that break out of me. I do not know the happiness of those who receive. (*TSZ*, 2:9)

Very seldom if ever in the history of thought has such extravagance of self-exaltation been wedded so intimately to such luxuriance of self-pity. To the degree that the pathos is real and not a sham, the condition of having nothing to love beyond one's own value-creating light is desperate.[1] The self-exaltation must seem like a compensation for the pain of this condition. Man, then, must transcend his need to revere simply because there is nothing to revere but "esteeming" itself, "the most estimable treasure" (*TSZ*, 1:15), if also a treasure doomed to frustration. Intellectual honesty then becomes a virtue worth boasting about. It must be admitted, however, that the claim that "man is a reverent animal," so far from crowning the genetic reduction of theism, sweeps it aside. For that claim is nothing other than the basic contention of Judaeo-Christian anthropology; and a reduction of faith to the fundamental fact with which faith, on its own interpretation of things, reckons is less than compellingly reductive.

That the pathos of the "Night Song" is genuine may be true enough. Nietzsche quoted it, at greater length than I have done, in *Ecce Homo*, describing it as "the immortal lament at being condemned by the overabundance of light and power, by his [Zarathustra's] sun-nature, not to love" (*EH, TSZ*, 7). That "being condemned ... not to love" should surely be emphasized. It raises the possibility that Nietzsche was jealous of lovers. But he also presented plenty of evidence to indicate that the will to power usurps its place *as* the sun, that its self-exaltation is not compensatory, but the original moving force, as, for reasons already given, he was bound to do. "I desire that your conjectures should not reach beyond your creative will. Could you *create* a god? Then do not speak to me of any gods." "God is a conjecture; but I desire that your conjectures should be limited by what is thinkable. Could you *think* a god? But this is what the will to truth should mean to you: that everything be changed into what is thinkable for man, visible for man, feelable by man" (*TSZ*, 2:2). The will to truth, according to this passage, is not what Nietzsche elsewhere claimed it was, a vestige of piety, but the direct outgrowth of the will to power, which *converts* what is into what human power can grasp, and willingly and willfully denies that there is or could be anything else. After this, the famous assertion of only a few lines later can come as no surprise: "But let me reveal my heart to you entirely, my friends: *if* there were gods, how could I endure not to be a god! *Hence* there are no gods. Though I drew this conclusion, now it draws me."

A much later note amplifies these suggestions.

> The belief that the world as it ought to be *is*, really exists, is a belief of the unproductive who do *not desire to create a world* as it ought to be. They posit it as already available, they seek ways and means of reaching it. "Will to truth"—*as the impotence of the will to create....*
> It is a measure of the degree of strength of will to what extent one can do without meaning in things, to what extent one can endure to live in a meaningless world *because one organizes a small portion of it oneself.* (*WP*, #585)

Especially in light of the last quotation from *Zarathustra*, one can see that it is difficult to separate the strength to live in a meaningless world *because* one organizes a small portion of it oneself from the will to live in a meaningless world *in order to* savor the greatest feeling of power in organizing a small portion of it oneself. A large part of Nietzsche's onslaught against religion was undertaken with the aim of restoring, or rather, creating, a sense of human proprietary pride, which had been opposed, in varying degrees of intensity and directness, by Judaeo-Christian faith. The creativity lavished on God had to be claimed for man; more, the value bestowed on God had to be claimed for the value-bestowing powers of man.

> All the beauty and sublimity we have bestowed upon real and imaginary things I will reclaim as the property and product of man: as his fairest apology. Man as poet, as thinker, as God, as love, as power: with what regal liberality he has lavished gifts upon things so as to impoverish himself and make himself feel wretched! His most unselfish act hitherto has been to admire and worship and to know how to conceal from himself that it was he who created what he admired.[2]

Why, one wonders, must this most "unselfish act," the fairest ground of all other unselfish acts, be undone? Zarathustra's "Night Song" reminds us, the moralism of unselfishness aside, that this generosity on man's part can cause something other than feelings of wretchedness, and that feelings of wretchedness can be caused, instead, by reclaiming one's "gift." Nietzsche was sensitive to the damage caused by feelings of guilt, but not sensitive enough to see that engaging in proprietary squabbles with the deity may be the least noble, the least effective, perhaps the most guilt-ridden, and not impossibly the most dishonest way of repairing such damage.

The moral implications of this Feuerbachian aspect of Nietzsche's "transvaluation of all values," especially when taken together with his desire to maintain, rather than simply abolish, the noble lack of complacency demanded by the very religions he opposed in his indictment of guilt-inducing ideas, constitute the heart of the problem that his philosophy raises. In order to see this problem as clearly as possible, I must ask the reader's indulgence for one last, rather lengthy, comparative excursus, on the relation between Nietzsche's doctrines and some of those of specifically *Pauline* Christianity. This comparison suggests itself for a number of reasons. Pauline Christianity was the religion in which Nietzsche, as a Lutheran pastor's son, was himself raised. Furthermore, Nietzsche's contempt for Paul and Augustine was particularly fierce, and his feelings about Luther were only slightly more ambivalent because of his admiration for Luther's achievement in helping to form the modern German language; and one can suspect that where the smoke of his contempt is densest, much of value and of special relevance for the understanding, as well as the evaluation, of Nietzsche himself may be concealed.

More important, however, are two more specific issues. First, if one of the most important facets of Nietzsche's antitheological prejudice was the desire to reclaim mankind's "fairest apology" for mankind itself, the Pauline tradition has, of all theological traditions, perhaps been the one that has most insisted upon the reverse principle, "Thine be the glory." Second, both Paul and Nietzsche appear at times to have an ambivalence toward the very idea of moral law, which makes the comparison most particularly intriguing. It remains only to add, by way of introduction, that Paul is as controversial a figure as Nietzsche, and that nothing like a general summary, or a general defense, of Pauline theology is attempted here.

Morality and Pride

Nietzsche's most important and lengthy treatment of Paul is aphorism #68, "The first Christian," in *Daybreak*. Paul's writings, he contended, serve to "expose" Christianity if we read them, *"really read"* them, "not as the revelations of the 'Holy Spirit', but with a free and honest exercise of one's own spirit and without thinking all the time of our personal needs...." That the need to expose Christianity may be a personal need, and just as corrupting as credulity, is not considered. (But can it be that Nietzsche was not aware of this, and not aware, in general, of how easily so much that he wrote can be turned around?)

Originally, Nietzsche observed, Paul had been "at once the fanatical defender and chaperone of the God and his law, and was constantly combating and on the watch for transgressors and doubters, harsh and malicious towards them and with the extremest inclination for punishment." He continued:

And then he discovered in himself that he himself—fiery, sensual, melancholy, malevolent in hatred as he was—*could* not fulfil the law, he discovered indeed what seemed to him the strangest thing of all: that his extravagant lust for power was constantly combating and on the watch for transgressors and goad. Is it really "carnality" which again and again makes him a transgressor? And not rather, as he later suspected, behind it the law itself, which *must* continually prove itself unfulfillable and with irresistible magic lures on to transgression? But at that time he did not yet possess this way out of his difficulty. Many things lay on his conscience— he hints at enmity, murder, sorcery, idolatry, uncleanliness, drunkenness and pleasure in debauch—and however much he tried to relieve his conscience, and even more his lust for domination, through the extremest fanaticism in revering and defending the law, there were moments when he said to himself: "It is all in vain! The torture of the unfulfilled law cannot be overcome." ... The law was the cross to which he felt himself nailed: how he hated it! how he had to drag it along! how he sought about for a means of *destroying* it—and no longer to fulfil it!

Possessed with this hatred, Paul was ready for his vision of Christ, which gave him the instrument for "perfect revenge" against the law.

> Sick with the most tormented pride, at a stroke he feels himself recovered.... To die to evil—that means also to die to the law; to exist in the flesh—that means also to exist in the law!... Even if it is still possible to sin, it is no longer possible to sin against the law: "I am outside the law." ... [N]ow not only has all guilt been taken away, guilt as such has been destroyed; now the law is dead, now the carnality in which it dwelt is dead—or at least constantly dying away.... [h]e arises with Christ, participates with Christ in divine glory.... With that the intoxication of Paul is at its height, and likewise the importunity of his soul—with the idea of becoming one with Christ all shame, all subordination, all bounds are taken from it, and the intractable lust for power reveals itself as an anticipatory revelling in *divine* glories.

One of the curious features of this account is that it is in part based upon what Paul wrote, in part on a travesty of what Paul wrote, and in part on Nietzsche's own psychologizing, from someone who did not disclaim an intimate acquaintance with the "lust for power." By not making any distinction between these, however, Nietzsche obscured the difference between confessions by Paul, made with a purpose, and that which seems to penetrate beneath what Paul himself thought and can serve to cast aspersions on him and his thought in their entirety. And by obscuring this distinction Nietzsche could avoid raising the question whether Paul's struggle with the law was at all related to the most legitimate aspects of his own "immoralism," if aspects that were often obscured by Nietzsche himself.[3]

That Paul was harsh in persecuting Christianity, Paul himself tells us. That Paul hated the law and sought vengeance against it is Nietzsche's own, highly improbable, insight. (I shall return to this shortly.) That Paul could be viewed, both in his struggles with the law and in his redemptive faith, as revealing a lust for power may be true, if all effort for total fulfillment can be described by that catch-all term, here used as abuse; but it is also true that Paul's writings contain a formidable critique of that very lust.

The center of Nietzsche's charge, however, is that Paul could not fulfill the law. The catalogue of Paul's sins, it must be noted first of all, is pure calumny, one which must stagger any imagination that tries to conceive of what an avowedly *moralistic* Nietzsche would have been like. Paul did not hint at "enmity, murder, sorcery, idolatry," and so forth. "[A]s to the righteousness under the law [I was] blameless" (Phil. 3:6), Paul wrote, and no evidence survives to contradict him. Nietzsche's catalogue seems to have been suggested by various Pauline lists of what Christians must not do, particularly Galatians 5:19–21, in a context which invites no thought whatever that Paul was confessing or even "hinting" at anything about his own conduct, past or present. One should add that it is a generally accepted belief that Paul continued to observe the Jewish law throughout his life, though not as one bound to it for the salvation of his soul.[4]

Various passages in Nietzsche suggest the idea that he who overthrows a law can be justified only by acting in the name of a higher scale of values.[5] By calumniating Paul, presumably, Nietzsche evidently wished to maintain that Paul's spiritual struggles did not merit this justification (which other aspects of Nietzsche would suggest to be superfluous.) Paul simply wanted to overthrow what had given a deeply humiliating sense of failure to him. Paul, however, had specifically written that his aim was to set the law "on a firmer footing" (Rom. 3:31) and Nietzsche's entire campaign against Christian guilt-feeling would have been completely otiose if it had been otherwise. The paradox is that Nietzsche and Paul both complained against the destructiveness of guilt and sought the power of "righteousness," differently defined, of course, by each. But where Nietzsche oscillated between these two aims, and very rarely, if ever, brought them together successfully, Paulinism tried to deal with both at once in an intelligible dialectic.

Paul, of course, did write about the law as an intensifier of sin. The real culprit, however, was precisely "carnality" in the broad sense of *sin*, conceived in quasi-substantial terms, not the law, which Paul stated flatly was "good," and recognized as such by the "inmost self" (Rom. 7:23). The law did not work any "irresistible magic" in luring to transgression. Sin found in the law the means to its excitation: "sin found its opportunity in the commandment, seduced me, and through the commandment killed me" (Rom. 7:11). The crucial problem is what was meant by these words. Their suggestiveness has been infinitely fruitful, but this very suggestiveness makes the task of interpreting what their original author meant by them far from easy, perhaps impossible. That Paul was thinking here, not in autobiographical terms, but of the seduction of Eve by the serpent, is likely and widely recognized. Even more certain is that only through the commandment, on Paul's view, could sin become conscious of itself, thus becoming "mortal."

Most interesting, however, is the hint of a mechanism by which the scrupulousness engendered by the desire to fulfill the law actually increased the difficulty, if not of following particular ordinances, at least of being certain of the "purity" of one's heart. The most valuable thing in Nietzsche's own account of Paul is relevant here: "his extravagant lust for power was constantly combating and on the watch for transgressors and goad." It would be more valuable if Nietzsche had distinguished here between externalized and internalized moralistic "aggression." "Transgressors" points one way, seeming to refer to Paul's persecuting zeal, and "goad" another. Paul said nothing that unambiguously justifies the idea of scrupulousness as itself productive of destructive guilt-feeling. But he did write that the law was given that "sin might more abound," and this idea of sins and sinfulness multiplying under the pressure of the law was later regarded, especially by Luther, as the destructive power of the scrupulous self-consciousness, which, endeavoring to fulfill the law, must maintain a relentless and ultimately destructive vigilance, destructive because no powers of introspection could suffice to clear the conscience. On the contrary, the act of relentless introspection would perpetually feed on itself. This would only undermine the self, and goodness, by threatening despair. The mystery is why Nietzsche, who was to attack Jewish and Christian morality, as we have been, as "the evil eye for all things," should have attacked Paul, at the very least the original inspirer of all insight into the baneful effects of excessive scrupulosity in the history of Western man.[6]

Behind scrupulosity, however, is often something else, which traditionally had been called "pride" and which Nietzsche, of course, dubbed the will to power. But the theme of pride in relation to the law has two aspects, one of which is related to the scrupulous conscience, the other being, or appearing to be, its reverse. This is the phenomenon of "defiance," which I shall treat first.

Augustine, in explication of Romans, wrote that the "law, however good in itself, only augments the evil desire by forbidding it," and noted that "in some strange way the very object which we covet becomes all the more pleasant when it is forbidden."[7] Surely an obvious parallel with the psychological presuppositions of the doctrine of the will to power presents itself. Sin, the radically self-centered will to power, is augmented by the challenge of the law. The law is then analogous to the Nietzschean obstacle, without which there is no sin in the crucial sense of defiance, or will to power in the crucial sense of self-conscious self-assertion against an alien will. But just as, for Paul and Augustine alike, there would be no sin without an evil possibility, which the law only crystallizes, so in Nietzsche there would be no will to power without a desire to *use* the obstacle, however it be defined, as a challenge to be met for the greater glory of the self. It should be noted in passing that Nietzsche could specifically advocate exploiting the charm exercised by the "forbidden" as such.[8]

A law that provokes defiance is one which threatens to humiliate, that indeed does humiliate by the very claim that man stands in need of it. It was thus given, in Pauline language, "for reasons of sin." But this provocation, in which unfaith reads its own condemnation and reacts defiantly out of its own offended pride, might be greatly lessened if the law were expressed in terms more inviting and less humiliating to its recipient. It was doubtless with such considerations in mind that Nietzsche wrote: "Jesus said to his

Jews: 'The law was for servants—love God as I love him, as his son! What are morals to us sons of God!'" (*BGE*, #164), a complete aphorism that appears to be complimentary to Jesus and his aim. Yet if we assume here that the derogation of "morals" refers to the spirit of pained subordination, not to conduct animated by love,[9] then this aim attributed to Jesus alone was thoroughly Pauline. Paul saw in the Gospel a new revelation of the father-hood of God, one that liberated from "servility" in the very clarity with which it mainfested the divine love. (Whether Judaism actually stood in need of this new clarity is a question that will not be discussed here.[10]) "For all who are moved by the Spirit of God are sons of God. The Spirit you have received is not a spirit of slavery leading you back into a life of fear, but a Spirit that makes us sons, enabling us to cry 'Abba! Father!'" (Rom. 8:14–15). "To prove that you are sons, God has sent into our hearts the Spirit of his Son, crying 'Abba! Father!' You are therefore no longer a slave but a son" (Gal. 4:6–7).

Notwithstanding his emphasis on the fatherhood of God, Paul, of course, condemned pride, and it is this condemnation, when taken in its total con-text, which has been one of the most psychologically suggestive parts of his doctrine. Again, it should be noted that there may be a difference between what Paul meant and what has been read into his epistles. According to one recent interpretation, Paul was not especially vexed by the pride of "works righteousness" at all, but simply by the pride he discerned in the resistance of Jews to the universalization of salvation through the Gospel, a univer-salization that was his principal aim.[11] But Paul was thought to mean, as he still normally is, that the law served to inflate pride, not merely for those who defied it, but also for those who fulfilled it. Such pride was particularly destructive of the proper relationship people should have to their Creator. Paul certainly believed that the law could encourage pride in some fashion, and implied pretty clearly that it did in his own case. Faith, by contrast, being specifically faith in God's goodness rather than the adequacy of one's own works, excluded pride. "What room then is left for human pride? It is excluded. And on what principle? The keeping of the law would not exclude it, [a claim that it is not unreasonable to suppose was based upon personal experience and to suppose, as well, was meant to be understood as such] but faith does. For our argument is that a man is justified by faith quite apart from success in keeping the law" (Rom. 3:27–28). Thus Nietzsche's attack on Paul in *Daybreak* is partly based on what Paul confesses, an arrogance in which sin used the law for its own purposes. But this attack is no better for that. On the contrary. Since the entire gravamen of the charge against the law as perverted by sin was the crux of Pauline theology and the crux, as well, of the psychological-theological perils that the Pauline tradition addressed, Nietzsche's act of "exposing" Paul is, where it is not simply calumny, an abortive exposition of Paul. But it is an *abortive* exposition because it uses the theme of pride to cast aspersions on the total meaning of Paul's doctrine and his personality, rather than seeing it as a stage in a developing self-awareness and piety. For Paul, pride was overcome by the recognition of the necessity of dependence upon grace and divine forgiveness, as well as by the availability of salvation to all who would take it, which completely destroyed pride in any comparative sense of the term. Nietzsche, by contrast, charged that "Religion has debased the concept 'man'; its ultimate consequence is that everything good, great, true is superhuman and bestowed only through an act of grace" (*WP*, #136). This is nothing but another version of the offended pride that Nietzsche had accused Paul of having been obsessed by; and it is made, if we take this note in the total context of Nietzsche's thought, not in defense of man as such, but the superior man.

Paul could regard love as the fulfillment of the law, not merely because the ethical component of the law was included in the gospel of love, as Jesus had maintained, but also because law and love alike pointed to human fulfillment as consisting in reconciliation with God and one's fellows. As a consequence, we may say, both law and love implicitly placed crucial weight upon the realm of the interpersonal and condemned as evil what inflated the self at the other's expense. They condemned likewise, as a subtler but no less serious evil, a mode of obedience to morality that was at bottom self-reflexive, using virtue itself to isolate and glorify the self and the sense of self, rather than seeing it as the mode of positively relating to the other.

If Paul condemned the misuse of the law for the inflation of self, Nietzsche's own reduction of morality to will to power depended upon reviving and radicalizing the very misuse Paul had condemned. In a long note from the period of the *Genealogy*, he brought out the full force of his equation of morality with the desire for the feeling of power. He discerned a long historical development in which moralists and moral psychologists had struggled against the "egoistic" aspect of moral motivation, a struggle carried on under the influence of Christianity and philosophies of the "herd." Then, in modern times, he noted, correctly enough, there were frequent efforts to attain a moderate justification of the egoistic in the total economy of man in society. The ultimate revelation attained by this process of development, however, was his own contribution:

> one grasps that altruistic actions are only a species of egoistic actions—and that the degree to which one loves, spends oneself, proves the degree of individual power and personality. In short, *that when one makes men more evil, one makes them better*—and that one cannot be one without being the other—....
>
> *Consequences:* there are *only* immoral actions and intentions; the so-called moral ones must be shown to be immoral. (*WP*, #787)

Nietzsche's complaints against "altruism" amounted, in part, to the claim that altruism was impossible because the self would, at the least, prove its own power and personality in its very love. In fairness it should be added that he sometimes implied a moral gain in this self-consciousness. Zarathustra asked his friends to grow weary of saying "what makes an act good is that it is unselfish," adding: "Oh, my friends, that your self be in your deed as the mother is in her child—let that be *your* word concerning virtue!" (*TSZ*, 2:5) All virtue, at any rate all Christian virtue, had been regarded as an ultimate giving of self which presupposed that the self be in its deed. Yet one realizes, however reluctantly, that this exhortation is apparently meant to be shocking, as if selfishness of this kind had ever been proscribed.

A mode of selfishness in which the self puts itself into its deed as the mother in her child thus lends itself to so innocent a reading that one must wonder how the discovery that altruism is at bottom a kind of "egoism" could ever be regarded by Nietzsche as tantamount to the discovery that "there are *only* immoral actions...." The answer surely lies in the teleological principle behind conduct that Nietzsche came to assume. It is not simply that in love and self-expenditure one "proves the degree of individual power and personality." One loves and expends oneself *in order to* prove such power. A note written shortly after this one makes this explicit. "That one stakes one's life, one's health, one's honor, is the consequence of high spirits and an overflowing, prodigal will: not from love of man but because every great danger challenges our curiosity about the degree of our strength and our courage" (*WP*, #949).

The attempt to abolish the distinction between egoistic and nonegoistic is, needless to say, ambiguous. Two forms of this ambiguity, together with their relation to Christian doctrine, should be discussed. First, Christianity, by promising salvation and fulfillment, exhibited will to power for Nietzsche; but he mocked the Christian promise of "reward." "'For if ye love them which love you, what reward have ye?' ... The principle of 'Christian love': in the end it wants to be *paid* well" (*A*, #45). The language of reward has, of course, been frequently used in both Jewish and Christian exhortations, biblical and postbiblical. Nevertheless, real love of God and the good was understood as love of them "for their own sake." The Talmud, Augustine, and Luther had all been equally clear on this point, and Augustine and Luther had added that doing the good for any other reason was "servile," the product of fear of punishment.[12] The very difficulty, however, of transcending self-centered motivation was the ground for the necessity of the belief in grace, which enabled the individual to see God and the good as lovable for their own sake. To see this theory of grace as the product of the will to belittle man is, I suggest, extremely crude. The doctrine of grace is based upon the experience of the loved as intrinsically lovable, that is, as having its value in itself rather than bestowed *upon* it by the lover, as on

Nietzsche's view. The lovability of the loved is then experienced as a gift of the loved. "Reward" then became less something added to grace than the effect of the higher state of being that grace had bestowed. Nietzsche, on the other hand, held out the feeling of power as the psychological telos and moving force of morality, which must be regarded as "reward" in a particularly gross sense. One might still wish to maintain that the very ferocity of Nietzsche's attacks on Paul for wanting "power" (which were repeated in the *Antichrist*) means that Nietzsche really wished to affirm a kind of self-transcendence, but could only make this intelligible on his own premises by his psychological reduction. This may be true, but the view that the "superabundant" man cannot love except what he bestows remains characteristically Nietzschean, and the reduction remains a reduction. The self-understanding of "goodness" as the desire for the feeling of power simply eliminates the possibility of seeking to love without thought of "reward." That means that love is not love, and that is why all actions are "immoral" at bottom. If so, the grounds of the entire reclamation project are lacking. Rather, the act of reclaiming destroys man's "fairest apology," his ability to love without thinking that this very ability was primarily significant in what it revealed about *man*.

The second ambiguity follows from this, but brings out its serious moral, or anti-moral, dimension. If one understands goodness as one *form* of the will to power, with a view, not to distinguish this form from others, but instead with the aim of drawing the inference that "there are *only* immoral actions and intentions," then the psychological reduction is indistinguishable from a moral destruction. It becomes impossible then to distinguish "noble" pride from brutal pride, since the emphasis is upon pride, on consciousness of egocentric power and delight in that consciousness as an ultimate value. This must threaten to lead to the abolition of any humanity that cannot be used to reinforce the pride of power. Actions not undertaken from "love of man" could then as easily be diametrically opposed to such love in their *effects* as well as their motivation. Pride then becomes not merely theologically, but also humanistically disastrous. Nietzscheanism lives and moves and has its being in this ambiguity. On the one hand, his immoralism was frequently the call for the emancipation of pride, specifically aristocratic pride, in its most avowedly repressive and brutally self-centered forms. It is on the basis of the psychological teleology of the quest for the feeling of power that we can understand how Nietzsche could praise giving in the most whole-hearted fashion in *Zarathustra* while simultaneously sliding imperceptibly toward the praise of aristocratic egotism in the later books. On the other hand, since pride itself required some sort of "objective" sanction, the feeling of power could not always be understood by Nietzsche as strictly egocentric, since it could only be attained in its intensest form in relation to some principle that justified it. *Machtgefühl*, after all, at least in its "sublimated" form, demands something objective, some "shadow of God," something to which to rise and something by which to condemn. (For this reason Nietzsche could criticize any teleology that placed a form of consciousness as the supreme end, since this "debased" "life and the enhancement of its power ... to a means" when it was, on the contrary, the supreme end) (*WP*, #707). If, however, this shadow is not to induce guilt and condemn pride, but rather enhance pride and the ferocious self-righteousness in which pride finds its greatest intensity, it must be treated very carefully, with a remarkable mixture of honesty in defending pride and dishonesty about the means with which this dubious task is performed.

Nietzsche was often capable of rising to this formidable challenge. It can be said, and for once in defense of his consistency, that the "objective" purpose he conceived was not one that subordinated the self and its pride, or threatened to induce guilt, at least in himself. Nietzsche, we may say, substituted "life" for God. "Life," this most nebulous of abstractions, was a cause which made a direct appeal to the noble, that is, the strong, that is, the *vital* man: he could claim it as his very own, yet seek to rise to its demands as to a cause larger than himself.

The complex and ambiguous character of Nietzsche's "solution" to the problem of how to synthesize the feeling of power with a freedom beyond the possibility of guilt, in other words, how to synthesize the camel, the lion, and the child, is exquisitely expressed in a draft of a letter to his sister written just before his collapse. "The task which is imposed *upon* me is, all the same, my nature—so that only now do I comprehend what was my predestined good fortune. I play with the burden which would crush any other mortal...."[13] The demand must be imposed *upon* him in order for there to be any glory in not being crushed by it, and in order for it to have a significance wider than himself. But it must be his nature in order for it to proceed gloriously out of himself, as a reflection of how much vitality he possessed. And finally, since he *plays* with what would crush others, he seems to have combined the blitheness of the self-enclosed child with the noble grandeur of those assuming enormous burdens. The letter is so transparently a painful pose that to quote it seems gratuitously cruel. But Nietzsche *had* to pose in this way. The whole "logic" of his thought is revealed in this pose as in nothing else.

Yet there is still an ambiguity. For Nietzsche praised the egocentric vitality that is not concerned with any alien burdens, as well as an objective concern for life, as a valuable way in which life itself could be preserved in its liveliness. This very judgment, of course, presupposes a step "beyond" the narrowly egocentric to a "total" view that is alien to those who are vital in an unsublimated sense. Nietzsche's vitality was sublimated, with a view of "life." Yet he objected strenuously to the man who, "like a camel," "lets himself be well loaded." Especially the strong, reverent spirit that would bear much: he loads too many *alien* grave words and values on himself, and then life seems a desert to him" (*TSZ*, 3:11, 2) If "life" is not to be an alien, grave word, a harmony is presupposed between life and the personal values of the individual. If, however, such a harmony between the demands of "life," whatever they are, and the values of the individual does not obtain, then life itself becomes an alien abstraction.

It is presumably the sublimated, the "creators" of values, those who are "responsible" to life, who must determine what, after all, life itself does not determine adequately according to the very premises of Nietzschean responsibility. Yet this very sublimation means that the creator, or ruler, can have no "innocence" and perforce must, like Nietzsche himself, become formidably *judgmental*. He could still claim, to be sure, that his sublimation proceeded from his own vitality, as well as from the history of "asceticism," which he both represented and transcended. As a result, however, of the magnitude of his task, the recreation of the world, all pretense of play became grostesque. One can play only with a task that has no intrinsic importance, *or* with a task of which one is fully a *master*, for only then is "playfulness" psychologically appropriate. When, shortly after his collapse into madness, Nietzsche wrote the following to Burckhardt, he was probably more honest than in his near-mad letter to his sister just cited. "In the end I would much rather be a Basel professor than God; but I have not dared push my private egoism so far as to desist for its sake from the creation of the world. You see, one must make sacrifices however and wherever one lives."[14]

How grotesque it was for Nietzsche to have posed as one who played with his task (cf. *EH*, 2:10), how self-righteous was the judgmentalism which the magnitude of his task seemed to endorse, and thus how formidable were the pressures which found their purest and certainly their most charming expression in this mad letter, can be gathered from the following very late note.

This universal love of men is in practice the *preference* for the suffering, underprivileged, degenerate: it has in fact lowered and weakened the strength, the responsibility, the lofty duty to sacrifice men. All that remains, according to the Christian scheme of values, is to sacrifice oneself: but this residue of human sacrifice that Christianity concedes and even advises has, from the standpoint of general breeding, no meaning at all. The prosperity of the species is unaffected by the self-sacrifice of this or that individual (—whether it be in the monkish and ascetic manner or, with the aid of crosses, pyres, and scaffolds, as "martyrs" of error). The species requires that the ill-constituted, weak, degenerate, perish: but it was precisely to them that Christianity turned as a conserving force; it further enhanced that instinct in the weak, already so powerful, to take care of and preserve themselves and sustain one another. What is "virtue" and "charity" in Christianity if not just this mutual preservation, this solidarity of the weak, this hampering of selection? What is Christian altruism if not the mass-egoism of the weak, which divines that if all care for one another each individual will be preserved as long as possible?

If one does not feel such a disposition as an extreme immorality, as a crime against life, one belongs with the company of the sick and possesses its instincts oneself—

Genuine charity demands sacrifice for the good of the species—it is hard, it is full of self-overcoming, because it needs human sacrifice. And this pseudo humaneness called Christianity wants it established that no one should be sacrificed. (*WP*, #246)

This theme, of course, has been treated before. But its relevance in the present context requires the repetition. The substitution of life for God did not create a new innocence in any humane sense of the word. It did not abolish condemnation, self-righteousness, indignation, or destruction. How important is it, therefore, that Nietzsche substituted "human sacrifice" for "punishment"? What kind of an "advance" does it constitute? None at all.

The Christianity that Nietzsche attacked for being insufficiently sacrificial was also, of course, the Christianity he attacked for being overly sacrificial. To this we now turn.

Gratitude and Goodness

Paul is mentioned by name only in the most passing fashion in the *Genealogy* (1:16); but the climax of Nietzsche's denunciation of the bad conscience and self-degradation through the idea of God was surely meant to evoke Pauline theology.

> —suddenly we stand before the paradoxical and horrifying expedient that afforded temporary relief for tormented humanity, that stroke of genius on the part of Christianity: God himself sacrifices himself for the guilt of mankind, God as the only being who can redeem man from what has become unredeemable for man himself—the creditor sacrifices himself for his debtor, out of *love* (can one credit that?), out of love for his debtor!— (*G*, 2:21)

This is the emotional climax of an analysis of the bad conscience and religion as the accumulation of debt and consciousness of debt. It was in relation to this analysis that Nietzsche had endeavored to clarify the distinction between late Jewish and Christian faith and all others. For other peoples, he had noted, being at once dogmatic and irritatingly nonspecific, the sense of debt *increased* with the power of the group, and decreased as the power of the group decreased, presumably because the group was convinced that their gods had not kept their part of the bargain. But the bad conscience internalizes indebtedness, and then the aim becomes to "preclude, pessimistically, once and for all, the prospect of a final discharge," so that guilt recoils back upon the *debtor*. Nietzsche was doubtless thinking of the tendency of Israel, in her prophets, to blame herself for misfortunes. In the *Antichrist* we read that when the old god was no longer able to do what once he could, the people "should have let him go" (*A*, #25). But they did not, holding onto him at the price of making him a god of "demands," as we have seen in an earlier chapter. In the *Genealogy*, Nietzsche contrasted the humiliating god with the gods of the Greeks, who did not hold sins against men, who took upon themselves, as the inspirers of evil actions, as the "deceivers" of men, "not the punishment, but, what is *nobler*, the guilt" (*G*, 2:23). Typically, Nietzsche ignored almost all of what did not fit into his neat antitheses. The tendency to blame the gods rather than themselves was criticized by Greeks.[15] But we need not press this point.

More important is to investigate the relevance of this thesis of indebtedness to Judaeo-Christian faiths. Much would seem to confirm that relevance. Man, according to the Bible, owes God everything in the most radical sense since God is presented as Creator. Furthermore, Israel's faith was based upon a Covenant, which seems clearly relevant to a relation which, if it is hardly to be called "commercial," nevertheless can suggest ideas of indebtedness. Then, too, the idea of the "suffering servant," when Christianized as the Passion, could be interpreted as a "payment" of God to Himself, since nothing else would do, precisely as Nietzsche said. Finally, Judaism and Christianity had emphasized that man's goodness is a response, a reaction, to God's goodness, that man *owes* his goodness to God.

But all of this is misleading in the most radical ways. That man in one sense "owes" God everything makes nonsense of the idea of indebtedness itself, since man could not pay God back, and this was clear from the beginning of human history. That was why, for Paul, and not for Paul alone, Abraham was "justified by his faith." Mankind was created in free love, not a love needing repayment, with interest. The covenant was not such a transaction, but God's condescension. This condescension calls forth the elevation of man. "Ye shall be a holy people." The covenant thus entered into obligated Israel, an obligation only intensified by the idea that for the sake of this covenant the world was created. But the relation of love transcended all legal limits and all questions of literal "indebtedness." The question was only, would mankind live up to the dignity of the relationship or not? To the degree that man could not do so without developing a pride that destroyed the relation of love altogether, which would, in turn, destroy the dignity of the relationship, to that degree, on the Pauline interpretation, God had to make it clear, as it were, that man must only pay back his "debt" by *acknowledging that he had received love as a gift, not a debt.* Paul's theology was designed to clarify just that and, in the process, to universalize the salvation promised to the Jews. In light of this, while it is indisputably true that Jesus' sacrifice has sometimes been regarded moralistically as a payment to the demands of God's "justice," there is very little good evidence to attribute this view to Paul any more than to Jesus himself.[16] Pauline "expiation" is not payment. It was a sacrifice making love manifest, lifting the curse on sin by wiping it away. Saving faith then became faith in the order of the world as love, not as will to power.

But this means that the final item of "indebtedness" mentioned above is real, is, in fact, essential: man owes his "goodness" to God. He gives only as a result of what he is given, from life to the forgiveness of sins. The self is, and must be, "reactive," for it finds itself in a world it did not make, living under conditions it did not choose, and free only within limits. Its crucial choice, then, is to be grateful or resentful, to respond to love with love or to refuse love because it is interpreted as something else.

By emphasizing the Judaeo-Christian God as the supreme ideal that induces a purely destructive guilt rather than as an ideal that ennobles and in which God gave humanity the opportunity for a very real, if certainly dependent, dignity, Nietzsche pointed to a radical lifting of the burden of guilt as the promise of atheism.

> The advent of the Christian God, as the maximum god attained so far, was ... accompanied by the maximum feeling of guilty indebtedness on earth. Presuming we have gradually entered upon the *reverse* course, there is no small probability that with the irresistible decline of faith in the Christian God there is now a considerable decline in mankind's feeling of guilt; indeed, the prospect cannot be dismissed that the complete and definitive victory of atheism might free mankind of this whole feeling of guilty indebtedness toward its origin, its *causa prima*. Atheism and a kind of *second innocence* belong together. (*G*, 2:20)

Unfortunately, the abolition of the "whole feeling of guilty indebtedness" toward the origin comes perilously close to destroying the foundations of what was best in the teaching of *Zarathustra*.

> This is the manner of noble souls: they do not want to have anything for nothing; least of all, life. Whoever is of the mob wants to live for nothing; we others, however, to whom life gave itself, we always think about what we might best give in return. And verily, that is a noble speech which says, "What life promises us, we ourselves want to keep to life."
> One shall not wish to enjoy where one does not give joy. And one shall not *wish* to enjoy! For enjoyment and innocence are the most bashful things: both do not want to be sought. One shall *possess* them—but rather *seek* even guilt and suffering. (*TSZ*, 3:12, 5)

This is one of the noblest passages in Nietzsche's works. In context, the seeking of suffering need not be read as morbid, the seeking of guilt need not be read as "evil." And the notion of the bashfulness of enjoyment and innocence is beyond praise, if hardly original with Nietzsche.

But is it not in complete contradiction to the spirit of the prophecy and hope voiced later in the *Genealogy*? In a literal sense, perhaps the answer must be in the affirmative. It will not do to say that the *Genealogy* looks to the abolition of guilty indebtedness while Zarathustra wants grateful indebtedness. The two cannot be distinguished in that fashion. The mob who are not "noble" are *mob*. The substitution of one word for another, of a sneer for condemnation, does not seem to matter.

Yet even if this be true, the difference in terminology is revealing, and helps remove the apparent contradiction. What was really offensive to Nietzsche in the concept of *guilty* indebtedness? One possible answer would be that such indebtedness does not proceed from love, but merely from an externally imposed burden, and that consequently Nietzsche was condemning an unhappy and depressed state in the debtor that of necessity precluded an ennobling and fulfilling gratitude. If so, however, then Nietzsche was simply maligning once again the religious tradition that had sought to eliminate the unhappy depression of guilt. But there is another explanation. Nietzsche recognized that "guilty indebtedness," to the degree that it is a reasonable phrase for the condition of believers at all, was a condition *imposed upon all*, that all were to respond to love with love. But this robs virtue of the "aristocratic magic" that Nietzsche complained it lost whenever virtue was proclaimed as the obligation of all. The noble, then, could have no consciousness of a special merit in doing what only the noble would think of doing if what they did was what God had demanded of all. This means, however, that Zarathustra at his noblest cannot be sharply separated from the Nietzsche who demanded "human sacrifices," for the concept of a universal obligation that dignifies the obligated and thus might protect them, is not available as a shield for the many. Instead, the noble man is in a position of being able to use "life" and his own gratitude to "life" to sacrifice right and left. And since, moreover, this "life" makes no demands except "vitality," the distinction between sacrificing for life and sacrificing for one's own *Machtgefühl* and *to* one's own *Machtgefühl* threatens to lose all meaning, and with it, the distinction between the sublimated and the unsublimated. "At the risk of displeasing innocent ears I propose: egoism belongs to the nature of a noble soul—I mean that unshakable faith that to a being such as 'we are' other beings must be subordinate by nature and have to sacrifice themselves" (*BGE*, #265).

Faith

Because Pauline faith was a reaction to God's goodness, it was to inspire goodness. And since the goodness demanded was, like God's, an agape that ought to flow toward one's fellows irrespective of all self-serving considerations, including the feeling of power, the moral task became sharper and more difficult in the light of faith. It became more difficult, as well, because the ideal goodness was one so internalized, so much a part of the grace-given nature of the believer, that it could be considered the fulfillment of the famous prophecy of Jeremiah, which has often been viewed as an important part of the background to Pauline faith.

> But this is the covenant that I will make with the house of Israel after those days, saith the Lord, I will put My law in their inward parts, and in their heart will I write it; and I will be their God, and they shall be My people; and they shall teach no more every man his neighbor, saying: 'Know the Lord'; for they shall all know Me, from the least of them unto the greatest of them, saith the Lord; for I will forgive their iniquity, and their sin will I remember no more. (31:33–34)

The more inward the law becomes, the less alienated it is, the more it is one's own. As a result, this consummation becomes the perfection and fulfillment of the individual as well as his "moralization."

But the Pauline tradition has normally recognized that man's condition is not one of perfect possession of faith and grace, and the moral unity that is the fruit of both. The task of internalization, therefore, was precisely that, a task, one which the self could not complete upon its own, but toward which it strove to the measure of its faith and love. From this point of view, the doctrine of faith as specifically belief in the remission of sins and the availability of reconciliation could be considered as a lightening of the moral burden placed upon man by the law, but with the specific proviso that this alleviation should have the effect, when interpreted in the proper spirit, of encouraging agape and making it more powerful by placing "moral striving" upon a positive footing of love rather than a negative one of fear. As Calvin put this issue:

> See how our works lie under the curse of the law if they are tested by the standard of the law. But how can unhappy souls set themselves with alacrity to a work from which they cannot hope to gain anything in return but cursing? On the other hand, if freed from this severe exaction, or rather from the whole rigor of the law, they hear themselves invited by God with paternal lenity, they will cheerfully and alertly obey the call, and follow his guidance.[17]

Nietzsche criticized sharply the doctrine that faith was the basis of moral elevation. By claiming that there was no substitute for works and that faith too often did not lead to works at all (*D*, #22), he sounded, perhaps unwittingly, very reminiscent of Kant, not normally a philosopher he echoed on moral subjects. His main point, however, depended on the view that faith was merely a state of consciousness, something of the "fifth rank" in comparison to "the value of the instincts," as he put it (*A*, #39).

This judgment on faith from the late Nietzsche helps to explain the remarkable equation between Lutheran faith and knowledge in the specifically Socratic-Platonic sense that he had given years before, in *Daybreak*, an equation that is surely absurd. Because Pauline faith was a mystical doctrine that referred to the whole man, it was not analogous at all to merely considering something to be true. At bottom, in fact, there is a clear analogy, though obviously no identity, between the Pauline doctrine of works flowing from faith and the Nietzschean doctrine of graciousness flowing from power and self-acceptance, the power *of* self-acceptance, discussed in the second chapter of this study. One can add that should one harden that Nietzschean doctrine into a more dogmatic position than it ever perhaps was, and say that true strength results in kindness and gentleness, then this view stands upon exactly the same empirical basis of irrefutability and unprovability as the Pauline doctrine that true faith leads to works. One could say of both that he who is not kind and gentle is not *really* strong, or does not *really* possess faith, regardless of how he may consciously view himself. Nietzsche's "instinct" was merely biological terminology for "grace."[18]

Nietzsche never gave any sign of recognizing the analogy between his own most edifying doctrine and the doctrines of Paul. In one important passage, however, he discussed "faith," not with the interests of kindness and gentleness specifically in mind, but in order to define the noble man considered apart from all questions of behavior; and in this passage he referred to religious faith as something shallower:

—What is noble? What does the word "noble" still mean to us today? What betrays, what allows one to recognize the noble human being, under this heavy, overcast sky of the beginning rule of the plebs that makes everything opaque and leaden?

It is not actions that prove him—actions are always open to many interpretations, always unfathomable—nor is it "works." Among artists and scholars today one finds enough of those who betray by their works how they are impelled by a profound desire for what is noble; but just this need *for* what is noble is fundamentally different from the needs of the noble soul itself and actually the eloquent and dangerous mark of its lack. It is not the works, it is the *faith* that is decisive here, that determines the order of rank—to take up again an ancient religious formula in a new and more profound sense: some fundamental certainty that a noble soul has about itself, something that cannot be sought, nor found, nor perhaps lost. *The noble soul has reverence for itself.* (*BGE*, #287)

This noble soul is depicted as beyond striving, if not beyond activity. His self-certainty *is*. Yet how seriously can we take this as the depiction, not of a transcendent ideal, but of a reality? This certainty is rooted, in Nietzsche's view, presumably in the body, in "health" broadly conceived. But it is also conscious and self-conscious, for the noble man "has reverence for itself." The more self-conscious this reverence is, however, the more it must be subject to being lost, found, sought, at any rate, intensified or diminished. Otherwise, the strong man could not regard "every danger," to recall a previous quotation, as something that "challenges our curiosity about the *degree* [emphasis added] of our strength and our courage." Once again the contrast between acting for power and acting from power reappears. If, however, we recall Zarathustra's complaint against the most despicable man, he who is incapable of despising himself, and use it, not as a contradiction, but as a much-needed qualification, of this soul that has reverence for itself, we can say that Nietzsche attempted a synthesis of the strength beneath consciousness and will, deriving from sources anterior to both, and the strength of self-conscious self-certainty, which is subject to augmentation. There is great depth, one can readily acknowledge, in the attempt at just such a synthesis as this.

The position is nevertheless extremely awkward. The reclamation project requires, not merely that the noble soul have reverence for *himself*, but *reverence* for himself, and one cannot combine such reverence with despising oneself without drastically altering the character of reverence and despising alike. If the reverence in question is regarded as based upon the capacity of the noble soul for lofty ideals, as the reclamation project would suggest, then it is an inadequate ground for reverence unless the noble soul lives up to these demands. But if his ideal is merely the conceptual formulation of what he already is, then he deserves no reverence for his capacity to conceive ideals that urge him beyond himself. As a result, the reclamation project lowers the possibility of conscious guilt and pained inadequacy, but at the price of lowering the ideal and inviting an antinomian interpretation. Antinomianism, to be sure, was also a danger in Pauline theology, but one against which Paul, like Luther after him, guarded much more carefully than Nietzsche ever did.

The religious "projection" of the ideal onto God, while at the same time conceiving it as one's original "unfallen" nature and one's eventual goal, taken together with the interpretation of "strength" as "faith," had the effect of avoiding the oscillation between invulnerable self-certainty and self-despising striving characteristic of Nietzsche. The positive symbols of God,

Creation out of love and grace, and the Kingdom of God, when combined with the negative symbols of fall, death, and sin, emphasize the importance of spiritual movement away from the latter and toward the former. The positive symbols draw their power from the belief in a reality superior to human will; but they function as ciphers of completion to energize as well as to direct the human will. Faith and action were to be mutually reinforcing. The more one acted in faith and love, the more one would "see" the reality of love and the more certain one would become of one's faith.

The superiority of the noble soul consists in his not needing symbols of consummation (unless one regards eternal recurrence as one such symbol) because he is consummated already. In fact, however, his ability to dispense with the symbol of what transcends him is too often intelligible, all-too intelligible, in terms of his reliance upon realities *beneath* him. Sometimes, as we have so often seen, these realities are ordinary people. They can also be the lower elements of the soul, which the higher ones self-consciously rule. In the following passage it is very definitely both, the presence of the vulgar being indispensable to give a vivid sense of superiority to the abstract self-domination which is praised.

> To live with tremendous and proud composure; always beyond—. To have and not to have one's affects, one's pro and con, at will; to condescend to them for a few hours; to *seat* oneself on them as on a horse, often as on an ass—for one must know how to make use of their stupidity as much as of their fire. To reserve one's three hundred foregrounds; also the dark glasses; for there are cases when nobody may look into our eyes, still less into our "grounds." And to choose for company that impish and cheerful vice, courtesy. And to remain master of one's four virtues: of courage, insight, sympathy, and solitude. For solitude is a virtue for us, as a sublime bent and urge for cleanliness which guesses how all contact between man and man—"in society"—involves inevitable uncleanliness. All community makes men—somehow, somewhere, sometime "common." (*BGE*, #284)

This is by no means entirely unattractive. Richard Schacht quoted this passage at the conclusion of his laudatory treatment of Nietzsche's morality, minus the last two sentences.[19] But those sentences are crucial, throwing a disturbing light on both the near self-alienation of the ideal of mastery evoked here and the "impish and cheerful vice, courtesy," which, in context, looks like nothing but unconcealed contempt. As a replacement for looking up, the defining act of *homo religiosus*, and not looking at all, but "blinking," the activity of the last man, Nietzsche could only offer the alternative of looking down. One may believe that, in truth, there is no fourth alternative, and be thankful enough to Nietzsche for posing the choices at once so neatly and so passionately. That thankfulness, however, need not require that one make his choice one's own.

To refuse to do so is certainly not to commit oneself to denying any validity whatever to Nietzsche's critique of religious symbolism, all questions of religion's verifiable truth aside, which, we have seen, is of very dubious relevance to Nietzsche's reclamation project in any case. The Judaeo-Christian religious tradition has known two basic derailments, one into aestheticism and the other into moralism.

The aspect of Nietzsche's philosophy that most directly concerns religious aestheticism provides a critique of it that cannot be lightly dismissed. Religious symbols can be misused in a fashion that entails transforming them from inspirers of creative action into the replacement of creativity by pure contemplation. The very idea of God has, of course, been conceived, usually with no small help from Greek philosophy, as the perfect "object" of vision, one that perfectly "satisfies," fills up, its beholder. Predicates of desire-gratifying infinity and beauty are heaped upon God with such abandon that nothing is then left for man to do *except* look up. Religion has too often met this threat simply moralistically, as the Puritans did. But this scarcely reaches the heart of Zarathustra's question "What could one create if gods existed?" (*TSZ*, 2:2). Behind this question is a view, less of *gods*, than of God conceived as the total monopolist of all value, for whom Creation adds nothing except the manifestation of what He already possesses prior to all manifestation. As a result, it is not merely the moral activity of men, but their creative activity in general that appears threatened.

It is, in fact, not entirely surprising that it should have been Augustine, one of the profoundest of all Paulines, who should have been so crucial in the Platonization of God in the theological tradition, a Platonization that at times made all creativity into the mere play of shadows on the wall of the cave.[20] Augustine's definition of love as the desire to be filled with the sight of God was altogether harmonious with a tendency to insist upon the worthlessness of the self, except when dominated by that desire. If Augustine was not without all sense of a belief in man as a lesser partner in God's creation, it was not a theme he emphasized, and many have followed him in this underemphasis.[21]

Many, however, have not; and one can doubt whether this kind of theology is any more genuinely typical of the Christian tradition, to say nothing of the Jewish tradition, than the analogous aestheticism of eternal recurrence at its most retrospective and passive.[22] All religion must insist that there is something other than what Leo Strauss has called "the charm of competence"[23] (the hypertrophy of this charm being what is really meant by "God is dead"), but religions stressing interhuman responsibility and the "goodness of Creation" as much as Judaism and Christianity cannot be legitimately held to surrender the importance of all creative action.

One can suggest, in fact, that Nietzsche greatly oversimplified matters when he pointed to a dichotomy between living in a meaningful world and organizing a portion of it onself. On the contrary, the Nietzschean project for the control of history operates under the inspiration of deliverances from Mt. Sinai, as it is also that inspiration gone mad. It is surely not unreasonable to say that the Judaeo-Christian notion of a "meaningful" world is one that moderates pride and, above all, insists on the indispensable value of human community, by appealing to an antecedent order out of which and for which humanity emerged. But in order for this world to become meaningful to human beings, the imitation, on a lower level of power, of the creative and moral activity of God must be pursued by those human beings. That religion insisted that the highest does not await our efforts to bring Him into existence may have produced too much quietism in the past. On the other hand, the same insistence meant that the universe was rich enough to tolerate the continued existence of the weak.[24]

Religious moralism finds its most obvious expression in the sweeping contempt for, indeed, the positive fear of, all ritualistic, aesthetic, and contemplative elements in religion. This may result in a compulsive activism in which the end to be served appears far less in the forefront of the consciousness of the actor than the need to keep busy. This form of conduct has often been advocated as a means to "avoid temptation," but one would score too easy and cheap a victory over the spirit of moralism by emphasizing that. Far more important is the need to achieve a progressively more inward and thorough consciousness of faith itself. The serious point in all "Puritanism" against the aesthetic is that the beautiful offers an all-too convincing illusion of self-perfection. Because it is too convincing, the self does not need to strive, but merely feels, or thinks "impersonally." And because it may be an illusion, the actual moral character of the self may be thoroughly deficient, lazy, cowardly, selfish, and, for all of its aesthetically inspired enthusiasm, loveless.

But in his desire to avoid this form of self-centeredness, which takes itself for sublime devotion to the divine, the religious moralist who does not simply settle down to habits of endless self-alienated labor may, in his drive to ever-deeper levels of inwardness, concentrate on *negative feelings about himself*. Action, then, is not the joy of self-expression and not the joy of serving those one loves. At issue here is not "masochism" nor "oriental despotism," nor any other cheap anti-religious cliché, but something subtler. It is not a question of loving to be bullied and of enjoying, in recompense, the savor of the bully's power. Nor is it a question of really loving one's absolute self-abnegation, the wallowing in the consciousness of being the "chief of sinners." Rather, it is a question of so identifying God's *goodness* with His power to give grace to the unworthy that one must hold onto the most vivid sense of that unworthiness in order to sense that goodness with the maximum intensity. And that means to hold on to one's suffering for dear life, and to conceive of one's activity itself as a form of suffering and, under the need for this conception, actually making it so. That others may come to suffer for this may be true enough.

Nietzsche, however, preserved his own version of just this.

> The happiness and self-contentment of the Lazzaroni or the "bliss" of "beautiful souls" or the consumptive love of Herrnhuteristic pietists prove nothing regarding order of rank among men. As a great educator, one would have to scourge such a race of "blessed people" mercilessly into unhappiness. The danger of dwarfing, of relaxation is present at once:—against Spinozistic or Epicurean happiness and against all relaxation in contemplative states. But if virtue is the means to such a happiness, very well, *then one has to become master over virtue, too.* (WP, #910)

Even more revealing in this connection is a note from the period of the *Genealogy* itself, which so often appears anti-ascetic.

> *Type of my disciples.*—To those human beings who are of any concern to me I wish suffering, desolation, sickness, ill-treatment, indignities—I wish that they should not remain unfamiliar with profound self-contempt, the torture of self-mistrust, the wretchedness of the vanquished: I have no pity for them, because I wish them the only thing that can prove today whether one is worth anything or not—that one endures. (WP, #910)

The suffering, including the suffering of self-contempt, that makes the Puritan more certain of the graciousness of God makes the Nietzschean disciple more certain of his power to endure. But where the Puritan's faith creates a limit to his rejoicing in suffering by the very idea of the divine graciousness itself, he who is committed to Nietzsche's famous proposition that "what does not destroy me, makes me stronger" (T, Maxims, 7), scarcely possesses any *external* limiting idea at all. The limit, then, must be purely the limit of his own strength, which, of all limits, the Nietzschean himself must be most continuously tempted to transgress. For this reason Nietzsche had to write, at other times, in the most directly contrary way, and denounce Christianity for damaging the spontaneous joy of life. But since this oscillation does not constitute a doctrine of the mean, one could argue that Nietzscheanism is the intensification or the abolition of Christian asceticism with equal accuracy. At bottom Nietzsche could not synthesize the image of the complacent noble with the image of the noble whose nobility is dependent upon despising himself, still less with the noble whose strength was dependent upon his being *forced* to be strong.[25] Therefore he had to give expression to now one, now another, pole.

Both the aesthetic and the moralistic distortions of religion involve the misuse of religious symbols for the denial of the highest in the human rather than the elevation of the human to the divine. Zarathustra demanded that the disciples of the Redeemer "would have to look more redeemed" (*TSZ*, 2:4). So, it can be replied, should the author of so many paeans to suffering.

It can be maintained, however, that I have misunderstood Nietzsche in a fashion analogous to Nietzsche's misunderstanding of Christianity, and that it is by no means impossible to regard Nietzsche and the most subtle strand in the Judaeo-Christian tradition as a whole as pointing to the same thing, just as, by the same token, the most morbid strands of Judaeo-Christian faith and of Nietzsche point to the same thing. If we take Jeremiah's prophecy to exemplify that subtlest strand, and view it as pointing beyond all the alienation and, with it, the pomp and circumstance of religion, to an eschatological vision of wholeness, so that the very greatness of God ceases to "intimidate," we can then say that religion does not aim simply to replace pride by humility, but to transcend, eventually, the entire tangle of pride and humility, which Nietzsche was quite correct to regard as all too close to one another. Analogously, we can regard Nietzsche's child, if rescued from his solipsism, as pointing in the same direction. Finally, Nietzsche's critique of the man dissatisfied with himself need not be regarded as a demand to replace guilt by pride, but both by sober self-contentment, perhaps with some reverence for what transcends the self thrown in for good measure. The will to power would then be seen, either as a movement toward its own *abolition*, as *power*, as the law for Paul moved toward its abolition as *law*, or, alternatively, power would be regarded in so innocuous and innocent a light that one could allow Nietzsche the term, since he was so adamant about it, without feeling that anything of moral substance was lost. Such a view must rest on an interpretation of Nietzsche's personal psychology which holds that his expressions of brutality were less the expression of the desperate need for *Machtgefühl* than simply desperation itself, beneath which was a deeper current moving in decidedly Christian channels.[26] More important, it must rest on far fewer texts than it ignores. But it is not simply wrong. Scarcely anything one could say about Nietzsche is. That makes it all the harder, however, to believe that it is simply right.

Nietzsche's critique of Christianity derives its greatest force and dubiousness from the same phenomenon that the Pauline tradition had addressed, that of moral accusation.

> I want to learn more and more to see as beautiful what is necessary in things; then I shall be one of those who make things beautiful. *Amor fati*: let that be my love henceforth! I do not want to wage war against what is ugly. I do not want to accuse; *I do not even want to accuse those who accuse* [emphasis added]. *Looking away* shall be my only negation. And all in all and on the whole: some day I wish to be only a Yes-sayer. (*GS*, #276)

Self-absorbed though this passage is, there is no need to regard it as simply another "proof of strength." Surely it reflects a real humanity, even a real piety. But it was not a hope that was to be fulfilled, and Nietzsche was as inconsistent on the subject of accusation as on every other of supreme moral importance. "Would that you might invent for me the justice that acquits everyone," said Zarathustra a year later, "except him that judges" (*TSZ*, 1:19). "Dionysus is a *judge!*—Have I been understood?" (*WP*, #1051) runs a note of 1885, in a context in which Goethe, Beethoven, Shakespeare, and Raphael are apparently found wanting.

Most revealing of all, however, is a short paragraph from the *Antichrist*. "'But if ye forgive not men their trespasses, neither will your Father forgive your trespasses' (Matt. 6:15). Very compromising for said 'Father'" (#45). One need have no affection for any doctrine of damnation in order to find this flippancy far off the mark. The transcendence of accusation, if it is to have any serious meaning, can only be in the name of an order that unites mankind, an order that exists, not beyond good and evil, but in and for the good. Such an order, however, must, to say the very least, find it extremely difficult to include the one who would judge without being judged, who insists on wielding the terrible weapons of accusation, regardless of whether or not they are "morally" conceived, without any possibility that they might recoil upon himself.

And it was just that privilege which Nietzsche demanded, with his "crimes against life" and his description "human, all-too human," and his noble man who has reverence for himself and contempt for everything else. His inconsistency on judgment, like so many of his other inconsistencies, may be traced at times to the simple fact that he identified by turns with the oppressed and the oppressing, the judged and the judging, the victims of a "just God" and with God as creator of the world and controller of history, with the sacrificed and with the sacrificers, with the victims of pitying condescension and the bestower of condescending pity.[27]

Because of the depth of his sensitivity to guilt-feeling, his preternatural touchiness, which obliged him to accuse even those who did not like his books, he felt the tremendous force of accusation as few moral philosophers ever have. The great blond beasts of his imagination could have laughed it off, as he knew. But he could not. The will to power was then born as that which cannot be accused and does not need to accuse. But since the will to power was usually in its essence competitive, it could not dispense with accusation to deal with a world whose very competitiveness Nietzsche so often embraced. The result, however, was that accusation had to be available to the strong and not to the weak, to the upper class beset by a rising rabble, but not to those who "may" exist "only for service and the general advantage." His glimpses of self-enclosed innocence, in such a general context, are merely one dishonesty more, and that the worst: for it implies that one can ever be "justified" in one's own eyes alone, without need for a framework of meaning that links the self to the other. One can share Nietzsche's contempt for "vanity," conceived as dependence on the other's praise, and still find his whole pose of self-sufficiency a lie. The philosopher who looked down with condescension on those souls who, aided by religion, could find some contentment in the real order by viewing themselves as placed "in an illusory higher order of things" could, in the final analysis, "justify" himself only as the one who broke history in half,[28] an order at once illusory and moral, but the only escape from solipsism available to him.

To praise oneself as the one who breaks history in half is to endeavor to escape from solipsism into a wider network of human meaning. That which is most noble, as well as most histrionic and vainglorious in Nietzsche, is connected with this need for a wider meaning, which led him to criticize the last man. Modern liberalism can be legitimately criticized, at times, because its ethic can often lead to a solipsistic individuality, one which does not endeavor to rise, in morality, thought, or feeling, to any height. That may mean both that the individual is "ignoble" and also that he is unfulfilled. All legitimate complaints against hedonism boil down to the shallowness and hollowness of all purely narcissistic joys. Rather, one should say that all pure narcissism, which looks neither up nor down, is not joy at all, but, at its best, only pleasure; for it involves solely the self, and what involves solely the self is the body and the unsublimated feelings of the body. The joyful, by contrast, involves the spiritual self, which includes the other by aspiring to the inclusiveness of the universal.

"Creativity" must be understood, not as an act in which the self is incidental, a mere mouthpiece of the divine and the "objective," nor as an act in which the pure self manifests itself in its purity. The former is both too vain and too humble, too vain because most human creation is partly limited by the limitations of its creator, and also because, at its best, such creation proceeds from an "inspiration" that the "I" cannot claim purely as its "own" without fatuity. It is too humble because this "limitation" is partly the result of a positive power, the power to transform into "what is thinkable for man, visible for man, feelable by man," precisely as Zarathustra said. But the view that the pure self manifests itself in creation is also wrong. The spiritual self is an abstraction, one which cannot be extricated from "the fatality of all that is," in other words, from the concrete sociohistorical matrix of the individual's life. Nietzsche tended to deny the importance of that matrix, even to the point of attacking the self-alienation involved in consciousness itself, whenever he was not in the mood for the grand gestures of *amor fati*.

Finally, one can say that creativity involves communication as an essential, not an incidental, part of itself, a communication to the self and beyond the self. All joy wants to communicate itself, as one of the greatest principles of scholasticism has it. Nietzsche was profoundly aware of the difficulty of communication and struggled for it manfully throughout his career as an author. But his very failure to receive evidence of his success produced a strain for which he was only too ready to compensate himself; and his philosophy of the will to power was well suited to provide compensation in some of its doctrines. Success in communication could thus be viewed as merely a sign that one communicated low things to low people.[29] Correspondingly, incommunicability could be taken as a sign of elevation, and thus used as a vehicle of a manic self-conceit as an alternative to a depressive sense of failure. If we recall his best words on the subject, in which communication becomes the "gift-giving virtue" of Zarathustra, we can understand how Nietzsche at his best preserves a false emphasis that connects Nietzsche at his best to Nietzsche at his worst. For the same pride which could relish incommunicability as a tribute to one's superiority had to claim, in a slightly better mood, the "gift-giving virtue" to be the product of a pure, creative self rather than regard it as a good in which the self "participated" and, as a result of the joy of this participation, sought to share.

The hyperindividualistic terms of Nietzsche's reclamation project, of the "will to power" in general, required this proprietary attitude. And it was aided and abetted by his own need to glorify his solitude as a tribute to his superiority, a need which was intended to be a sign of his self-sufficiency and which was, instead, the clearest sign of its absence. And this attitude meant that his philosophy, colored by the pressures of these needs, evoked a conception of individual fulfillment that could be conceived equally well in terms of an utterly trivial pursuit of what is purely one's own, one which is made no less trivial by looking down on the rabble, or a terrible pursuit of the *Machtgefühl* that can come only when one involves the other in a competitive relation with oneself.

The principle of the enhancement of life does not abolish this tension between the terrible and the trivial, as we have seen; it merely reproduces it, serving as a cloak for both. If the individual must be stretched beyond himself to avoid becoming the last man, he should be stretched by grace or the aspiration to the gracious, rather than by the wrack of an abstraction that sacrifices the many while not even serving to ennoble the few, by the spirit of "By doing we forego," properly illuminated, rather than by the spirit of the desire for what "*forces* us to be strong." Nietzsche's appeal for force and his philosophical emancipation of individual force helped bring forth terrible men; and nothing helps so much to give the last man a good conscience as the thought that the only alternative to himself is the terrible man. The idea of "God" has done more than Nietzsche ever did to point beyond triviality and beyond terror alike because it lends itself to serving the twin aims of Nietzsche's own thought, self-perfection and self-transcendence, more coherently, less brutally, and with less dependence on the fatuities of the

competitive-comparative than does the "will to power." It also avoids in-
ducing the individual to fall prey to the equally gross absurdities of the "self-
sufficiency" Nietzsche extolled on the one hand or to an identification of the
good with any and every form of blind social conformity, which he attacked,
on the other. Finally, theism insists that the good is not simply identical with
social justice, still less with a social justice, whether of the right or the left,
inspired by murderous thoughts and realized by murderous deeds; but it
also insists that a social justice humanely conceived is an indispensable goal
of exertion for those with any pretense to a desire to remain faithful to the
earth, and not for them alone. None of this makes theism necessarily true;
but the mere memory of it reduces the philosophy of the will to power,
which is rather less necessarily true, to a *faute de mieux*. As such, by its own
implicit admission, it cannot stand.

None of this means that it is necessary to end this book on a note of
resounding accusation of Nietzsche and Nietzscheanism, and for reasons
that go far beyond the attractiveness of gracious gestures at the end of a
rather arduous journey. Nietzsche cannot be simply condemned, not merely
because of the wealth of his insights, but also because of the extraordinary
dividedness of the man and his philosophy. He himself tore fragments of
Christianity from one another so that they ceased to make any sense, and
were ripe for the misinterpretation he was not loath to provide. But the
fragments waged war in his own mind until *he* ceased to make any sense.
The author of paeans to the most ruthless conceptions of aristocratic
privilege denounced Christian "order of rank," "hierarchy of souls", and
everything, in short, which savored of Nietzscheanism, as false, as, in fact,
unworthy (KGA, 8:2, p. 398, cf. *A*, #40). The man who could, perhaps after
his collapse into madness, identify vivisection with "what guarantees spirit
and future,"[30] had collapsed into madness trying to protect a horse from its
master's whip. Most revealing of all, however, is a fragment from late in his
last creative year, so frequently marked by euphoria, which reads, in its
entirety: "—and if my philosophy is a hell, I will at least pave the way to
it with good sentences" (KGA, 8:3, p. 284). This is a line that should be
equally embarrassing to Nietzschephiles and Nietzschephobes alike who, in
whatever way, would impose a monolith on the awesome conflicts which
constitute his work. It indicates, and it is not unique in doing so, that Nietzsche can be completely exculpated from the bad taste of loving all of his own
philosophy.[31] It also indicates how false it would be to seize upon this or
that symbol of redemptive innocence and identify it *with* Nietzsche's philosophy.

To insist that Nietzsche was torn apart is not to deny the extraordinary,
perhaps the unique, educating power of his work. On the contrary, that
power may owe more to the depths of his unresolved conflicts than to anything else. But that power must also depend, or so it seems to me, upon one's

being willing to "fight" Nietzsche hard enough; and *enough* is, unfortunately, tooth and nail. It goes without saying that, in the process of this struggle, it is necessary to be on one's guard against becoming overfond of the fighting as an end in itself. Should that happen, then, of course, the worst side of Nietzsche wins, and, equally regrettable, one becomes blind to the roses scattered, here and there, amidst his thorns.

> Yes, my joy wants to delight,
> Every joy wants to delight.
> Would you like to pick my roses?
>
> You must stoop and stick your noses
> Between thorns and rocky views,
> And not be afraid of bruises.
>
> For my joy—enjoys good teases.
> For my joy—enjoys good ruses.
> Would you like to pick my roses?
>   (*GS*, "Prelude," #9)[32]

Notes

Introduction

1. The best-known of these, partly because of its intrinsic merits and partly because of the stature of its author, is Thomas Mann's "Nietzsche's Philosophy in the Light of Recent History," available in English in Thomas Mann, *Last Essays*, trans. Richard and Clara Winston (New York, 1958), pp. 141–77. Also worthy of note, but far less well known, is the study of Karl August Götz, *Nietzsche als Aussnahme: zur Zerstörung des Willens zur Macht* (Freiburg, 1949).

2. Two books in particular should be singled out for their refreshing opposition to Kaufmann's palliation of Nietzsche: Olivier Reboul's *Nietzsche Critique de Kant* (Presses Universitaires de France, 1974) and the very recent study of Ofelia Schutte, *Beyond Nihilism: Nietzsche without Masks* (Chicago and London, 1984). Schutte's book is vitiated by an unconvincing and very vague account of the will to power, which does not fit well either with most of Nietzsche's texts or with her own presentation of Nietzsche's politics. But that presentation makes many sound points. Also worthy of note are remarks of Walter H. Sokel: "What Nietzsche and Hitler have in common, for all the obviously enormous differences in substance as well as level, is precisely the aesthetic perspective on politics.... Kaufmann has given us an antiseptic image of [Nietzsche] which cannot remain credible for long. By trying too hard to make Nietzsche respectable, Kaufmann has done a disservice to the many brilliant insights which characterize his work in many other respects." "Political Use and Abuses of Nietzsche in Walter Kaufmann's Image of Nietzsche," *Nietzsche Studien* 12 (1984):441–42.

3. Reboul, *Nietzsche Critique*, p. 146, n. 1

Chapter 1. The Will to Power

1. For the best general treatment of the doctrine of the will to power, see Wolfgang Müller-Lauter, "Nietzsches Lehre vom Willen zur Macht," *Nietzsche Studien* 3 (1974):1–60.

2. For the most thorough presentation of Nietzsche's epistemology, see Rudiger Hermann Grimm, *Nietzsche's Theory of Knowledge* (Berlin and New York, 1977).

3. Walter Kaufmann, *Nietzsche: Philosopher, Psychologist, Antichrist*, 4th ed., (Princeton, N.J., 1974), chap. 9.

4. Even Bentham could grant the reality of what he termed the "pleasures of relief," but he did not make much of them, and the very phrase suggests a passive, or, as Nietzsche would say, "decadent" bias. *Principles of Morals and Legislation*, chap. 5, sec. 16.

5. Martin Heidegger, *Nietzsche*, vol. 1, *The Will to Power as Art*, trans. David Farrell Krell (New York, 1979), p. 53.

6. See Wolfgang Müller-Lauter's criticism of Heidegger in *Nietzsche: Seine Philosophie der Gegensätze und die Gegensätze seiner Philosophie* (Berlin and New York, 1971), pp. 30–31.

7. See *BGE*, #229, where Nietzsche emphasizes the role of cruelty in the appeal of tragedy.

8. René Girard, "Strategies of Madness—Nietzsche, Wagner, and Dostoevski," in *"To Double Business Bound": Essays on Literature, Mimesis, and Anthropology* (Baltimore and London, 1978), p. 72.

9. He referred to "rhythmic obstacles and resistances" in this same note.

Chapter 2. Caesar and Christ

1. Hans M. Wolff has interpreted this passage very narrowly as concerning only the ideals of the *knower*. *Friedrich Nietzsche: Der Weg Zum Nichts* (Bern, 1956), p. 202. This seems to me to be very doubtful. Instead, I am assuming it was intended to express a broad ethical ideal.

2. Kaufmann in particular deserves credit for discerning the importance of sublimation in Nietzsche's work. See chaps. 7 and 8 of his *Nietzsche: Philosopher, Psychologist, Antichrist*, 4th ed. (Princeton, N.J., 1974).

3. See Perry Miller, *The New England Mind: The Seventeenth Century* (Boston, 1939), pp. 253–55.

4. Thomas Aquinas, *Summa Theologica*, pts. 1–2, q. 24, art. 2.

5. Yer. Berakot, 4.9. As quoted in Joseph P. Schultz, *Judaism and the Gentile Faiths: Comparative Studies in Religion* (Rutherford, N.J., 1981), p. 345. Cf. George Foot Moore, *Judaism in the First Centuries of the Christian Era: The Age of the Tannaim* (Cambridge, Mass., 1927), 1:482–83.

6. Karl Jaspers, *Nietzsche and Christianity*, trans. E. B. Aston (Chicago, 1961), p. 93.

7. Walter Kaufmann, in his note to #983 of the *Will to Power*, pp. 513–14 n.59 (from his own article, "Jaspers' Relation to Nietzsche").

8. This interpretation of Kant is based upon my *Shaftesbury, Rousseau, and Kant* (Rutherford, N.J., 1980), pp. 112–62.

9. As quoted and translated by Walter Kaufmann, *Nietzsche*, p. 252.

10. Cf. H. A. Rayburn, *Nietzsche: the Story of a Human Philosopher* (London, 1948), pp. 413–14.

11. See *WP*, #382, cf. *BGE*, #270.

12. Nietzsche's supreme symbol of strength was a "Dionysian," "tragic" pessimism. It is exceedingly hard to read that into Goethe. It should be added that, in one of his notes, Nietzsche made it clear that the admiration for Goethe expressed in his writings was a mask. "We take our accidental positions (like Goethe, Stendhal), our experiences, as foreground and stress them to deceive about our depths" (*WP*, #132). Kaufmann placed great stress on Nietzsche's admiration for Goethe, but did not cite this note.

13. Emerson's the *Conduct of Life* has many ideas similar to some of Nietzsche's, and Nietzsche read it in his youth.

14. Similarly, Nietzsche used Mozart's "gracious, golden, seriousness and *not* the seriousness of a German Philistine" (*NCW*, "Wagner as a Danger," 2) to berate Wagner. When Mozart was considered in isolation, Nietzsche wrote about him in words of disgusting condescension, even hinting at weakness. "Mozart—a delicate and amorous soul, but entirely eighteenth-century, even when he is serious" (*WP*, #842).

15. Nietzsche could even say of himself, in a rare "confession" in the *Nachlass*, that he was not *healthy* enough for the power of Romantic music (*KGA*, 8:1, p. 293). But the taste for Romantic music, which never lost all of its attraction for Nietzsche notwithstanding this confession, was, also notwithstanding this confession, frequently a symptom of weakness for Nietzsche, as his endless polemics, occasionally astute, occasionally absurd, against Wagner

testify.

16. Heinz Röttges has observed the indistinguishability on many crucial points between the decadent "last man," who will be discussed later, and the "higher man" Nietzsche tried to promote. *Nietzsche und die Dialektik der Aufklärung* (Berlin and New York, 1972), pp. 231–32.

17. Werner J. Dannhauser, *Nietzsche's View of Socrates* (Ithaca and London, 1974), p. 220.

18. Cf. the notorious note #749 of *The Will to Power*: "The princes of Europe should consider carefully whether they can do without our support. We immoralists—we are today the only power that needs no allies in order to conquer: thus we are by far the strongest of the strong. We do not even need to tell lies.... [W]e shall conquer and come to power even without truth. The spell that fights on our behalf, the eye of Venus that charms and blinds even our opponents, is *the magic of the extreme*, the seduction that everything extreme exercises: we immoralists—we are the most extreme."

19. For relevant material, see John Andrew Bernstein, *Shaftesbury, Rousseau, and Kant*, passim.

Chapter 3. Affirmation, Self-Confirmation, and Selection

1. See, for example, Richard Schacht's *Nietzsche* (London, Boston, Melbourne, and Henley, 1983), pp. 261–66.

2. See Brend Magnus, *Nietzsche's Existential Imperative* (Bloomington and London, 1978), pp. 84–86.

3. See Georg Simmel, *Schopenhauer and Nietzsche*, 3d ed. (Munich and Leipzig, 1923), p. 183.

4. Cf. Ivan Soll, "Reflections on Recurrence: A Re-examination of Nietzsche's Doctrine, *Die ewige Wiederkehr des Gleichen*," in Robert C. Solomon, ed., *Nietzsche: A Collection of Critical Essays* (New York, Anchor paperback, 1973), pp. 329–32.

5. It was not merely Christian piety that led Karl Jaspers to condemn this entire line of thought in Nietzsche as unreasonable. See *Nietzsche: An Introduction to the Understanding of his Philosophical Activity*, trans. Charles F. Wallraff and Frederick J. Schmitz (Tucson, Ariz. 1965), pp. 325–27 and 432–33.

6. Ludwig Klages, *Die Psychologischen Errungenschaften Nietzsches* (Leipzig, 1926), p. 216.

7. See Peter Heller, *Dialectics and Nihilism: Essays on Lessing, Nietzsche, Mann, and Kafka* (University of Massachusetts Press, 1966), pp. 144 and 321, n. 82.

8. As Ofelia Schutte has put it, "it is possible, both logically and psychologically, to affirm the recurrence out of a sadomasochistic drive to torture others or oneself." *Beyond Nihilism: Nietzsche without Masks* (Chicago and London, 1984), p. 69.

9. Cf. Lev Shestov, *Athens and Jerusalem*, trans. and with intro. by Bernard Martin (New York, 1968), pp. 224–25.

Chapter 4. The Master and the Slave

1. "[H]e who is not induced to activity by any positive pain will always be affected by a negative one, namely boredom, perceived as a form of emptiness of sensation by the person accustomed to change of sensations. In trying to fill his life with something such a person will often feel compelled to do something harmful to himself rather than do nothing at all." Immanuel Kant, *Anthropology from a Pragmatic Point of View*, trans. Victor Lyle Dowdell, rev. and with intro. by Frederick P. Van De Pitte (Carbondale and Edwardsville, Ill., 1978), p. 133. Nietzsche almost certainly had not read this work. It is far from certain whether he read much Kant at all.

2. See the monumental work of Norman K. Gottwald, *The Tribes of Yahweh: A Sociology of the Religion of Liberated Israel, 1250–1050 B.C.E.* (Maryknoll, N.Y., 1979).

3. John Calvin, *Institutes of the Christian Religion*, bk. 3, chap. 10.

4. *City of God*, bk. 22, chap. 30. Trans. M. Dods in Whitney J. Oates, ed., *Basic Writings of Saint Augustine* (New York, 1948), 2:662.

5. Pts. 1–2, Q. 32, Art. 4.

6. Lucretius, *De Rerum Natura*, bk. 2, ll. 1–16. Trans. Rolfe Humphries. (London and Bloomington, 1969).

7. Hans Barth, *Wahrheit und Ideologie*, 2d ed., enl. (Erlenbach and Zürich, 1961), p. 266. See, however, *WP*, #216.

8. See the conclusion of the "Letter to Menoeceus."

9. David Hume, *A Treatise of Human Nature*, L. A. Selby-Bigge, ed. (Oxford, 1888), p. 411.

10. See Augustine's *Of Christian Doctrine*, bk. 3, chap. 16.

Chapter 5. The Critical Purpose of Nietzsche's Philosophy of History

1. The context of this sentence even hints at a moralizing of the human race, which Nietzsche here accepts, if not without ambiguity.

2. "The Use and Abuse of History," 8, and his vicious polemic, "David Strauss, the Confessor and Writer," 7.

3. Georg Wilhelm Friedrich Hegel, *The Philosophy of History*, trans. J. Sibree, intro. by C. J. Friedrich (New York, 1956), p. 289.

4. Again, this was something he once was willing to recognize explicitly. See *D*, #71.

5. Eckhard Heftrich claims that Nietzsche did not imagine that Christian morality would not be strong enough to prevent the misuse of his own slogans. *Nietzsches Philosophie: Identität von Welt und Nichts* (Frankfurt am Main, 1962), p. 200. There is excellent reason to doubt this, as I go on to show in the text.

6. Cf. Roger Hollinrake, *Nietzsche, Wagner, and the Philosophy of Pessimism* (London, 1980), pp. 45–46.

7. Jean-Jacques Rousseau, *Rousseau, Juge de Jean-Jacques*, in *Oeuvres Complètes*, ed. Gagnebin and Raymond (Paris, 1959), 1:846.

8. This interpretation of Rousseau is given, at greater length and with references, in my *Shaftesbury, Rousseau, and Kant* (Rutherford, N.J., 1980), pp. 61–112.

9. In the *Gay Science* (#354), Nietzsche had related the origin of consciousness and, therefore, presumably, language, to the need for communication, which he traced to human weakness. This served to denigrate communication and consciousness, which he presented in this aphorism as self-alienation, whereas the effort to assign language to noble *power* served to exalt language and, presumably, consciousness as well.

10. This is especially true of Walter Kaufmann, *Discovering the Mind*, vol. 2, *Nietzsche, Heidegger, and Buber* (New York, 1980), p. 76, where Kaufmann wrote that Nietzsche simply "tried to get as much scientific mileage as possible out of a psychological hypothesis," and that he just "occasionally wondered" whether that hypothesis could be extended to all life and to the inorganic.

Chapter 6. Foundations of Nietzschean Politics

1. See, for example, *T*, "Skirmishes," #44 and *WP*, #70.

2. See Gilles Deleuze, *Nietzsche and Philosophy*, trans. Hugh Tomlinson (New York, 1983), pp. 8–10 and pp. 80–82. Whether or not Nietzsche actually was thinking of Hegel's

"master and slave" in constructing his own view of the master, Deleuze is in a sense correct in contrasting Nietzsche with Hegel, for Nietzsche's noble does not seek recognition at all. On the other hand, the psychological verisimilitude of this sublime independence is open to question. I would add, also, that of all the famous books on Nietzsche written since the war, that of Deleuze is perhaps the most seriously misleading on the moral character of Nietzsche's philosophy. "One cannot overemphasize *the extent to which the notions of struggle, war, rivalry, or even comparison are foreign to Nietzsche and to his conception of the will to power.*" p. 82. Italics do not make this claim any truer.

3. Edmund Burke, "Appeal from the New to the Old Whigs," in *The Works of the Right Honorable Edmund Burke*, rev. ed. (Boston, 1866), 4:175.

4. See #56. On the other hand, in a note on Manu from around the same period as the *Antichrist*, Nietzsche seemed to criticize this very aspect of Manu. *WP*, #42.

5. In a note Nietzsche proclaimed that "the higher type" was "only possible through the repression [*Herunterdrückung*] of the lower to a function." *KGA*, 8:1, p. 94.

6. Scholars are in considerable disagreement about whether this renunciation can be demanded on *Platonic* premises, and whether or not Plato himself enjoined it.

7. Cf., in addition to material already quoted, the following note: "A declaration of war on the masses by *higher men* is needed! Everywhere the mediocre are combining in order to make themselves master! Everything that makes soft and effeminate, that serves the ends of the 'people' or the 'feminine,' works in favor of *suffrage universel*, i.e., the dominion of *inferior* men. But we should take reprisal and bring this whole affair (which in Europe commenced with Christianity) to light and to the bar of judgment" (*WP*, #861). To the bar of judgment!

8. See Erwin Panofsky, *The Life and Art of Albrecht Dürer*, 4th ed. (Princeton, N.J., 1955), p. 245.

9. "The vicious and unbridled: their depressive influence on the value of the desires. It was the dreadful barbarism of custom that, especially in the Middle Ages, compelled the creation of a veritable 'league of virtue'—together with an equally dreadful exaggeration of that which constitutes the value of men....

"... that which men of power and will are able to demand of themselves also provides a measure of that which they may permit themselves. Such natures are the antithesis of the vicious and unbridled: although they may on occasion do things that would convict a lesser man of vice and immoderation."

10. See George Brandes, *Friedrich Nietzsche*, trans. A. G. Chester (New York, n.d.), pp. 67 and 69 for both letters.

11. Karl Löwith has observed the contrast between Nietzsche's praise of creativity and the "imitation" of nature characteristic of the ideals of the classical antiquity he purported to admire above all else. *Meaning in History* (Chicago and London, 1949), pp. 221–22.

Chapter 7. Nietzsche and the Barbarians of the Twentieth Century

1. Nietzsche's influence on German political thought through the First World War, however, has been recently and interestingly treated by R. Hinton Thomas, *Nietzsche in German Politics and Society 1890–1918* (Manchester, 1983). Thomas stresses the diversity of Nietzsche's influence, and the way in which many people whom Nietzsche had vigorously condemned found his thought valuable, including anarchists and leaders of the women's movement. Two of the best-known works in English on the background of Nazi ideology seriously understate the relevance of Nietzsche: Peter Viereck's *Metapolitics: The Roots of the Nazi Mind*, rev. ed. (New York, 1965), and the very valuable study of Fritz Stern, *The Politics of Cultural Despair: A Study in the Rise of the Germanic Ideology*, Anchor paperback (New York, 1965).

2. See the article of Werner J. Dannhauser, "Friedrich Nietzsche," in Leo Strauss and

Joseph Cropsey, eds., *History of Political Philosophy*, 2d ed. (Chicago, 1972), p. 801.

3. For a good short treatment of Nietzsche's attitude toward the theater, see Jonas Barish, *The Antitheatrical Prejudice* (Berkeley, Los Angeles, London, 1981), pp. 400–417. A more nearly full-scale treatment, with different emphases, is provided by M. S. Silk and J. P. Stern, *Nietzsche on Tragedy* (Cambridge, 1981).

4. It should also be noted that even in *Zarathustra*, Nietzsche specifically praised obedience as such (1:10) and in *Twilight* he said in praise of modern Germany "here one still obeys without feeling that obedience humiliates." ("What the Germans Lack," 1) This is no less reasonable than the contrary proposition that obedience must necessarily humiliate, but is also hardly an attitude calculated to undermine the authority of any state. It was a central axiom of Nietzsche's that power is expressible in terms of either the ability to command *or* obey, weakness in terms of the ability to do neither.

5. In his notes Nietzsche praised Petronius repeatedly, as well as the *Antichrist* itself. (#46)

6. Proudhon and Sorel can be cited for the left. For the enthusiasm of thinkers for war in the late nineteenth and early twentieth centuries, the classic polemic of Julien Benda, *La Trahison des Clercs* (English translation, *The Treason of the Intellectuals*) remains worth reading. Also valuable is the more recent study of Roland N. Stromberg, *Redemption by War: the Intellectuals and 1914* (Lawrence, Kan., 1982).

7. Joachim C. Fest has emphasized the centrality of war in Hitler's idea of politics. *Hitler*, translated by Richard and Clara Winston (New York, 1974), pp. 607–8. But cf. Eberhard Jäckel, *Hitler's Weltanschauung: a Blueprint for Power*, trans. Herbert Arnold (Middleton, Conn., 1972), p. 94.

8. Kaufmann, *Nietzsche*, p. 315.

9. As Olivier Reboul has noted in criticism of Kaufmann. *Nietzsche Critique de Kant* (Presses Universitaires de France, 1974), p. 133.

10. Kaufmann, *Nietzsche*, p. 314, claimed that what "Nietzsche admired in Napoleon ... were not his military triumphs or his imperial crown." But since Nietzsche unquestionably admired Napoleon's capacity to *rule* (see *BGE*, #199, for example), the former is an irrelevance (and is unsupported); the latter is equally false. See *T*, "Skirmishes," #48. Kaufmann's claim that what Nietzsche admired, instead, was Napoleon in his capacity as "the antithesis of the German 'Wars of Liberation'" is partly true, but also seriously misleading. The Wars of Liberation were fought to overthrow Napoleonic rule!

11. In the *Genealogy* (1:16) Nietzsche viewed Napoleon as the incarnation of the aristocratic antithesis to the leveling of the French Revolution. This is very strange history. Napoleon, of course, restored order to France, created a new nobility, and made peace (of sorts) with the Church. But for public opinion in France and liberal opinion outside of France, he was anything but the embodiment of the slogan "supreme rights for the few," as Nietzsche would have us believe.

12. J. M. Thompson, *Napoleon Bonaparte: His Rise and Fall* (Oxford, 1952), p. 204.

13. Ibid., p. 202.

14. Herbert Kiesewetter regarded Nietzsche as rather pacifist in comparison with Hegel. *Von Hegel zu Hilter: eine Analyse der Hegelschen Machtsideologie und der politischen Wirkungsgeschichte der Rechthegelianismus* (Hamburg, 1974), p. 236 (for Nietzsche's "pacifism.")

15. Walter Kaufmann's translation of *The Genealogy of Morals* and *Ecce Homo* (New York, 1967), p. 344. The passage is quoted in its entirety.

16. Letter of Christmas 1887. *The Portable Nietzsche*, pp. 456–57.

17. See Blaise Pascal, *Pensées*, #571 in the Brunschvicg arrangement.

18. In Kaufmann's translation, the date for this note is given as 1884–88. But the *KGA* places it at the end of this period, in 1888. See 8:3, p. 173.

19. Uriel Tal, *Christians and Jews in Germany: Religion, Politics, and Ideology in the Second Reich, 1870–1914*, trans. Noah Jonathan Jacobs, (Ithaca and London, 1975), p. 278. The Mac-

cabees, of course, were earlier rebels than those referred to above. What the anti-Semites did with Bar-Kochba et al. I do not know.

20. Kaufmann has stressed this in *Nietzsche*, pp. 298–99.

21. Uriel Tal, *Christians and Jews*, p. 226. Tal, however, by no means stresses the importance of Nietzsche in the period with which he was concerned.

22. See his discussion in *Nietzsche contra Wagner*, #4.

23. It is worth noting that Nietzsche does not seem to have disagreed with the "natural" status of pity, his descriptions of the blond beast notwithstanding.

24. See, for example, *KGA*, 8:3, pp. 207, 402, which expressly deals with prohibiting the weak from reproducing (though Nietzsche withdrew it from the *Antichrist*, for which it was intended), and p. 413: "Transvaluation of all values: that *will be costly* (*kostspielig*), I promise it."

25. There is some evidence for this. See *KGA*, 8:3, p. 13.

26. See Sanford A. Lakoff, *Equality in Political Philosophy* (Boston, 1968), pp. 19–20.

27. Peter Koster has stressed the axiomatic character of Nietzsche's inegalitarianism in his excellent monograph, *Der Sterbliche Gott: Nietzsches Entwurf übermenschlicher Grösse* (Meisenheim am Glan, 1972), pp. 34–35. Cf. also Ofelia Schutte, *Beyond Nihilism*, pp. 141–42.

Chapter 8. Nietzsche and Nietzscheanism

1. *The Rebel: An Essay on Man in Revolt*, trans. Anthony Bower, with a foreword by Sir Herbert Read (New York, 1956), p. 75.

2. "Nietzsche's Philosophy in the Light of Recent History," in *Last Essays*, trans. Richard and Clara Winston (New York, 1959), p. 142.

3. Many of the most inhumane dicta in Nietzsche are from the section of *Beyond Good and Evil* entitled "What is Noble."

4. Walter A. Kaufmann, *Discovering the Mind*, 2:102.

5. R. J. Hollingdale, *Nietzsche: The Man and his Philosophy* (Baton Rouge, 1965), p. 216.

6. Wolfgang Müller-Lauter, *Nietzsche: Seine Philosophie der Gegensätze und die Gegensätze seiner Philosophie* (Berlin and New York, 1971), pp. 116ff.

7. Ibid., p. 123.

8. Strauss was wounded by Nietzsche's ferocious onslaught and died shortly thereafter. Nietzsche was initially troubled by this, but in notes written long afterward, he strove to convince himself that he was nothing of the kind. (See *KGA*, 7:3, pp. 416 and 423.)

9. Girard, "Strategies of Madness," pp. 70–71.

10. Translated by Helen Zimmern, in *Complete Works of Friedrich Nietzsche*, ed. Oscar Levy (London, 1909), 6.

11. Perhaps piety has had something to do with this. Thus Karl Jaspers wrote that, in his critique of Christian morality, Nietzsche "stopped short (an astonishing fact!) before the figure of Jesus." (Something of an overstatement, to be sure.) *Nietzsche: An Introduction to the Understanding of his Philosophical Activity*, p. 142.

12. Crane Brinton's remark that Nietzsche could "always see enough of himself in others to recognize their weaknesses" has more than a measure of truth. *Nietzsche*, rev. ed. (New York, 1965), p. 164.

13. Letter of 4 January 1889 to Peter Gast, in *The Portable Nietzsche*, p. 685.

14. "Let the world perish, let there be philosophy, let there be the philosopher, let there be me!"

15. Cf. the comments of Peter Heller, *Dialectics and Nihilism* (University of Massachusetts Press, 1966), p. 145.

16. Girard, "Strategies of Madness," p. 62.

Chapter 9. The Shadow of God

1. Cf. the analysis of the "Night Song" by Eric Voegelin in *Science, Politics, and Gnosticism* (Chicago, 1968), pp. 28–34.

2. An unnumbered note in the *Will to Power*, p. 85. The *KGA* gives its date as late 1887 or early 1888. 8:2, p. 283.

3. Paul Ricoeur has seen Nietzsche as essentially operating within the Pauline tradition, albeit unknowingly, in a passing reference in his *The Symbolism of Evil*, trans. Emerson Buchanan (New York, Evanston, and London, 1967), p. 140. My interpretation of the relationship is very different from what Ricoeur's appears to be, but it was this work that first suggested the comparison to me. Works on Nietzsche's critique of Christianity have generally dealt with Nietzsche's treatment of Paul, and the question of the resemblances between the two, very superficially.

4. W. D. Davies, *Paul and Rabbinic Judaism: Some Rabbinic Elements in Pauline Theology*, rev. ed. (New York, 1967), p. 321.

5. The famous passages that Nietzsche put into the mouths of "madmen." *D*, #14 and *GS*, #125, insist that the destroyers of the law and the murders of God, respectively, must be worthy of their deeds. "[I]f I am not *more* than the law I am the vilest of all men," as the *Dawn* madman says. That Nietzsche meant to distance himself from the desperation of this attitude is clear in the immediate context, far less clear in the context of his work as a whole. Cf. Zarathustra's "Are you one of those who had the *right* to escape from a yoke? There are some who threw away their last value when they threw away their servitude." (*TSZ*, 1:17). Precisely because a clear answer to Zarathustra's question may be completely unavailable, one can suggest, the frenzy of the madmen can easily develop to the degree that an answer is conscientiously sought.

6. For a very stimulating critique of the notion that Paul himself should be regarded as the father of the "introspective conscience," see Krister Stendahl, *Paul Among Jews and Gentiles and Other Essays* (Philadelphia, 1976), pp. 7–23 and 78–96. For one of the best discussions of the issues raised by the Pauline critique of the law, see the sympathetic essay by the Jewish philosopher Hans Jonas, "The Abyss of the Will: Philosophical Meditation on the Seventh Chapter of Paul's Epistle to the Romans," in *Philosophical Essays: From Ancient Creed to Technological Man* (Englewood Cliffs, N.J., 1974), pp. 335–48.

7. *On the Spirit and the Letter*, trans. P. Holmes, in *Basic Writings of Saint Augustine*, ed. Whitney J. Oates (New York, 1948), 1:464–65.

8. "I do not wish to promote any morality, but to those who do I give this advice ... say *that morality is something forbidden*. That way you might win over for these things the kind of people who alone matter: I mean those who are *heroic*" (*GS*, #292; cf. *WP*, #317). The heroic is not perhaps so identical with the adolescent as Nietzsche appears to have thought.

9. A likely enough assumption. "Whatever is done from love always occurs beyond good and evil" occurs in the same collection of epigrams. *BGE*, #153.

10. For the most scholarly discussion of Paul by a modern Jewish historian of religion, see H. J. Schoeps, *Paul*, trans. H. Knight (Philadelphia, 1961).

11. John G. Gager, *The Origins of Anti-Semitism: Attitudes Toward Judaism in Pagan and Christian Antiquity* (New York and Oxford, 1983), pp. 217 and 248–49.

12. The words of Luther may be taken as representative of the Christian formulation of this view: "man must ... first of all pray for grace that, changed in spirit, he will want to and will do everything from a cheerful and ready heart, not from slavish fear or puerile cupidity, but from a free and manly attitude of mind. But only the Spirit can bring this about." *Lectures on Romans, Library of Christian Classics*, 15, trans. and ed. Wilhelm Pauck (Philadelphia, 1961), pp. 195–96.

13. Turin, December 1888. *Selected Letters of Friedrich Nietzsche*, ed. and trans. Christopher

Middleton (Chicago and London, 1969), p. 340.

14. Letter of 6 January 1889, *The Portable Nietzsche*, p. 685.

15. Nietzsche himself cited the *Odyssey* 1, ll. 32ff. as something of an exception, which he extenuated by saying that Zeus rather good-naturedly blames human "foolishness, *not* sin!" But the aristocratic poet Theognis, about whom Nietzsche had written in his school days, wrote: "Everything's gone to the dogs and ruin! Still, / Karnos, we must not blame the blessed gods: / The violence of men, vile greed and pride / Have thrown us from our good luck into bad." *Hesiod, Theogony: Works and Days: Theognis, Elegies*, trans. Dorothea Wender (Harmondsworth, Eng.: Penguin, 1973), ll. 833–36. A fragment from Solon to a similar effect could be cited.

16. See the discussion of this point, which is admittedly very controversial, in John Ziesler, *Pauline Christianity* (Oxford and New York, 1983), pp. 89–90.

17. John Calvin, *Institutes of the Christian Religion*, trans. Henry Beveridge (Grand Rapids, Mich., 1966), p. 133.

18. Modern psychology substitutes terms different from both, referring, of course, to childhood experience, above all, the reception of love from one's parents as crucial in the "strengthening" of the individual. If anything, this is closer to Paul than to Nietzsche, since it insists upon the crucial importance of what the individual receives from others.

19. Schacht, *Nietzsche*, p. 474

20. For the classic treatment of the relation between Platonic and Christian love, see Anders Nygren, *Agape and Eros*, trans. Philip S. Watson (New York, 1969). Nygren stresses the role of Augustine in effecting a synthesis, of which he is highly critical, though not along the lines of the present discussion.

21. Jean Granier, in a brief critical appraisal of Nietzsche from a Christian perspective, supports Nietzsche on creativity and maintains that Christianity should accommodate an emphasis on human creativity. "Conclusion: Thinking with and Against Nietzsche," in *Nietzsche and Christianity*, ed. Claude Geffre and Jean-Pierre Jossua (Edinburgh and New York, 1981, p. 103.

22. Cf. Hans Pfeil, *Von Christus zu Dionysus: Nietzsches religiöse Entwicklung* (Meisenheim am Glan, 1975), pp. 200ff.

23. Leo Strauss, *Notes on Machiavelli* (Glencoe, Ill., 1958), p. 297.

24. In his own way, Nietzsche sought to conceive of the world as rich rather than needy. Thus he attacked Darwinism for mistaking "Malthus for nature," and in overemphasizing "the struggle for *existence*." (*T*, "Skirmishes," #14. Cf. *GS*, #349, where Darwinism is reduced to "English overpopulation"). But this line of thought, which can hardly be viewed as anything other than a remnant of cosmic piety, did nothing whatever for the "weak," as the aphorism from *Twilight of the Idols* makes clear.

25. See chapter 1, p. 32, above.

26. See Bernhard Welte, *Nietzsches Atheismus und das Christentum* (Darmstadt, 1958), especially pp. 56–62 for a related *rapprochement*.

27. Compare Nietzsche's mocking "interpretation" of the myth of the Fall, in which God is fearful of science and fearful that in man He "had created a rival for himself" (*A*, #48) with his remark, quoted in an earlier chapter, that "if one wants slaves, then one is a fool if one educates them to be masters."

28. "The uncovering of Christian morality is an event without parallel, a real catastrophe. He that is enlightened about that, is a *force majeure*, a destiny—he breaks the history of mankind in two. One lives before him, or one lives after him." *EH*, "Why I am a Destiny," 8.

29. A *leitmotiv* in his anti-Wagnerian polemics. See, for example, *Nietzsche contra Wagner*, "Wagner as a Danger," 2.

30. See the fragment in the appendix to Kaufmann's translation of *Ecce Homo*, p. 341. The context is an attack on his brother-in-law, but it is likely that some of Nietzsche's hostility to Wagner is also finding an outlet as well.

31. Cf. a letter to Overbeck, 2 July 1885: "My life is now governed by the wish that things are *not* as I see them...." *Nietzsche: a Self-Portrait from His Letters*, trans. and ed. Peter Fuss and Henry Shapiro (Cambridge, Mass., 1971), p. 87.

32. Translation has been slightly altered.

Works Cited

NIETZSCHE'S WORKS

German Editions

Kritische Gasamtausgabe. Edited by Giorgio Colli and Mazzino Montinari. 30 vols. Berlin and New York, 1967–78.

Musarionausgabe. 23 vols. Berlin, 1920–29.

Translations: Works and Notes

Beyond Good and Evil: Prelude to a Philosophy of the Future. Translated with commentary by Walter Kaufmann. New York, 1966.

Daybreak: Thoughts on the Prejudices of Morality. Translated by R. J. Hollingdale, introduction by Michael Tanner. Cambridge, 1982.

The Gay Science. Translated with commentary by Walter Kaufmann. New York, 1974.

On the Genealogy of Morals. Translated by Walter Kaufmann and R. J. Hollingdale, and *Ecce Homo*, translated by Walter Kaufmann. Commentary by Walter Kaufmann. New York, 1967. These two works are coupled together in one Vintage paperback.

The Portable Nietzsche. Includes *Thus Spoke Zarathustra, The Antichrist, Twilight of the Idols, Nietzsche contra Wagner,* and miscellaneous selections. Translated by Walter Kaufmann. New York, 1954.

The Will to Power. Translated by Walter Kaufmann and R. J. Hollingdale. Edited by Walter Kaufmann. New York, 1967.

Letters

Nietzsche: A Self-Portrait from His Letters. Translated and edited by Peter Fuss and Henry Shapiro. Cambridge, Mass., 1971.

Selected Letters of Friedrich Nietzsche. Translated and edited by Christopher Middleton. Chicago and London, 1969.

MISCELLANEOUS

Aquinas, Thomas. *Summa Theologica.* Translated by Fathers of the English Dominican Province. 3 vols. New York, 1947.

Augustine. *Basic Writings of Saint Augustine*. Edited and with an introduction by Whitney J. Oates. 2 vols. New York, 1948.

———. *Of Christian Doctrine*. Translated with an introduction by D. W. Robertson, Jr. Indianapolis and New York, 1958.

Barish, Jonas. *The Antitheatrical Prejudice*. Berkeley, Los Angeles, and London, 1981.

Barth, Hans. *Wahrheit and Ideologie*. 2d ed., enl. Erlenbach and Zürich, 1961.

Benda, Julien. *The Treason of the Intellectuals*. Translated by Richard Aldington. reprint ed. New York, 1969.

Bentham, Jeremy. *An Introduction to the Principles of Morals and Legislation*. Reprinted in *The Utilitarians*. New York, 1961.

Brandes, Georg. *Friedrich Nietzsche*. Translated by A. G. Chester. New York, n.d.

Bernstein, John Andrew. *Shaftesbury, Rousseau, and Kant: An Introduction to the Conflict Between Aesthetic and Moral Values in Modern Thought*. Rutherford, N.J., 1980.

Burke, Edmund. "Appeal from the New to the Old Whigs." *The Works of the Right Honorable Edmund Burke*. rev. ed. Boston, 1866. 4:61–215.

Calvin, John. *Institutes of the Christian Religion*. Translated by Henry Beveridge. 1845; reprint ed., Grand Rapids, Mich., 1966.

Camus, Albert. *The Rebel: An Essay on Man in Revolt*. Translated by Anthony Bower. Foreword by Sir Herbert Read. New York, 1956.

Dannhauser, Werner J. "Friedrich Nietzsche." In *History of Political Philosophy*, edited by Leo Strauss and Joseph Cropsey. 2d ed. Chicago, 1972. Pp. 782–803.

———. *Nietzsche's View of Socrates*. Ithaca and London, 1974.

Davies, W. D. *Paul and Rabbinic Judaism: Some Rabbinic Elements in Pauline Theology*. Rev. ed. New York, 1967.

Deleuze, Gilles. *Nietzsche and Philosophy*. Translated by Hugh Tomlinson. New York, 1983.

Fest, Joachim C. *Hitler*. Translated by Richard and Clara Winston. New York, 1974.

Gager, John D. *The Origins of Anti-Semitism: Attitudes Toward Judaism in Pagan and Christian Antiquity*. New York and Oxford, 1983.

Geffre, Claude, and Jean-Pierre Jossua, eds. *Nietzsche and Christianity*. Edinburgh and New York, 1981.

Girard, René. "Strategies of Madness—Nietzsche, Wagner, and Dostoevski." Reprinted in *"To Double Business Bound": Essays on Literature, Mimesis, and Anthropology*. Baltimore and London, 1978. Pp. 61–83.

Gottwald, Norman K. *The Tribes of Jahweh: A Sociology of the Religion of Liberated Israel, 1250–1050 B.C.E.* Maryknoll, N.Y., 1979.

Götz, Karl August. *Nietzsche als Aussnahme: zur Zerstörung des Willens zur Macht*. Freiburg, 1949.

Grimm, Rudiger Hermann. *Nietzsche's Theory of Knowledge*. Berlin and New York, 1977.

Heftrich, Eckhard. *Nietzsches Philosophie: Identität von Welt und Nichts*. Frankfurt am Mein, 1962.

Hegel, G. W. F. *The Philosophy of History*. Translated by J. Sibree. Introduction by C. J. Friedrich. reprint ed. New York, 1956.

Heidegger, Martin. *Nietzsche*, vol. 1, *The Will to Power as Art*. Translated by David Farrell Krell. New York, 1979.

Heller, Peter. *Dialectics and Nihilism: Essays on Lessing, Nietzsche, Mann, and Kafka*. University of Massachusetts Press, 1966.

Hollingdale, R. J. *Nietzsche: The Man and his Philosophy*. Baton Rouge, La., 1965.

Hollinrake, Roger. *Nietzsche, Wagner, and the Philosophy of Pessimism*. London, 1982.

Hume, David. *A Treatise of Human Nature*. Edited by L. A. Selby-Bigge. Oxford, 1888.

Jäckel, Eberhard. *Hitler's Weltanschauung: A Blueprint for Power*. Translated by Herbert Arnold. Middleton, Conn., 1972.

Jaspers, Karl. *Nietzsche and Christianity*. Translated by E. B. Aston. Chicago: Gateway ed., 1961.

———. *Nietzsche: An Introduction to the Understanding of His Philosophic Activity*. Translated by Charles F. Wallraff and Frederick J. Schmitz. Tucson, Arizona, 1965.

Jonas, Hans. "The Abyss of the Will: Philosophical Meditation on the Seventh Chapter of Paul's Epistle to the Romans." Reprinted in Hans Jonas, *Philosophical Essays: From Ancient Creed to Technological Man*. Englewood Cliffs, N.J., 1974.

Kant, Immanuel. *Anthropology from a Pragmatic Point of View*. Translated by Victor Lyle Dowdell, revised and with an introduction by Frederick P. Van De Pitte. Carbondale and Edwardsville, Ill., 1978.

Kaufmann, Walter A. *Discovering the Mind*, vol. 2, *Nietzsche, Heidegger, and Buber*. New York, 1980.

———. "Jaspers' Relation to Nietzsche." In *From Shakespeare to Existentialism*, pp. 283–319. Garden City, N.Y.: Anchor Books, 1960.

———. *Nietzsche: Philosopher, Psychologist, Antichrist*. 4th ed. Princeton, N.J., 1974.

Kiesewetter, Herbert. *Von Hegel zu Hitler: eine Analyse der Hegelschen Machtsideologie und der politischen Wirkungsgeschichte des Rechthegelianismus*. Hamburg, 1974.

Klages, Ludwig. *Die Psychologischen Errungenschaften Nietzsches*. Leipzig, 1926.

Koster, Peter. *Die Sterbliche Gott: Nietzsches Entwurf übermenschlicher Grösse*. Meisenheim am Glan, 1972.

Lakoff, Sanford A. *Equality in Political Philosophy*. Boston, 1968.

Löwith, Karl. *Meaning in History*. Chicago and London, 1949.

Lucretius. *De Rerum Natura*. Translated by Rolfe Humphries. London and Bloomington, Ind., 1969.

Luther, Martin. *Lectures on Romans*. Translated and edited by Wilhelm Pauck. Library of Christian Classics, 15. Philadelphia, 1961.

Magnus, Brend. *Nietzsche's Philosophical Imperative*. Bloomington and London, 1978.

Mann, Thomas. "Nietzsche's Philosophy in the Light of Recent History." In *Last Essays*, translated by Richard and Clara Winston. New York, 1958. Pp. 141–77.

Miller, Perry. *The New England Mind: The Seventeenth Century*. Boston, 1939.

Moore, George Foot. *Judaism in the First Centuries of the Christian Era: The Age of the Tannaim*. 3 vols. Cambridge, Mass., 1927.

Müller-Lauter, Wolfgang. "Nietzsches Lehre vom Willen zur Macht." *Nietzsche Studien* 3 (1974):1–60.

———. *Nietzsche: Seine Philosophie der Gegensätze und die Gegensätze seiner Philosophie*. Berlin and New York, 1971.

Nygren, Anders. *Agape and Eros*. Translated by Philip S. Watson. reprint ed. New York, 1969.

Panofsky, Erwin. *The Life and Art of Albrecht Dürer*. 4th ed. Princeton, N.J., 1955.

Pfeil, Hans. *Von Christus zu Dionysus: Nietzsches religiöse Entwicklung*. Meisenheim am Glan, 1975.

Rayburn, H. A. *Nietzsche: The Story of a Human Philosopher*. London, 1948.

Reboul, Olivier. *Nietzsche Critique de Kant*. Presses Universitaires de France, 1974.

Ricoeur, Paul. *The Symbolism of Evil*. Translated by Emerson Buchanan. New York, Evanston, and London, 1967.

Röttges, Heinz. *Nietzsche und die Dialektik der Aufklärung*. Berlin and New York, 1972.

Rousseau, Jean-Jacques. *Oeuvres Complètes*. vol. 1. Edited by Bernard Gagnebin and Marcel Raymond. Paris, 1959.

Schacht, Richard. *Nietzsche*. London, Boston, Melbourne, and Henley, 1983.

Schoeps, H. J. *Paul*. Translated by H. Knight. Philadelphia, 1961.

Schultz, Joseph P. *Judaism and the Gentile Faiths: Comparative Studies in Religion*. Rutherford, Madison, and Teaneck, N.J., 1981.

Schutte, Ofelia. *Beyond Nihilism: Nietzsche Without Masks*. Chicago and London, 1984.

Shestov, Lev. *Athens and Jerusalem*. Translated and with an introduction by Bernard Martin. New York, 1968.

Silk, M. S., and J. P. Stern. *Nietzsche on Tragedy*. Cambridge, 1981.

Simmel, Georg. *Schopenhauer und Nietzsche*. 3d ed. Munich and Leipzig, 1923.

Sokel, Walter H. "Political Use and Abuses of Nietzsche in Walter Kaufmann's Image of Nietzsche." *Nietzsche Studien* 12 (1984):436–42.

Solomon, Robert C., ed. *Nietzsche: a Collection of Critical Essays*. New York, 1973.

Stendahl, Krister. *Paul Among Jews and Gentiles and Other Essays*. Philadelphia, 1976.

Stern, Fritz. *The Politics of Cultural Despair: A Study in the Rise of the Germanic Ideology*. New York, 1965.

Strauss, Leo. *Notes on Machiavelli*. Glencoe, Ill., 1958.

Stromberg, Roland N. *Redemption by War: the Intellectuals and 1914*. Lawrence, Kans., 1982.

Tal, Uriel. *Christians and Jews in Germany: Religion, Politics, and Ideology in the Second Reich, 1870–1914*. Translated by Noah Jonathan Jacobs. Ithaca and London, 1975.

Theognis. *Elegies*. In *Hesiod, Theogony: Works and Days: Theognis, Elegies*. Translated by Dorothea Wender. Harmondsworth, Eng.: Penguin, 1973.

Thomas, R. Hinton. *Nietzsche in German Politics and Society 1890–1918*. Manchester, 1983.

Thompson, J. M. *Napoleon Bonaparte: His Rise and Fall*. Oxford, 1952.

Viereck, Peter. *Metapolitics: The Roots of the Nazi Mind*. Rev. ed. New York, 1965.

Voegelin, Eric. *Science, Politics, and Gnosticism*. Chicago, 1968.

Welte, Bernhard. *Nietzsches Atheismus und das Christentum*. Darmstadt, 1958.

Wolff, Hans M. *Friedrich Nietzsche: Der Weg zum Nichts*. Berne, 1956.

Ziesler, John. *Pauline Christianity*. Oxford and New York, 1983.

Index